REPRODUCTION
IN EDUCATION, SOCIETY
AND CULTURE

Theory, Culture & Society

Theory, Culture & Society caters for the resurgence of interest in culture within contemporary social science and the humanities. Building on the heritage of classical social theory, the series examines ways in which this tradition has been reshaped by a new generation of theorists. *Theory, Culture & Society* will also publish theoretically informed analyses of everyday life, popular culture, and new intellectual movements.

EDITOR: Mike Featherstone, *Teesside Polytechnic*

SERIES EDITORIAL BOARD
Roy Boyne, *Newcastle upon Tyne Polytechnic*
Mike Hepworth, *University of Aberdeen*
Scott Lash, *University of Lancaster*
Roland Robertson, *University of Pittsburgh*
Bryan S. Turner, *University of Essex*

Also in this series

The Tourist Gaze
Leisure and Travel in Contemporary Societies
John Urry

Global Culture
Nationalism, Globalization and Modernity
edited by Mike Featherstone

Theories of Modernity and Postmodernity
edited by Bryan S. Turner

Reproduction in Education, Society and Culture

Pierre Bourdieu
and
Jean-Claude Passeron

translated from the French by
Richard Nice

with a Foreword by
Tom Bottomore

Preface to the 1990 edition by
Pierre Bourdieu

Sage Publications
London · Thousand Oaks · New Delhi
in association with *Theory, Culture & Society*

SAGE Publications Ltd
6 Bonhill Street
London EC2A 4PU

SAGE Publications Inc
2455 Teller Road
Thousand Oaks, California 91320

SAGE Publications India Pvt Ltd
32, M-Block Market
Greater Kailash – I
New Delhi 110 048

published in association with *Theory, Culture & Society*, Department of
Administrative and Social Studies, Teesside Polytechnic

British Library Cataloguing in Publication Data

Bourdieu, Pierre
    Reproduction in education, society and culture. – (Theory,
    culture and society).
    1. Socialisation. Role of educational institutions
    I. Title   II. Passeron, Jean-Claude   III. Series   IV. La
    reproduction. *English*
    370.19

    ISBN 0-8039-8319-0
    ISBN 0-8039-8320-4 pbk

Library of Congress catalog card number 90-060265

Printed in Great Britain

CONTENTS

List of Tables

List of Figures

ACADEMIC ORDER AND SOCIAL ORDER
Preface to the 1990 edition

Reproduction, I am told, has made its way among the most widely cited books:[1] the 'author's vanity' would incline me to accept this consecration without further ado . . . if the lucidity of the sociologist, based on a few cases of direct encounter, did not lead me to surmise that a number of the references to it were purely classificatory, and, for some, negative, so that it may be that this book obtained in part for wrong reasons the recognition which it perhaps had every right reason to beget.

Among the causes of the success of this study – which hopefully will no longer be read in complete isolation from those of my other works to which it is closely linked [2] – the most obvious is arguably, along with the timing of its publication in the midst of a period of academic upheaval, its title, which quickly made it the emblem of a new current of analysis. The counterpart for this more or less acknowledged position of theoretical leadership that critics, and particularly the most critical and simplistic of them,[3] thrust upon the book by falling for the effect of label, however, was an extraordinary simplification – if not outright distortion – of the scientific thesis it propounded and of the empirical inquiries it contained (in a language which, I must concede, did at times reach peaks of density and difficulty, particularly in the first part devoted to a tentative exposition, *more geometrico*, of a theory of symbolic violence). Its advocates and adversaries alike have frequently joined in reducing an involved analysis of the extremely sophisticated mechanisms by which the school system *contributes* to reproducing the structure of the distribution of cultural capital and, through it, the social structure (and this, only to the extent to which this relational structure itself, as a system of positional differences and distances, depends upon this distribution) to the ahistorical view that society reproduces itself mechanically, identical to itself, without transformation or deformation, and by excluding all individual mobility. It was no doubt easier, once such a mutilation had been effected, to charge the theory with being unable to accommodate change or to take it to task for ignoring the resistance of the dominated – so many (mis)interpretations that I have explicitly and repeatedly rejected, and which a close reading of the book, along with the empirical research in which it was grounded, should suffice to put aside.

To explain such misreadings, I could be content to invoke those interests and passions that are commonly called political: analyses guided by the will to know and explain, at the cost of a constant effort to surmount the passions, often contradictory, that the academic institution necessarily instills in those who are its product and who live off it, if not for it, are thus read in the logic of the trial, perceived through initial prejudice, for or against, as mere political theses inspired by an originary bias for denunciation or legitimation. Owing to the philosophical mood of the moment, such "political" readings were also often compounded with a "theoretical" or, to be more precise, a theoreticist reading: when the English translation of the book appeared (nearly a decade after the French original), the British intellectual universe was under the sway of the Grand Theory of Althusserian philosophers who had amplified the simplified "theses" they had read in *The Inheritors* and *Reproduction* by "generalizing" them under the idiom of the Ideological State Apparatuses.

None of this helped to attract the reader's attention to the painstaking empirical research and to the concrete field descriptions in which the theoretical propositions were rooted and which qualified and nuanced them from numerous angles. Thus in a series of studies published in 1965 under the title *Pedagogical Relation and Communication*, and which are still unavailable in full English translation to this day,[4] we developed a perspective on classroom interactions and on negotiations over the production and the reception of language which anticipated, and stands much closer to, ethnomethodological constructivism (and in particular to a book such as *Language Use and*

School Performance by Aaron Cicourel and his colleagues published some ten years later)[5] than to the kind of structuralism that *Reproduction* is routinely associated with. In this work, we examined the social construction of the multilevel social relation of classroom understanding in and through misunderstanding to reveal the process whereby students and teachers come to agree, by a sort of tacit transaction tacitly guided by the concern to minimize costs and risks in a situation that neither controls fully, on a minimal working definition of the situation of communication. Also, in another related study entitled 'The Categories of Professorial Judgment' published a few years before the English translation of *Reproduction*,[6] we attempted to retrace the social genesis and functioning of the practical taxonomies, inseparably social and academic, through which professors fabricate an image of their students, of their school performance and of their academic value, and act to (re)produce, via forms of cooptation based on these categories, the faculty as an institution. This indicates how much the labelling of *Reproduction* as a stucturalist work owes to ignorance of the empirical work which underlays it.[7]

To appraise justly the effort of rupture that resulted in *Reproduction*, one must bear in mind what the dominant theoretical climate of the 1960s was:[8] the notion of "mutation" had become the buzzword of many a sociologist, especially among those who claimed to dissect the effects of the new mass media;[9] others prophesied the vanishing of social differences and 'the end of ideology;' others still, firm believers in the extraordinary 'mobility' of American society, proclaiming the demise of class, held that ascription was finally and for ever giving way to 'achievement.' Against all these notions, *Reproduction* sought to propose a model of the social mediations and processes which tend, behind the backs of the agents engaged in the school system – teachers, students and their parents – and often *against their will*, to ensure the transmission of cultural capital across generations and to stamp pre-existing differences in inherited cultural capital with a meritocratic seal of academic consecration by virtue of the special symbolic potency of the *title* (credential). Functioning in the manner of a huge classificatory machine which inscribes changes within the purview of the structure, the school helps to make and to impose the legitimate exclusions and inclusions which form the basis of the social order. In my most recent book *The State Nobility*,[10] which brings together the results of a whole array of investigations on the relations between elite schools, professorial practices, and what we may want to designate by the short-hand term of the ruling class, some of which were undertaken well prior to writing this 'work of youth' that *Reproduction* is, I have shown that educational titles credentials fulfil, in a different historical context, a social function quite analogous to that which befell nobility titles in feudal society. The specific symbolic efficacy of educational titles lies in that it not only guarantees technical competency but also, as the public attestation of 'gifts' or individual 'merits,' consecrates a true *social essence*. Whence the ambiguity of the 'progress' which has taken us from the collective and hereditary statuses of the nobility *stricto censu* to today's school nobility: if the degree of achievement and of technical proficiency actually required of the dominant has no doubt never been higher, it nevertheless remains that it continues to stand in very close statistical relationship to social origins, to birth, that is, to ascription. And, in societies which claim to recognize individuals only as equals in right, the educational system and its modern nobility only contribute to disguise, and thus legitimize, in a more subtle way the arbitrariness of the distribution of powers and privileges which perpetuates itself through the socially uneven allocation of school titles and degrees.

But one must go beyond the misunderstandings that were inscribed in the challenge that *Reproduction* represented, at least in intention, for the great antinomies that structure the understanding of the academic sociologist, those which oppose theory and research, internal and external analysis, objectivism and subjectivism, and so on. To come to a correct measure of the change of perspective (or, to use a more pompous term, of paradigm) to which *Reproduction* contributed, it is more fruitful to focus, not on the so-called theoretical issues and polemics that owe much of their existence and of their persistence to the logic of academic reproduction, but rather on the range of works that have emerged since and have entirely renewed our knowledge and understanding of the school, in both the United States and Great Britain. Such studies, at once empirical and theoretical, as Cookson and Persell's *Preparing for Power: America's Elite Boarding Schools*, Jeannie Oakes' *Keeping Track*, Brint and Karabel's historical sociology of community colleges or Michelle Fine's ongoing research on ghetto schools, to name but a few,[11] have made us aware that American society, which was almost invariably described, in the sixties, i.e., at the time when we began our first research on education, as the promised land of social fluidity and individual achievement (in contradistinction to the older European societies ensconced in the conservatism and social rigidities of their nobilities and bourgeoisies), also has its "elite schools" and its lesser educational institutions equally devoted, like their European counterparts, to the perpetuation and legitimation of social hierarchies. Thus we now know that, in America no less than in Europe, credentials contribute to ensuring the reproduction of social inequality by safeguarding the preservation of the structure of the distribution of powers through a constant re-distribution of people and titles characterized, behind the impeccable appearance of equity and meritocracy, by a systematic bias in favour of the possessors of inherited cultural capital. This empirical validation of the model outlined in *Reproduction* in the very society that was for so long held up as its living refutation would appear to be worth all the proofs and procedures of conventional empiricist methodology. And we shall not despair that America loses yet another parcel of its 'exceptionalism' when this loss contributes to the greater unity of social science.

Pierre Bourdieu
Collège de France, Paris, May 1989
(Translation by Loïc J.D. Wacquant)

NOTES

1. [Translator's Note] This new paperback edition of the book marks the nomination of the book as a "Citation Classic" by the Institute for Scientific Information which puts out the Social Science Citation Index (see *Current Contents/Social and Behavioral Sciences* 21(8), 20 February 1988).

2. Among others, *The Inheritors* (with J.-C. Passeron, Chicago, The University of Chicago Press, 1979 [1964]); *L'amour de l'art* (Paris, Editions de Minuit, 1966); *Distinction: A Social Critique of the Judgement of Taste* (London, Routledge and Kegan Paul; Cambridge, MA, Harvard University Press, 1984 [1979]); and especially *Outline of A Theory of Practice* (Cambridge, Cambridge University Press, 1977).

3. I have in mind here, among others, the book by Stanley Aronowitz and Henri A. Giroux, *Education Under Siege: The Conservative, Liberal, and Radical Debate Over Schooling* (London, Routledge and Kegan Paul, 1985), whose subtitle alone reveals a petition of methodological principle that immediately voids the claim of sociology to the autonomy of science by adopting, as with classes, a purely political taxonomy, and furthermore a purely Anglo-American one.

4. Pierre Bourdieu, Jean-Claude Passeron et Monique de Saint Martin (eds), *Rapport pédagogique et communication* (Paris and The Hague, Mouton, 1965). Portions of this volume appeared as: Pierre Bourdieu and Jean-Claude Passeron, "Language and Pedagogical Situation," and Pierre Bourdieu, Jean-Claude Passeron and Monique de Saint Martin, "Students and the Language of Teaching," in D. McCallum and U. Ozolins (eds) *Melbourne Working Papers 1980*, (Melbourne, University of Melbourne, Department of Education, 1980, pp. 36–77 and pp. 78–124).

5. A.V. Cicourel, K.H. Jennings, S.H.M. Jennings, K.C.W. Leiter, R. McKay, H. Mehan, and D.R. Roth, *Language Use and School Performance* (New York, Academic Press, 1974).

6. Pierre Bourdieu and Monique de Saint Martin, "Les catégories de l'entendement professoral," *Actes de la recherche en sciences sociales*, 3 (May 1975), pp. 68–93 (ec. "The Categories of Professorial Judgment," in Pierre Bourdieu, *Homo Academicus*, Cambridge, Polity Press, and Stanford, Stanford University Press, 1988 [1984], pp. 194–225). An even earlier piece was Pierre Bourdieu, "Systems of Education and Systems of Thought," *International Social Science Journal*, 19(3), (1967), pp. 338–358.

7. For an early examination of the scientific contribution and limits of structuralism, see Pierre Bourdieu, "Structuralism and Theory of Sociological Knowlege," *Social Research*, 35(4), (Winter 1968), pp. 681–706. See also Pierre Bourdieu, "From Rules to Strategies," *Cultural Anthropology*, 1-1 (February 1986), pp. 110–120, and "Social Space and Symbolic Power," *Sociological Theory*, 7-1 (Spring 1989), pp. 14–25.

8. Indeed, a full appreciation of the place of *Reproduction* among works in the sociology of education which proliferated rapidly, especially in the United States

during the 1970s, in the direction it had charted (e.g. Randall Collins, "Functional and Conflict Theories of Educational Stratification," *American Sociological Review* 36, 1971, pp. 1002–1019, and Samuel Bowles and Herbert Gintis, *Schooling in Capitalist America: Educational Reform and the Contradictions of Economic Life*, New York, Basic Books, 1976), requires that one pays notice to the original date of publication of this book and of its companion volume *The Inheritors* (1970 and 1964 respectively).

9. Pierre Bourdieu and Jean-Claude Passeron, "Sociologues des mythologies et mythologies de sociologues," *Les temps modernes*, 211 (December 1963), pp. 998–1021.

10. Pierre Bourdieu, *La noblesse d'Etat: Grandes Ecoles et esprit de corps* (Paris, Editions de Minuit, 1989).

11. Peter W. Cookson, Jr., and Carolyn Hodges Persell, *Preparing for Power: America's Elite Boarding Schools* (New York, Basic Books, 1985); Jeannie Oakes, *Keeping Track: How Schools Structure Inequality* (New Haven, Yale University Press, 1985); Steven Brint and Jerome Karabel, *The Diverted Dream: Community Colleges and the Promise of Educational Opportunity in America, 1900–1985* (New York, Oxford University Press, 1989); Michelle Fine, "Silencing in Public Schools," *Language Arts*, 64-2, 1987, pp. 157–174. See also Randall Collins, *The Credential Society: A Historical Sociology of Education and Stratification* (New York, Academic Press, 1976); Julia Wrigley, *Class, Politics, and Public Schools, Chicago 1900–1950* (New Brunswick, Rutgers University Press, 1982); Michael W. Apple, *Teachers and Texts: A Political Economy of Class and Gender Relations in Education* (London, Routledge and Kegan Paul, 1986).

FOREWORD

The work of Pierre Bourdieu and his colleagues at the *Centre de sociologie européenne* in Paris is already well known to some English speaking sociologists and cultural historians, and perhaps especially to those who have been investigating the context and development of working class culture. But it has not previously been fully accessible to the larger audience of those whose studies may involve, in a less direct way, problems concerning the maintenance of a system of power by means of the transmission of culture. The appearance of an English translation of *La reproduction*, by Pierre Bourdieu and Jean-Claude Passeron, is therefore particularly welcome; for in this book the theoretical ideas which have guided the research on cultural reproduction over the past decade or so are clearly and comprehensively expounded, and some of the important results of that research are communicated. The two parts of the book, theoretical and empirical, as the authors make clear in their foreword, are very closely connected, the theoretical propositions arising on one side from the needs of research, and on the other side being constructed or elaborated in order to make possible empirical testing.

The first important characteristic of this work, then, can be seen in the continuous interplay between theory and research; the overcoming in an ongoing collective enterprise of that division between the construction of theoretical models by 'thinkers' and the use of such models, in a derivative way, by 'researchers', which has so often been criticized as a major failing of sociology as a science. It may well be that the division can only be transcended effectively by this kind of long-term involvement in the exploration of a particular broad domain of social life, by a group of researchers who acquire to some extent the qualities of a 'school' of thought. In the present case this characteristic is evident not only in the books that Bourdieu and his colleagues have published, but especially in the recently established journal *Actes de la recherche en sciences sociales* which seems to convey even in its title the notion of a continuing process of theoretical-empirical investigation. I am sure, at any rate, that this kind of permanent and systematic organization of research activities will prove more fruitful than the intermittent launching even of large scale research projects, though these too have as one of their most valuable features — over a limited period of time — an inescapable interaction between, and merging of, the activities of theoretical construction and empirical study.

The principal theoretical proposition from which this work begins is that 'every power which manages to impose meanings and to impose them as legitimate by concealing the power relations which are the basis of its force, adds its own specifically symbolic force to those power relations'. To put this in the context of the theory from which it derives, and which it develops powerfully in new directions, we can say that not only are 'the ruling ideas, in every age, the ideas of the ruling class', but that the ruling ideas themselves reinforce the rule of that class, and that they succeed in doing so by establishing themselves as 'legitimate', that is, by concealing their basis in the (economic and political) power of the ruling class. From this initial proposition Bourdieu and Passeron go on to formulate others, concerning especially 'pedagogic action' (that is, education in the broadest sense, encompassing more than the process of formal education) which is defined as the 'imposition of a cultural arbitrary (an arbitrary cultural scheme which is actually, though not in appearance, based upon power) by an arbitrary power'. The concept of pedagogic action is then developed in a series of further propositions and commentaries, which bring out, with a great wealth of detail, the diverse aspects of this action which need to be analyzed. Perhaps the most important conceptions that should be mentioned here are those which concern the significant part that the

reproduction of culture through pedagogic action plays in the reproduction of the whole social system (or social formation), and those dealing
with the 'arbitrary' character of culture, which is arbitrary not simply
in its content, but also in its form, since it is imposed by an arbitrary
power, not derived from general principles as a product of thought.

In the second part of the book these theoretical propositions are not
'applied' to empirical reality (to say this would be to distort the
relation between theory and research that is embodied, as I have
indicated, in this investigation); rather, we are shown how, in analysing
a particular system of pedagogic action (primarily, in this case, the
formal educational system) in France, the theoretical propositions can
give rise to empirically testable propositions, while the confrontation
with an empirical phenomenon stimulates the construction or modifica-
tion of theoretical propositions. There is much that is original in this
analysis, but perhaps what is most notable is its breadth; it is not
confined to an examination of the social selection of students at
different levels of the educational system, nor to a discussion of class
differences in linguistic codes (here expressed more comprehensively as
'linguistic and cultural capital'), but observes closely the actual process
of pedagogic action, especially in the universities, and sets all these
phenomena in a wider framework of the historical transformations of
the educational system. It would undoubtedly be of the greatest interest to have similar investigations in other societies, and in due course
the possibility of comparisons which might reveal still more clearly the
diverse ways in which cultural reproduction contributes to maintaining
the power of dominant groups.

There is an important theoretical question posed by this study which
deserves further consideration. In the first part of the book the authors
refer frequently to the imposition of an arbitrary cultural scheme, and
of a particular type of pedagogic action, by 'dominant groups and
classes', and in the second part they make use of social class categories
in examining social selection in the educational system. These propositions and analyses evidently presuppose a theory of classes and 'dominant groups' (fractions of classes or elites), both in the sense of a

general conception of the division of societies into such groups and classes which results in the imposition of a culture and in pedagogic action as symbolic violence, and in the narrower sense of a set of derived propositions which define the dominant classes and groups in a particular society and thus link the specific manifestations of pedagogic action with the basic characteristics of a determinate social structure.

From another aspect, of course, it may be said that the analysis of pedagogic action, and of the whole process of cultural reproduction, itself generates or modifies theoretical conceptions of the structure of dominant and subordinate classes and groups. Hence, this kind of research may lead, as in the studies contained in the second part of the book, to a confirmation (or in some cases a questioning) of a theory of class relations initially taken for granted. It would be interesting to pursue further the examination of such problems: to ask, for example, what changes in cultural reproduction occur with changes (if there are such) in the composition of dominant classes and groups, or with the growth in size of the middle classes (in whatever way this is to be conceived theoretically), or with changes in the nature and situation of the working class, or sections of it. The authors mention occasionally the pedagogic action of 'dominated classes', with which we could associate the notion of a 'counter-culture', and this aspect of their subject is doubtless one that will be developed more fully in the future, along with the theoretical discussion of class relations.

Thus this whole project of continuing research reveals new features in the analysis of social classes and political power. Arising probably from the intense interest in cultural dominance and cultural revolution that emerged in radical movements a decade ago, these investigations connect cultural phenomena firmly with the structural characteristics of a society, and begin to show how a culture produced by this structure in turn helps to maintain it.

Tom Bottomore
University of Sussex, 1976

FOREWORD TO THE FRENCH EDITION

The arrangement of this work in two books, at first sight very dissimilar in their mode of presentation, should not suggest the common conception of the division of intellectual labour between the piecemeal tasks of empirical inquiry and a self-sufficient theoretical activity. Unlike a mere catalogue of actual relations or a summa of theoretical statements, the body of propositions presented in Book I is the outcome of an effort to organize into a system amenable to logical verification on the one hand propositions which were constructed in and for the operations of our research or were seen to be logically required as a ground for its findings, and on the other hand theoretical propositions which enabled us to construct, by deduction or specification, propositions amenable to direct empirical verification.[1]

After this process of mutual rectification, the analyses in Book II may be seen as the application, to a particular historical case, of principles whose generality would support other applications, although those analyses were in fact the starting point for the construction of the principles stated in Book I. Because the first book gives their coherence to studies which approach the educational system from a different angle each time (dealing in succession with its functions of communication, inculcation of a legitimate culture, selection, and legitimation), each chapter leads, by various routes, to the same principle of intelligibility, i.e. the system of relations between the educational system and the structure of relations between the classes, the focal point of the theory of the educational system which progressively constituted itself as such as its capacity to construct the facts was affirmed in our work on the facts.

The body of propositions in Book I is the product of a long series of transformations, all tending to replace existing propositions with other, more powerful ones which in turn generated new propositions linked to the principles by more and closer relations. Our memory of that process would suffice to dissuade us from putting forward the present state of formulation of this system of principles as a *necessary* one — though they are linked by necessary relations — did we not know that this is true of every body of propositions — and even theorems — considered at a moment in its history. The guidelines which determined how far we pursued our enquiries were implied in the very project of writing the book: the uneven development of its various moments can only be justified in terms of our intention of pursuing the regression towards the principles or the specification of consequences as far as was necessary in order to relate the analyses in Book II to their theoretical basis.

Setting aside the incongruous option of devising an artificial language, it is impossible to eliminate completely the ideological overtones which all sociological vocabulary inevitably awakens in the reader, however many warnings accompany it. Of all the possible ways of reading this text, the worst would no doubt be the moralizing reading, which would exploit the ethical connotations ordinary language attaches to technical terms like 'legitimacy' or 'authority' and transform statements of fact into justifications or denunciations; or would take objective effects for the intentional, conscious, deliberate action of individuals or groups, and see malicious mystification or culpable naivety where we speak only of concealment or misrecognition.[2] A quite different type of misunderstanding is liable to arise from the use of terms such as 'violence' or 'arbitrariness'[3] which, perhaps more than the other concepts used in this text, lend themselves to multiple readings because they occupy a position at once ambiguous and pre-eminent in the ideological field, by virtue of the multiplicity of their present or past uses or, more exactly, the diversity of the positions occupied by their past or present users in the intellectual or political fields. We must claim the right to use the term arbitrariness to designate that and only that which is yielded by the definition we give it, without being obliged to deal with all the problems directly or indirectly evoked by the concept, still less to enter into the twilight debates in which all philosophers can think themselves scientists and all scientists philosophers, and the neo-Saussurian or para-Chomskian discussions of the arbitrariness and/or necessity of the sign and/or sign system or the natural limits of cultural variations, discussions and debates which owe most of their success to the fact that they revamp the dreariest topics[4] of the school tradition, from *phusei* and *nomo* to nature and culture. When we define a 'cultural arbitrary' by the fact that it cannot be deduced from any principle, we simply give ourselves the means of constituting pedagogic action in its objective reality,[5] by recourse to a logical construct devoid of any sociological or, a fortiori, psychological referent. We thereby pose the question of the social conditions capable of excluding the logical question of the possibility of an action which cannot achieve its specific effect unless its objective truth as the imposition of a cultural arbitrary is objectively misrecognized. This question can in turn be specified as the question of the institutional and social conditions enabling an institution to declare its pedagogic action explicitly as such, without betraying the objective truth of its practice. Because the term arbitrariness applies, in another of its uses, to pure de facto power, i.e. another construct equally devoid of any sociological referent, thanks to which it is possible to pose the question of the social and institutional conditions capable of imposing misrecognition of this de facto power and thereby its recognition as legitimate authority, it has the advantage of continually recalling to mind the primordial relationship between the arbitrariness of the imposition and the arbitrariness of the content imposed. The term 'symbolic violence', which explicitly states the break made with all spontaneous representations and spontaneist conceptions of pedagogic action, recommended itself to us as a means of indicating the theoretical unity of all actions characterized by the twofold arbitrariness of symbolic imposition; it also signifies the fact that this general theory of actions of symbolic violence (whether exerted by the healer, the sorcerer, the priest, the prophet, the propagandist, the teacher, the psychiatrist or the psychoanalyst) belongs to a general theory of violence and legitimate violence, as is directly attested by the interchangeability of the different forms of social violence and indirectly by the homology between the school system's monopoly of legitimate symbolic violence and the State's monopoly of the legitimate use of physical violence.

Those who choose to see in such a project only the effect of a political bias or temperamental irredentism will not fail to suggest that one has to be blind to the self-evidence of common sense to seek to grasp the social functions of pedagogic violence and to constitute symbolic violence as a form of social violence at the very time when the withering-away of the most 'authoritarian' mode of imposition and the abandonment of the crudest techniques of coercion would seem more than ever to justify optimistic faith in the moralization of history by the sheer effects of technical progress and economic growth. That would be to ignore the sociological question of the social conditions which must be fulfilled before it becomes possible to state scientifically the social functions of an institution: it is no accident that the moment of transition from ruthless methods of imposition to more subtle methods is doubtless the most favourable moment for bringing to light the objective truth of that imposition. The social conditions which require the transmission of power and privileges to take, more than in any other society, the indirect paths of academic consecration, or which prevent pedagogic violence from manifesting itself as the social violence it objectively is, are also the conditions which make it possible to state explicitly the objective truth of pedagogic action, whatever the degree of harshness of its methods. If 'there is no science but of the hidden', it is clear why sociology is allied with the historical forces which, in every epoch, oblige the truth of power relations to come into the open, if only by forcing them to mask themselves yet further.

NOTES

1. The theory of pedagogic action presented here is grounded in a theory of the relations between objective structures, the habitus and practice, which will be set out more fully in a forthcoming book by Pierre Bourdieu (see Translator's Note).

2. I.e. 'méconnaissance', the process whereby power relations are perceived not for what they objectively are but in a form which renders them legitimate in the eyes of the beholder. The (admittedly 'artificial') term 'misrecognition' has been adopted because it preserves the link with 'recognition' (*reconnaissance*) in the sense of 'ratification', and is consistent with the usage of other translators (trans.).

3. *arbitraire*: translated, according to context, as 'arbitrariness' or 'arbitrary' (as in 'cultural arbitrary') (trans.).

4. *les plus tristes topiques*: a passing shot at Claude Lévi-Strauss, author of *Tristes tropiques* (trans.).

5. I.e. the action of teaching or educating considered as a general social process, neither limited to the school nor even necessarily perceived as education. In this translation the word 'pedagogy' is to be understood in the sense of educative practice, whose principles may or may not be explicitly formulated (trans.).

TRANSLATOR'S NOTE

The availability of *Reproduction* in English is an event of some importance for Anglo-American sociology – and not only the 'sociology of education'. The remarks which follow, which seek to relate this book to its context in the collective research led by Pierre Bourdieu at the Centre for European Sociology (CES), in no way detract from its significance: on the contrary, by refusing to see *Reproduction* as a 'last word', but situating it in the process of research in which it represents a moment of provisional stock-taking, they should only enhance its utility.

Appended to this volume is a selective list of works on aspects of the sociology of education and culture, produced since 1964 by members of the CES; they are referred to by date and number here and in the notes to the text. Some of these works offer complementary applications and analyses, others carry further the theoretical analyses presented here, and others help to ground and rectify the general theory of symbolic power, of which the sociology of education is only one dimension.

Areas of specifically educational activity which *Reproduction* maps out more than it explores – scientific and technical education – are dealt with more fully by Claude Grignon (1971, 1; 1975, 11; 1976, 4) and Monique de Saint Martin (1971, 2). Other areas which have been studied more intensively include the *classes préparatoires* (1969, 1), religious education (1974, 4) and classroom disorder (1972, 4).

A point of reference to which *Reproduction* constantly returns is the structural homology between the school system and the Church. This homology is expounded more fully by Pierre Bourdieu in two articles on Weber's sociology of religion (1971, 5; 1971, 6). Religion and education, considered sociologically, constitute 'fields' – of forces

— comparable in their functioning to magnetic fields. This concept has been elaborated and applied in other areas in Pierre Bourdieu's subsequent work: see in particular 1971, 4 (on the intellectual field); 1973, 2 (the market in symbolic goods); 1975, 3 (the intersection of literature and power), 1975, 4 (philosophy and power); 1976, 1 (the scientific field). Recent articles by Luc Boltanski (1975, 1) and Bourdieu (1975, 8) explore fields (the strip cartoon, *haute couture*) marginal to the sphere of high culture but where a similar logic prevails. The studies of Flaubert, Amiel and Heidegger (1975, 3; 1975, 2; 1975, 4) seek to show at the level of the 'author' how individual strategy comes to terms with the objective structures of the field. Those who suppose that the methodological use of the 'cultural arbitrary' implies a selling-short of scientific culture will find that the article on the scientific field (1976, 1) specifies the conditions in which the play of interests and strategies within a field can nonetheless work to the advancement of scientific knowledge.

The agents involved in a given field share a 'misrecognition' of the true relations between the structure of that field and the structures of economic and political power; in the religious field this misrecognition is the foundation of *belief*, a concept amenable to transfer into the analysis of other fields. The process of misrecognition, formulated in a relatively abstract way in *Reproduction*, is grasped more concretely in 1975, 9, an analysis of the way in which teachers' judgements on their pupils transmute social classifications into school classifications (and, in a very different cultural context, in Bourdieu's anthropological studies in Kabyle society, in 1977, 1). These analyses may also be read in relation to the discussion of the institutional and social positions of the various categories of teachers which predispose them towards specific ideologies and practices (Chapter 4). Analyses of the situation of the teaching profession in the relationship between the school system and the economy, dealing more fully with the dynamics of that relationship, are to be found, in particular, in 1971, 9; 1973, 5; 1974, 3.

The role of class linguistic 'codes' is analysed further in 1975, 7, which contains a fuller discussion of the work of Basil Bernstein in relation to the work of W. Labov, and a fuller exposition of the theory of language which underpins the research in Chapter 2. The discourse of teaching, the 'language of authority', is dealt with further in 1975, 5, where there is a critique of J. L. Austin's notion of the 'illocutionary force' of utterances, arguing that the power of the speech act resides in the social authority delegated to a legitimate spokesman.

Thus the theory set out in *Reproduction* has been developed in ways which have constantly augmented its explanatory power and which dispel the vestiges of functionalism or abstract objectivism which the residual one-sidedness of some of the expositions in *Reproduction* may have allowed to remain. The central concept of the *habitus* receives its fullest development in 1972, 1 (the work referred to in the Foreword, note 1). The forthcoming English translation (*Outline of a Theory of Practice*, 1977, 1) contains additional chapters on 'practical logic', symbolic capital, and the different modes of domination. The analysis in Chapter 3 of *Reproduction* of the dialectic of objective class future and subjective experience is taken further in 1974, 1. On the social origin of the 'pure' aesthetic capability and the competence required for decoding a work of art, see 1971, 3 (cf. also 1968, 1). Habitus as 'taste' is anatomized in 1976, 3.

The Appendix contains an account of the 'translation' of the structure of objective educational chances which, while itself remaining relatively 'objectivist', at least makes it possible to pose the question of the role which individual and class strategy play in this process. As subsequent studies by Bourdieu and Boltanski (1971, 9; 1973, 4; 1975, 6) have shown, this process results from the play of antagonistic interests competing on the terrain of symbolic production, especially for command of the educational system and the profits it gives. Enlargement of the field — without any change in its *structure* — integrates previously excluded classes, enabling and constraining them to engage in competition in which the definition of the stakes and the possible modes of struggle (the range of strategies) proper to that field are themselves at stake in the struggle. See, for example, 1972, 2 (on marriage strategies); 1973, 4 (reconversion of economic into symbolic

capital), 1975, 6 (the inflation of qualifications). The task of sociology
in bringing these mechanisms to light is defined as one of 'deconsecra-
tion' (*Actes de la recherche en sciences sociales*, 1, p. 2).

The term 'misrecognition' epitomizes the translator's quandary; in
French *méconnaissance* is a simple word though given a specific
scientific sense. Here as elsewhere a clouding of the original text seems
unavoidable. It is hoped that recurrence and context will give
familiarity to terms which have often been preferred to the use of too
readily recognizable 'native' notions. Thus the term 'pedagogy' is no
wilful gallicism but the sign of the break with merely psychological
accounts of the teacher-pupil relation (see also the English translation
of Durkheim's *Education and Sociology*). Such French usages as have
been retained, whether for the sake of brevity (for the names of
institutions, see Glossary) or merely inadvertently, will not, it is hoped,
obscure the relevance of *Reproduction* to our own educational systems.
Those who suppose this work treats only of France should remember
Marx's admonition to his German readers when writing on England: *De
te fabula narratur.*

Richard Nice
Birmingham, UK, 1976

ABOUT THE AUTHORS
and Translator

PIERRE BOURDIEU was born in 1930 in France. After study at the Ecole Normale Supérieure, he became agrégé in Philosophy. He lectured in the Faculty of Letters in Algeria 1959-60, at the University of Paris 1960-62, and at the University of Lille 1962-64. He is presently Director of Studies at the Ecole des Hautes Etudes and Director of the Centre for European Sociology, Paris. He is the Editor of the journal *Actes de la Recherche en Sciences Sociales*, and is the author of *Sociologie de l'Algérie* (1958), *The Algerians* (1962), *Travail et travailleurs en Algérie* (1964), *Le Déracinement* (with Abdel Malek Sayad, 1964), *Les étudiants et leurs études* (with Jean-Claude Passeron, 1964), *Les Héritiers* (with Jean-Claude Passeron, 1964), *Un Art moyen* (1965), *L'Amour de l'art* (with A. Darbel, 1966), *Le Métier de sociologue* (with Jean-Claude Passeron and Jean-Claude Chamboredon, 1968), *Esquisse d'une théorie de la pratique* (1972), and numerous articles on the sociology of education.

JEAN-CLAUDE PASSERON was born in 1930 in France, and also became agrégé in Philosophy after study at the Ecole Normale Supérieure. He has taught at the Sorbonne in Paris, and at the University of Nantes. Since 1968 he has been at the experimental University of Vincennes, where he set up and directed the Sociology Department. Since 1960 he has collaborated in work at the Centre for European Sociology with Pierre Bourdieu, particularly in directing research in the sociology of education and in the publication of work arising from it, notably in *Les Héritiers* (with Pierre Bourdieu, 1964) and *La Reproduction* (with Pierre Bourdieu, French edition, 1970). He has also published *La Réforme de l'Université* (with G. Antoine, 1966), and has prefaced and directed translations, in particular that of Richard Hoggart's *The Uses of Literacy* (French edition, 1970).

RICHARD NICE was born in 1948 in London, and took his B.A. in English at King's College, Cambridge. He has taught for four years in the French educational system — at the University of Paris, the Ecole Normale Supérieure, and elsewhere in Paris, and also in Brittany. He now teaches French at the University of Surrey, UK.

Le capitaine Jonathan,
Etant âgé de dix-huit ans,
Capture un jour un pélican
Dans une île d'Extrême-Orient.
Le pélican de Jonathan,
Au matin, pond un oeuf tout blanc
Et il en sort un pélican
Lui ressemblant étonnamment.
Et ce deuxième pélican
Pond, à son tour, un oeuf tout blanc
D'où sort, inévitablement,
Un autre qui en fait autant.
Cela peut durer très longtemps
Si l'on ne fait pas d'omelette avant.

ROBERT DESNOS

Chantefleurs, Chantefables

Book I

FOUNDATIONS OF A THEORY
OF SYMBOLIC VIOLENCE

Prolixity and rigmarole might be somewhat curtailed if every orator were required to state at the beginning of his speech the point he wishes to make.

J.-J. Rousseau,

Le gouvernement de Pologne

The legislator, being unable to appeal either to force or to reason, must resort to an authority of a different order, capable of constraining without violence and persuading without convincing. This is what has, in all ages, compelled the fathers of nations to have recourse to divine intervention.

J.-J. Rousseau,

The Social Contract

Abbreviations used in Book I

PA   :   pedagogic action
PAu :   pedagogic authority
PW   :   pedagogic work
SAu :   school authority
ES   :   educational system
WSg :   the work of schooling

The purpose of these graphical conventions is to remind the reader that the concepts they stand for are themselves a shorthand for systems of logical relations which could not be set out in full in each proposition, although they were required for the construction of these propositions and are the precondition for an adequate reading. This device has not been extended to all the 'systemic' concepts used here (e.g. cultural arbitrary, symbolic violence, relation of pedagogic communication, mode of imposition, mode of inculcation, legitimacy, ethos, cultural capital, habitus, social reproduction, cultural reproduction), but only because we wished to avoid making the text unnecessarily difficult to read.

O. Every power to exert symbolic violence, i.e. every power which manages to impose meanings and to impose them as legitimate by concealing the power relations which are the basis of its force, adds its own specifically symbolic force to those power relations.

Gloss 1: To refuse this axiom, which states simultaneously the relative autonomy and the relative dependence of symbolic relations with respect to power relations, would amount to denying the possibility of a science of sociology. All the theories implicitly or explicitly constructed on the basis of other axioms lead one either to make the creative freedom of individuals the source of symbolic action, considered as autonomous from the objective conditions in which it is performed, or to annihilate symbolic action as such, by refusing it any autonomy with respect to its material conditions of existence. One is therefore entitled to regard this axiom as a principle of the theory of sociological knowledge.

Gloss 2: One only has to compare the classical theories of the foundations of power, those of Marx, Durkheim and Weber, to see that the conditions which enable each of them to be constituted exclude the possibility of the object-construction carried out by the other two. Thus, Marx is opposed to Durkheim in that he sees the product of a class domination where Durkheim (who most clearly reveals his social philosophy when dealing with the sociology of education, the privileged locus of the illusion of consensus) sees only the effect of an undivided social constraint. In another respect, Marx and Durkheim are opposed to Weber in that by their methodological objectivism they counter the temptation to see in relations of force inter-individual relations of influence or domination and to represent the different forms of power (political, economic, religious, etc.) as so many sociologically undifferentiated modalities of one agent's predominance (*Macht*) over another. Finally, because his reaction against artificialist conceptions of the social order leads Durkheim to emphasize the externality of constraint, whereas Marx, concerned to reveal the relations of violence underlying the ideologies of legitimacy, tends in his analysis of the effects of the dominant ideology to minimize the real efficacy of the symbolic strengthening of power relations (*rapports de force*) that is implied in the recognition by the dominated of the legitimacy of domination, Weber is opposed to both Durkheim and Marx in that he is the only one who explicitly takes as his object the specific contribution that representations of legitimacy make to the exercise and perpetuation of power, even if, confined within a psycho-sociological conception of those representations, he cannot, as Marx does, inquire into the functions fulfilled in social relations by misrecognition (*méconnaissance*) of the objective truth of those relations as power relations.

1. THE TWOFOLD ARBITRARINESS OF PEDAGOGIC ACTION

1. All **pedagogic action** *(PA) is, objectively, symbolic violence insofar as it is the imposition of a cultural arbitrary by an arbitrary power.*

Gloss: The propositions which follow (up to and including those of the third degree) refer to all PAs, whether exerted by all the educated members of a social formation or group (diffuse education), by the family-group members to whom the culture of a group or class allots this task (family education) or by the system of agents explicitly mandated for this purpose by an institution directly or indirectly, exclusively or partially educative in function (institutionalized education), and, unless otherwise stated, whether that PA seeks to reproduce the cultural arbitrary of the dominant or of the dominated classes. In other words, the range of these propositions is defined by the fact that they apply to any social formation, understood as a system of power relations and sense relations between groups or classes. It follows that in the first three sections, we have refrained from extensive use of examples drawn from the case of a dominant, school PA, to avoid even implicitly suggesting any restrictions on the validity of the propositions concerning all PAs. We have kept for its logical place (fourth degree propositions) specification of the forms nd effects of a PA carried on within the framework of a school institution; only in the last proposition (4.3.) do we expressly characterize the school PA which reproduces the dominant culture, contributing thereby to the reproduction of the structure of the power relations within a social formation in which the dominant system of education tends to secure a monopoly of legitimate symbolic violence.

1.1. PA is, objectively, symbolic violence first insofar as the power relations between the groups or classes making up a social formation are the basis of the arbitrary power which is the precondition for the establishment of a relation of pedagogic communication, i.e. for the imposition and inculcation of a cultural arbitrary by an arbitrary mode of imposition and inculcation (education).

Gloss: Thus, the power relations which constitute patrilineal and matrilineal social formations are directly manifested in the types of PA corresponding to each successional system. In a matrilineal system, where the father has no juridical authority over his son and the son no rights over his father's goods and privileges, the father has only affective or moral sanctions to back up his PA (although the group will grant him its support in the last instance, if his prerogatives are threatened) and cannot have recourse to the juridical assistance which he is guaranteed when, for example, he seeks to affirm his right to the sexual services of his spouse. By contrast, in a patrilineal system, in which the son, enjoying explicit, juridically sanctioned rights over his father's goods and privileges, stands in a competitive and even conflictual relation to him (as the nephew does, vis-à-vis the maternal uncle, in a matrilineal system), the father 'represents the power of society as a force in the domestic group' and so is able to make use of juridical sanctions in imposing his PA (cf. Fortes and Goody) Although there can be no question of ignoring the specifically biological dimension of the relation of pedagogic imposition, i.e. biologically conditioned childhood dependence, it is not possible to leave out of account the social determinations which specify in every case the adult-child relationship, including those cases in which the educators are none other than the biological parents (e.g. the determinations deriving from the structure of the family or the family's position in the social structure).

1.1.1. Insofar as it is a symbolic power which, by definition, is never reducible to the imposition of force, PA can produce its own specifically symbolic effect only to the extent that it is exerted within a relation of pedagogic communication.

1.1.2. Insofar as it is symbolic violence, PA can produce its own specifically symbolic effect only when provided with the social conditions for imposition and inculcation, i.e. the power relations that are not implied in a formal definition of communication.

1 1.3. In any given social formation, the PA which the power relations between the groups or classes making up that social formation put into the dominant position within the system of PAs is the one which most fully, though always indirectly, corresponds to the objective interests (material, symbolic and, in the respect considered here, pedagogic) of the dominant groups or classes, both by its mode of imposition and by its delimitation of what and on whom, it imposes.

Gloss: The symbolic strength of a pedagogic agency is defined by its weight in the structure of the power relations and symbolic relations (the latter always expressing the former) between the agencies exerting an action of symbolic violence. This structure in turn expresses the power relations between the groups or classes making up the social formation in question. It is through the mediation of this effect of domination by the dominant PA that the different PAs carried on within the different groups or classes objectively and indirectly collaborate in the dominance of the dominant classes (e.g. the inculcation by the dominated PAs of knowledges or styles whose value on the economic or symbolic market is defined by the dominant PA).

1.2. PA is, objectively, symbolic violence in a second sense, insofar as the delimitation objectively entailed by the fact of imposing and inculcating certain meanings, treated by selection and by the corresponding exclusion as worthy of being reproduced by PA, re-produces (in both senses) the arbitrary selection a group or class objectively makes in and through its cultural arbitrary.

1.2.1 The selection of meanings which objectively defines a group's or a class's culture as a symbolic system is arbitrary insofar as the structure and functions of that culture cannot be deduced from any universal principle, whether physical, biological or spiritual, not being linked by any sort of internal relation to 'the nature of things' or any 'human nature'.

1.2.2. The selection of meanings which objectively defines a group's or a class's culture as a symbolic system is socio-logically necessary insofar as that culture owes its existence to the social conditions of which it is the product and its intelligibility to the coherence and functions of the structure of the signifying relations which constitute it.

Gloss: The 'choices' which constitute a culture ('choices' which no one makes) appear as arbitrary when related by the comparative method to the sum total of present or past cultures or, by imaginary variation, to the universe of possible cultures; they reveal their necessity as soon as they are related to the social conditions of their emergence and perpetuation. Misunderstandings over the notion of arbitrariness (particularly confusion between arbitrariness and gratuitousness) derive, at best, from the fact that a purely synchronic grasp of cultural facts (such as anthropologists are generally condemned to) necessarily induces neglect of all that these facts owe to their social conditions of existence, i.e. the social conditions of their production and reproduction, with all the restructurings and reinterpretations connected with their perpetuation in changed social conditions (e.g. all the degrees distinguishable between the quasi-perfect reproduction of culture in a traditional society and the reinterpretative reproduction of the Jesuit colleges' humanist culture, suited to the needs of a salon aristocracy, in and through the academic culture of the nineteenth century bourgeois *lycées*). Thus the genesis amnesia which finds expression in the naive illusion that things have always been as they are', as well as in the substantialist uses made of the notion of the cultural unconscious, can lead to the eternizing and thereby the 'naturalizing' of signifying relations which are the product of history.

1.2.3. In any given social formation the cultural arbitrary which the power relations between the groups or classes making up that social formation put into the dominant position within the system of cultural arbitraries is the one which most fully, though always indirectly, expresses the objective interests (material and symbolic) of the dominant groups or classes.

1.3. The objective degree of arbitrariness (in the sense of proposition 1.1.) of a PA's power of imposition rises with the degree of arbitrariness (in the sense of proposition 1.2) of the culture imposed.

Gloss: The sociological theory of PA distinguishes between the arbitrariness of the imposition and the arbitrariness of the content imposed, only so as to bring out the sociological implications of the relationship between two logical fictions, namely a pure power relationship as the objective truth of the imposition and a totally arbitrary culture as the objective truth of the meanings imposed. The logical construct of a power relation manifesting itself nakedly has no more sociological existence than does the logical construct of meanings that are only cultural arbitrariness. To take this twofold theoretical construction for an empirically observable reality would be to condemn oneself to naive belief either in the exclusively physical force of power, a simple reversal of idealist belief in the totally autonomous might of right, or in the radical arbitrariness of all meanings, a simple reversal of idealist belief in 'the intrinsic strength of the true idea'. There is no PA which does not inculcate some meanings not deducible from a universal principle (logical reason or biological nature): authority plays a part in all pedagogy, even when the most universal meanings (science or technology) are to be inculcated. There is no power relation, however, mechanical and ruthless which does not additionally exert a symbolic effect. It follows that PA, always objectively situated between the two unattainable poles of pure force and pure reason, has the more need to resort to direct means of constraint the less the meanings it imposes impose themselves by their own force, i.e by the force of biological nature or logical reason.

1.3.1 The PA whose arbitrary power to impose a cultural arbitrary rests in the last analysis on the power relations between the groups or classes making up the˙ social formation in which is carried on (by 1.1 and 1 2) contributes, by reproducing the cultural arbitrary which it inculcates towards reproducing the power relations which are the basis of its power of arbitrary imposition (the social reproduction function of cultural reproduction).

1.3.2. In any given social formation the different PAs, which can never be defined independently of their membership in a system of PAs subjected to the effect of domination by the dominant PA, tend to reproduce the system of cultural arbitraries characteristic of that social formation, thereby contributing to the reproduction of the power relations which put that cultural arbitrary into the dominant position.

Gloss: In traditionally defining the 'system of education' as the sum total of the institutional or customary mechanisms ensuring the transmission from one generation to another of the culture inherited from the past (i.e. the accumulated information), the classical theories tend to sever cultural reproduction from its function of social reproduction, that is, to ignore the specific effect of symbolic relations in the reproduction of power relations. Such theories which, as is·seen with Durkheim, simply transpose to the case of class societies the representation of culture and cultural transmission most widespread among anthropologists, rely on the implicit premiss that the different PAs at work in a social formation collaborate harmoniously in reproducing a cultural capital conceived of as the jointly owned property of the whole 'society'. In reality, because they correspond to the material and symbolic interests of groups or classes differently situated within the power relations, these PAs always tend to reproduce the structure of the distribution of cultural capital among these groups or classes, thereby contributing to the reproduction of the social structure. The laws of the market which fixes the economic or symbolic value, i.e. the value qua cultural capital, of the cultural arbitraries produced by the different PAs and thus of the products of those PAs (educated individuals), are one of the mechanisms — more or less determinant·according to the type of social formation — through which social reproduction, defined as the reproduction of the structure of the relations of force between the classes, is accomplished.

2. PEDAGOGIC AUTHORITY

2. Insofar as it is a power of symbolic violence, exerted within a relation of pedagogic communication which can produce its own, specifically symbolic effect only because the arbitrary power which makes imposition possible is never seen in its full truth (in the sense of proposition 1.1); and insofar as it is the inculcation of a cultural arbitrary, carried on within a relation of pedagogic communication which can produce its own, specifically pedagogic effect only because the arbitrariness of the content inculcated is never seen in its full truth (in the sense of proposition 1.2) — PA necessarily implies, as a social condition of its exercise, **pedagogic authority *(PAu) and the* relative**

autonomy *of the agency commissioned to exercise it.*

Gloss 1: The theory of PA produces the concept of PAu in the very operation by which, in identifying the objective truth of PA as violence, it brings out the contradiction between that objective truth and the agents' practice, which objectively manifests the misrecognition of that truth (whatever the experiences or ideologies accompanying those practices). Thus the question is posed: what are the social conditions for the establishment of a relation of pedagogic communication concealing the power relations which make it possible and thereby adding the specific force of its legitimate authority to the force it derives from those relations? The idea of a PA exercised without PAu is a logical contradiction and a sociological impossibility; a PA which aimed to unveil, in its very exercise, its objective reality of violence and thereby to destroy the basis of the agent's PAu, would be self-destructive. The paradox of Epimenides the liar would appear in a new form: either you believe I'm not lying when I tell you education is violence and my teaching isn't legitimate, so you can't believe me; or you believe I'm lying and my teaching is legitimate, so you still can't believe what I say when I tell you it is violence.

To draw out all the implications of this paradox we only have to think of the vicious circles awaiting anyone who might seek to base his pedagogic practice on the theoretical truth of all pedagogic practice: it is one thing to teach 'cultural relativism', that is, the arbitrary character of all culture, to individuals who have already been educated according to the principles of the cultural arbitrary of a group or class; it would be quite another to claim to be giving a relativistic education, i.e. actually to produce a cultivated man who was the native of all cultures. The problems posed by situations of early bilingualism or biculturalism give only a faint idea of the insurmountable contradictions faced by a PA claiming to take as its practical didactic principle the theoretical affirmation of the arbitrariness of linguistic or cultural codes. This is a proof *per absurdum* that every PA requires as the condition of its exercise the social misrecognition of the objective truth of PA.

Gloss 2: PA necessarily gives rise, in and through its exercise, to experiences which may remain unformulated and be expressed only in practices, or may make themselves explicit in ideologies. but which in either case contribute towards masking the objective truth of PA: the ideologies of PA as non-violent action — whether in Socratic and neo-Socratic myths of non-directive teaching, Rousseauistic myths of natural education, or pseudo-Freudian myths of non-repressive education — reveal in its clearest form the generic function of educational ideologies, in evading, by the gratuitous negation of one of its terms, the contradiction between the objective truth of PA and the necessary (inevitable) representation of this arbitrary action as necessary ('natural').

2.1. Insofar as it is an arbitrary power to impose which, by the mere fact of being misrecognized as such, is objectively recognized as a legitimate authority, PAu, a power to exert symbolic violence which manifests itself in the form of a right to impose legitimately, reinforces the arbitrary power which establishes it and which it conceals.

Gloss 1: To speak of recognition of the legitimacy of PA is not to enter the problematic of the psychological genesis of representations of legitimacy to which Weber's analyses are liable to lead; still less is it to engage in an attempt to ground sovereignty in any principle whatsoever, whether physical, biological or spiritual, in short, to legitimate legitimacy. We are simply drawing out the implications of the fact that PA implies PAu, i.e. that it 'is accepted', in the sense in which a currency is accepted, and also, more generally, a symbolic system such as a language, an artistic style or even a style of dress. In this sense, recognition of PA can never be completely reduced to a psychological act, still less to conscious acquiescence, as is attested by the fact that it is never more total than when totally unconscious. To describe recognition of PA as a free decision to allow oneself to be cultivated or, conversely, as an abuse of power inflicted on the natural self, i.e. to make recognition of legitimacy a free or extorted act of recognition, would be just as naive as to go along with the theories of the social contract or the metaphysics of culture conceived as a logical system of choices, when they situate the arbitrary selection of signifying relations constitutive of a culture in an original, hence mythical, locus.

Thus, to say that certain agents recognize the legitimacy of a pedagogic agency is simply to say that the complete definition of the power relationship within which they are objectively placed implies that these agents are unable to realize the basis of that relationship although their practices, even when contradicted by the rationalizations of discourse or the certainties of experience, objectively take account of the necessity of the relations of force (cf. the outlaw who objectively grants the force of law to the law he transgresses in the mere fact that, by hiding in order to transgress it, he adapts his conduct to the sanctions which the law has the force to impose on him).

Gloss 2: The weight of representations of legitimacy, particularly of the legitimacy of the dominant PA, within the system of the instruments (symbolic or not) securing and perpetuating the domination of one group or class over others is historically variable. The relative strength of the reinforcement given to the balance of power between the groups or classes by symbolic relations expressing those power relations rises with (1) the degree to which the state of the balance of power hinders the dominant classes from invoking the brute fact of domination as the principle legitimating their domination; and (2) the degree of unification of the market on which the symbolic and economic value of the products of the different PAs is constituted (e.g. the differences in these two respects between the domination of one society over another and the domination of one class over another within the same social formation, or, in the latter case, between feudalism and bourgeois democracy with the continuous increase in the weight of the school within the system of the mechanisms of social reproduction).

Recognition of the legitimacy of a domination always constitutes a — historically variable — force which strengthens the established balance of power because, in preventing apprehension of the power relations *as* power relations, it tends to prevent the dominated groups or classes from securing all the strength that realization of their strength would give them.

2.1.1. Power relations are the basis not only of PA but also of the misrecognition of the truth about PA, a misrecognition which amounts to recognition of the legitimacy of PA and, as such, is the condition for the exercise of PA.

Gloss 1: Thus, as the chief instrument of the transubstantiation of power relations into legitimate authority, PA presents a privileged object for analysis of the social basis of the paradoxes of domination and legitimacy (e.g. the part played in the Indo-European tradition by the brute fact of sexual, warlike or magical potency as evidence of legitimate authority can be seen in the structure of genesis myths and in the ambivalences of the vocabulary of sovereignty).

Gloss 2: We leave it to others to decide whether the relations between power relations and sense relations are, in the last analysis, sense relations or power relations.

2.1.1.1. Power relations determine a PA's characteristic mode of imposition, defined as the system of the means required for the imposition of a cultural arbitrary and for the concealment of the twofold arbitrariness of the imposition, i.e. as a historical combination of the instruments of symbolic violence and the instruments of concealment (i.e. legitimation) of that violence.

Gloss 1: The link between the two senses of the arbitrariness inherent in PA (as in proposition 1.1 and 1.2) can be seen, inter alia, in the fact that the likelihood of the arbitrariness of a given mode of imposing a cultural arbitrary being at least partially revealed as such, rises with the degree to which (1) the cultural arbitrary of the group or class undergoing that PA is remote from the cultural arbitrary which the PA inculcates; and (2) the social definition of the legitimate mode of imposition rules out recourse to the most direct forms of coercion. The experience a category of agents has of the arbitrariness of PA depends not only on its characterization in this twofold respect but also on the convergence of these characterizations (e.g. the attitude of the Confucian literati to a cultural domination based on the colonizers' military force) or their divergence (e.g. in present-day France, the detached attitude working-class children manifest towards school sanctions, both because their distance from the culture inculcated tends to make them feel the arbitrariness of the inculcation as inevitable, and, in another respect, because the cultural arbitrary of their class has less room for moral indignation at forms of repression which anticipate the sanctions most probable for their class).

Every cultural arbitrary implies a social definition of the legitimate mode of imposing cultural arbitrariness and, in particular, of the degree to which the arbitrary power which makes PA possible can reveal itself as such without annihilating the specific effect of PA. Thus, whereas in certain societies recourse to techniques of coercion (smacking or even giving 'lines') is sufficient to disqualify the teaching agent, corporal punishments (the English public school's cat-o'-nine-tails, the schoolmaster's cane or the Koran school teacher's *falaqa*) appear simply as attributes of teacherly legitimacy in a traditional culture where there is no danger of their betraying the objective truth of a PA of which this is the legitimate mode of imposition.

Gloss 2: Awareness of the arbitrariness of a particular mode of imposition or a given cultural arbitrary does not imply apprehension of the twofold arbitrariness of PA. On the contrary, the most radical challenges to a pedagogic power are always inspired by the self-destructive Utopia of a pedagogy without arbitrariness or by the spontaneist Utopia which accords the individual the power to find within himself the principle of his own 'fulfilment'. All these Utopias constitute an instrument of ideological struggle for groups who seek, through denunciation of a pedagogic legitimacy, to secure for them-selves the monopoly of the legitimate mode of imposition (e.g. in the eighteenth century, the role of discourse on 'tolerance' in the critique with which the new strata of intellectuals strove to destroy the legiti-macy of the Church's power of symbolic imposition). The idea of a 'culturally free' PA, exempt from arbitrariness in both the content and the manner of its imposition, presupposes a misrecognition of the objective truth of PA in which there is still expressed the objective truth of a violence whose specificity lies in the fact that it generates the illusion that it is not violence.

It would therefore be pointless to counterpose to the definition of PA the experience which the educators and the educated may have of PA, particularly of those modes of imposition most capable (at a given moment in time) of masking the arbitrariness of PA (non-directive teaching): this would be to forget that 'there is no liberal education' (Durkheim) and that one must not take for an abolition of the twofold arbitrariness of PA the form it assumes when resorting, for example, to 'liberal' methods in order to inculcate 'liberal' dispositions.[1] The 'soft approach' may be the only effective way of exercising the power of symbolic violence in a determinate state of the power relations, and of variably tolerant dispositions towards the explicit, crude manifestation of arbitrariness.

If some people are nowadays able to believe in the possibility of a PA without obligation or punishment, this is the effect of an ethno-centrism which induces them not to perceive as such the sanctions of the mode of imposition characteristic of our societies. To overwhelm one's pupils with affection, as American primary school teachers do, by the use of diminutives and affectionate qualifiers, by insistent appeal to an affective understanding, etc. is to gain possession of that subtle instrument of repression, the withdrawal of affection, a pedagogic technique which is no less arbitrary (in the sense of proposition 1.1) than corporal punishment or disgrace. The objective truth of this type of PA is harder to perceive because, on the one hand, the techniques employed conceal the social significance of the pedagogic relation under the guise of a purely psychological relationship and, on the other hand, their place in the system of authority techniques making up the dominant mode of imposition helps to prevent agents formed by this mode of imposition from seeing their arbitrary character. Indeed, the simultaneity of the changes in authority relationships which accompany a change in power relations capable of bringing about a rise in the threshold of tolerance for the explicit, crude manifestation of arbitrariness, and which in social universes as different as the Church, the school, the family, the psychiatric hospital or even the firm or the army, all tend to substitute the 'soft approach' (non-directive methods, 'invisible pedagogy', dialogue, participation, 'human relations') for the 'strong arm', reveals the interdependence which constitutes into a system the techniques for imposing symbolic violence characteristic of the traditional mode of imposition as well as those of the mode which tends to take its place in the same function.

2.1.1.2. In any given social formation, the agencies which objectively lay claim to the legitimate exercise of a power of symbolic imposition and, in so doing, tend to claim the monopoly on legitimacy, necessarily enter into relations of competition, i.e. power relations and symbolic relations whose structure expresses in its own logic the state of the balance of power between the groups or classes.

Gloss 1: This competition is sociologically necessary because legitimacy is indivisible: there is no agency to legitimate the legitimacy-giving agencies, because claims to legitimacy derive their relative strength, in the last analysis, from the strength of the groups or classes whose material and symbolic interests they directly or indirectly express.

Gloss 2: Although the relations of competition between the different agencies obey the specific logic of the field of legitimacy considered (e.g. political, religious or cultural), the relative autonomy of the field never totally excludes dependence on power relations. The specific form taken by the conflicts between the legitimacy-claiming agencies in a given field is always the symbolic expression, more or less trans-figured, of the relations of force which are set up in this field between these agencies and which are never independent of the relations of force external to the field (e.g. the dialectic of excommunication, heresy, and challenges to orthodoxy in literary, religious or political history).[2]

2.1.2. Insofar as the relation of pedagogic communication within which PA is carried on presupposes PAu in order to be set up, it is not reducible to a pure and simple relation of communication.

Gloss 1: Contrary to common-sense prejudice and various scholarly theories which make attention conditional on understanding, in real learning situations (including language learning) recognition of the legitimacy of the act of transmission, i.e. of the PAu of the transmitter, conditions the reception of the information and, even more, the accomplishment of the transformative action capable of transforming that information into a mental formation (training).

Gloss 2: PAu so strongly marks all aspects of the relation of pedagogic communication that this relationship is often experienced or conceived along the lines of the primordial relation of pedagogic communication, i.e. the relationship between parents and children or, more generally, between generations. The tendency to re-establish with any person invested with PAu the archetypal relationship with the father is so strong that anyone who teaches, however young, tends to be treated as a father; e.g. *The Laws of Manu*: 'That brahmana who is the giver of spiritual birth and the teacher of the prescribed duties becomes by law the father of an aged man, even though he himself be a child'; and Freud: 'We understand now our relations with our teachers. These men, who were not even fathers themselves, became for us paternal substitutes. That is why they struck as so mature, so inaccessibly adult, even when they were still very young. We transferred onto them the respect and hopes the omniscient father of our childhood inspired in us, and we started to treat them as we used to treat our father at home.'

2.1.2.1. Insofar as every PA that is exerted commands a PAu from the outset, the relation of pedagogic communication owes its specific characteristics to the fact that it is entirely dispensed from the necessity of producing the conditions for its own establishment and perpetuation.

Gloss: The professional ideology which transmutes the relation of pedagogic communication into an elective encounter between the 'master' and the 'disciple' induces teachers to misrecognize in their professional practice or deny in their discourse the objective conditions of that practice, and to behave objectively, as Weber says, like 'little prophets in the pay of the State'. Contrary to what is proclaimed by such ideology, the relation of pedagogic communication differs from the various forms of communicative relation set up by agents or agencies which, seeking to exert a power of symbolic violence in the absence of any previous, permanent authority, are obliged to win and endlessly rewin the social recognition that PAu confers from the outset, once and for all. This explains why agents or institutions who, without commanding a PAu from the outset, presume to exercise the power of symbolic violence (propagandists, publicists, scientific popularizers, healers, etc.), tend to seek social respectability by usurping the direct or inverted appearances of legitimate practice, like the sorcerer, whose action stands in a homologous relation to the PA of the priest (e.g. the 'scientific' or 'educational' guarantees invoked by publicity and even scientific popularization).

2.1.2.2. Because every PA that is exerted commands by definition a PAu, the pedagogic transmitters are from the outset designated as fit to transmit that which they transmit, hence entitled to impose its reception and test its inculcation by means of socially approved or guaranteed sanctions.

Gloss 1: The concept of PAu clearly has no normative content. To say that the relation of pedagogic communication presupposes the PAu of the pedagogic agency (agent or institution) in no way prejudges the value intrinsically attached to that PAu, since PAu has precisely the effect of ensuring the social value of the PA, regardless of the 'intrinsic' value of the agency exerting it, and whatever, for example, the degree of technical or charismatic qualification of the transmitter. With the concept of PAu we are able to escape the pre-sociological illusion of crediting the person of the transmitter with the technical competence or personal authority which is, in reality, automatically conferred on every pedagogic transmitter by the traditionally and institutionally guaranteed position he occupies in a relation of pedagogic communication.

Gloss 2: Because the sending of a message within a relation of pedagogic communication always transmits at least the affirmation of the value of the PA, the PAu which guarantees the communication always tends to eliminate the question of the informative efficiency of the communication. Proof that the relation of pedagogic communication is irreducible to a formally defined relation of communication and that the informational content of the message does not exhaust the content of the communication, may be seen in the fact that the relation of pedagogic communication can be maintained as such even when the information transmitted tends towards zero, as in the limiting case of initiatory teaching or, closer to home, in some literary education.

2.1.2.3. Because every PA that is exerted commands by definition a PAu, the pedagogic receivers are disposed from the outset to recognize the legitimacy of the information transmitted and the PAu of the pedagogic transmitters, hence to receive and internalize the message.

2.1.2.4. In any given social formation, the specifically symbolic force of the sanctions, physical or symbolic, positive or negative, juridically guaranteed or not, which ensure, strengthen and lastingly consecrate

the effect of a PA, is greater the more the groups or classes to which they are applied are disposed to recognize the PAu which imposes them.

2.1.3. In any given social formation the legitimate PA, i.e. the PA endowed with the dominant legitimacy, is nothing other than the arbitrary imposition of the dominant cultural arbitrary insofar as it is misrecognized in its objective truth as the dominant PA and the imposition of the dominant culture (by 1.1.3 and 2.1).

Gloss: The monopoly on the dominant cultural legitimacy is always the object of competition between institutions or agents. It follows from this that the imposition of a cultural orthodoxy corresponds to a particular form of the structure of the field of competition, whose particularity becomes fully apparent only when compared with other possible forms such as eclecticism and syncretism, the academic answer to the problems raised by competition for legitimacy in the intellectual or artistic field and competition between the values and ideologies of different fractions of the dominant classes.

2.2. Insofar as it is invested with a PAu, PA tends to produce mis-recognition of the objective truth of cultural arbitrariness because, being recognized as a legitimate agency of imposition, it tends to produce recognition of the cultural arbitrary it inculcates as legitimate culture.

2.2.1. Insofar as every PA that is exerted commands a PAu from the outset, the relation of pedagogic communication within which PA is carried on tends to produce the legitimacy of what it transmits, by designating what it transmits – by the mere fact of transmitting it legitimately – as worthy of transmission, as opposed to what it does not transmit.

Gloss 1: This is the basis of the sociological possibility of PA, which inquiry into the absolute beginning of PA — an inquiry as fictitious in its own way as the speculation which runs into the dead-ends of the social contract or the 'pre-linguistic situation' — would lead one to regard as logically impossible, as is shown by the paradox of the *Euthydemus,* which rests on the hidden postulate of a PA without PAu: what you know, you don't need to learn; what you don't know, you can't learn, because you don't know what you need to learn.

Gloss 2: If one reduces the relation of pedagogic communication to a pure and simple relation of communication, one is unable to understand the social conditions of its specifically symbolic and specifically pedagogic efficacy which lie precisely in concealment of the fact that it is not a simple relation of communication; by the same token one is obliged to assume a 'need for information' in the receivers, a need, moreover, informed as to the information fit to satisfy it and pre-existing the social and pedagogic conditions of its production.

2.2.2. In any given social formation, legitimate culture, i.e. the culture endowed with the dominant legitimacy, is nothing other than the dominant cultural arbitrary insofar as it is misrecognized in its objective truth as a cultural arbitrary and as the dominant cultural arbitrary (by 1.2.3 and 2.2).

Gloss: The cultural arbitraries reproduced by the different PAs can never be defined independently of their place in a system of cultural arbitraries more or less integrated depending on the social formation but always subject to the domination of the dominant cultural arbitrary. Failure to recognize this fact is the source of the contradictions both of ideology concerning the culture of dominated classes and nations and of drawing-room chatter about cultural 'alienation' and 'dis-alienation'. Blindness to what the legitimate culture and the dominated culture owe to the structure of their symbolic relations, i.e. to the structure of the relation of domination between the classes, inspires on the one hand the 'culture for the masses' programme of 'liberating' the dominated classes by giving them the means of appropriating legitimate culture as such, with all it owes to its functions of distinction and legitimation (e.g. the curricula of the *Universités populaires*[3] or the Jacobin defence of the teaching of Latin); and on the other hand the populist project of decreeing the legitimacy of the cultural arbitrary of the dominated classes as constituted in and by the fact of its dominated position, canonizing it as 'popular culture'. This antinomy of the dominated ideology, which is directly expressed in the practice and discourse of the dominated classes (in the form, for example, of alternation between a sense of cultural unworthiness and aggressive depreciation of the dominant culture) and which spokesmen, whether or nor mandated by these classes, reproduce and amplify (complicating it with the contradictions of their own relation to the dominated classes and their contradictions, e.g. *proletkult*), can outlive the social conditions which produce it, as is attested by the ideologies and even the cultural policies of formerly dominated classes or nations, which oscillate between the aim of recovering the cultural heritage bequeathed by the dominant classes or nations and the aim of rehabilitating the survivals of the dominated culture.

2.3. Every agency (agent or institution) exerting a PA commands PAu only in its capacity as the mandated representative of the groups or classes whose cultural arbitrary it imposes in accordance with a mode of imposition defined by that arbitrary, i.e. as the delegated *holder of the right to exercise symbolic violence.*

Gloss: 'Delegation of authority' does not imply the existence of an explicit agreement, still less a codified contract, between a group or class and a pedagogic agency, although, even in the case of the family PA of a traditional society, the pedagogic agency's PAu may be juridically recognized and sanctioned (cf. Gloss on proposition 1.1). Even when certain aspects of the agency's PAu are explicitly codified (e.g. the codification of the right of violence on which patria potestas is based, or the juridical limitations on paternal PAu in modern societies,

or again the delimitation of the syllabus and legal conditions of employment in an educational institution), 'all is not contractual in the
contract' of delegation. To speak of delegation of authority is simply to
name the social conditions for the exercise of a PA, i.e. cultural
proximity between the cultural arbitrary imposed by that PA and the
cultural arbitraries of the groups or classes subjected to it.

In this sense, any action of symbolic violence which succeeds in
imposing itself (i.e in imposing misrecognition of the violence which is
its objective truth) objectively presupposes a delegation of authority.
Thus, contrary to popular or semi-learned representations which credit
publicity or propaganda and, more generally, the messages conveyed by
the modern media, with the power to manipulate if not to create
opinions, these symbolic actions can work only to the extent that they
encounter and reinforce predispositions (e.g the relationship between a
newspaper and its readers). There is no 'intrinsic strength of the true
idea'; nor do we see grounds for belief in the strength of the false idea,
however often repeated. It is always power relations which define the
limits within which the persuasive force of a symbolic power can act
(e.g. the limits on the efficacy of any revolutionary preaching or
propaganda applied to the privileged classes).

Similarly, prophetic action, i.e. an action which, like that of the
religious prophet, an *auctor* claiming to find the source of his *auctoritas*
within himself must apparently constitute the transmitter's PAu ex
nihilo and progressively win the adherence of his public, succeeds only
to the extent that it rests on a prior (though virtual and tacit) delegation of authority. If one is not to resort to the miracle of an absolute
beginning (which the Weberian theory of charisma tends to require), it
is necessary to posit that the successful prophet is the one who
formulates for the groups or classes he addresses a message which the
objective conditions determining the material and symbolic interests of
those groups have predisposed them to attend to and take in. In other
words, the apparent relationship between prophecy and its audience
must be reversed: the religious or political prophet always preaches to
the converted and follows his disciples at least as much as they follow him,

since his lessons are listened to and heard only by agents who, by everything they are, have objectively mandated him to give them lessons. Though one must not forget the effects of prophetic quasi-systematization, with its allusions and ellipses conducive to pseudo-understanding and misunderstanding, the fact remains that the likelihood of success for the prophetic message cannot be deduced from the intrinsic properties of the message (cf. the relative spread of Christianity and Islam). A verbalization which, simply by stating them, consecrates, i.e. sanctifies and sanctions, the expectations it meets, can add its own specifically symbolic strength to the pre-existing power relations only because it draws its strength from the tacit delegation it is granted by the groups or classes involved in those power relations.

2.3.1. A pedagogic agency commands the PAu enabling it to legitimate the cultural arbitrary that it inculcates, only within the limits laid down by that cultural arbitrary, i.e. to the extent that both in its mode of imposing (the legitimate mode) and in its delimitation of what it imposes, those entitled to impose it (the legitimate educators) and those on whom it is imposed (the legitimate addressees), it reproduces the fundamental principles of the cultural arbitrary that a group or class produces as worthy of reproduction, both by its very existence and by the fact of delegating to an agency the authority required in order to reproduce it.

Gloss: It is all too easy to perceive the limitations inherent in the delegation when they are explicitly defined, as they are whenever PA is exerted by an academic institution; but they are also observed in the case of the PA of the family group (both in the dominant and in the dominated groups or classes). The definition of the legitimate educators, the legitimate scope of their PA and its legitimate mode of imposition, takes very different forms, for example, depending on the kinship structure and the mode of succession, considered as a mode of transmission of power and economic goods (e.g. the different forms of division of pedagogic labour among the kin in patrilineal or matrilineal societies, or in the different classes of the same social formation). It is no accident that the children's upbringing is the object of conflicting representations and a source of tension or conflict whenever families cohabit or whenever lineages or generations belonging to different classes cohabit within the same family (for example, the extreme case of conflicts over the right of adults from one family to exert a PA, especially physical repression, on the children of another family; this conflict over the legitimate boundaries of family PA always owes its specific form to the relative position in the class structure of the family groups involved).

2.3.1.1. The delegation of the right of symbolic violence which estab- lishes the PAu of a pedagogic agency is always a limited *delegation; i.e. the delegation to a pedagogic agency of such authority as it requires in order to inculcate a cultural arbitrary legitimately, in accordance with the mode of imposition defined by that arbitrary, entails the impossi- bility for that agency of freely defining the mode of imposition, the content imposed and the public on which it imposes it (the principle of the limited autonomy of pedagogic agencies).*

2.3.1.2. In any given social formation the sanctions, material or sym- bolic, positive or negative, juridically guaranteed or not, through which PAu is expressed, and which ensure, strengthen and lastingly consecrate the effect of a PA, are more likely to be recognized as legitimate, i.e. have greater symbolic force (by 2.1.2.4), when they are applied to groups or classes for whom these sanctions are more likely to be confirmed by the sanctions of the market on which the economic and social value of the products of the different PAs is determined (the reality principle or law of the market).

Gloss 1: The recognition a group or class objectively accords a peda- gogic agency is always (whatever the psychological or ideological varia- tions of the corresponding experience) a function of the degree to which the market value and symbolic value of its members depend on

their transformation and consecration by that agency's PA. It is therefore understandable that the medieval nobility should have had little
interest in Scholastic education and that, in contrast, the ruling classes
of the Greek city-states should have had recourse to the services of the
Sophists or rhetors; and again, that in modern societies the middle
classes, and more precisely those middle-class fractions whose ascension
most directly depends on the School, differ from the working classes by
an academic docility which is expressed in, among other things, their
particular sensitivity to the symbolic effect of punishments or rewards
and more precisely to the social-certification effect of academic qualifications.

Gloss 2: The more unified the market on which the value of the
products of the different PAs is determined, the more the groups or
classes which have undergone a PA inculcating a dominated cultural
arbitrary are likely to have the valuelessness of their cultural attainment
brought home to them both by the anonymous sanctions of the labour
market and by the symbolic sanctions of the cultural market (e.g. the
matrimonial market), not to mention academic verdicts, which are
always charged with economic and symbolic implications. These calls to
order tend to produce in them, if not explicit recognition of the
dominant culture as the legitimate culture, then at least an insidious
awareness of the cultural unworthiness of their own acquirements.
Thus, by unifying the market on which the value of the products of the
different PAs is determined, bourgeois society (as compared, for
example, with feudal society) has multiplied the opportunities for
subjecting the products of the dominated PAs to the evaluative criteria
of the legitimate culture, thereby affirming and confirming its dominance in the symbolic order. In such a social formation, the relation
between the dominated PAs and the dominant PA can thus be under
stood by analogy with the relation set up, in a dualistic economy,
between the dominant mode of production and the dominated modes
of production (e.g. traditional agriculture and crafts), whose products
are subjected to the laws of a market dominated by the products of the

capitalist mode of production. At the same time, the unification of the symbolic market, however far advanced, in no way prevents the dominated PAs from imposing recognition of their legitimacy, at least for a time and in certain areas of practice, on those who undergo them, although their products are destined to discover that the cultural arbitrary whose worth they have had to recognize in order to acquire it is worthless on an economic or symbolic market dominated by the cultural arbitrary of the dominant classes (e.g. the conflicts accompanying acculturation into the dominant culture, whether for the colonized intellectual – the man the Algerians call *m'turni* – or for the intellectual of dominated-class origin, condemned to reassess paternal authority, with all the renunciations, repressions or accommodations this involves).

2.3.1.3. The more directly a pedagogic agency reproduces, in the arbitrary content that it inculcates, the cultural arbitrary of the group or class which delegates to it its PAu, the less need it has to affirm and justify its own legitimacy.

Gloss: In this respect, the PA exerted in a traditional society contitutes a limiting case since, in relaying an undifferentiated and therefore indisputable and undisputed social authority, it is accompanied neither by an ideological justification of PAu as such, nor by technical reflexion on the instruments of PA. The same is true when a pedagogic agency has the principal if not sole function of reproducing the lifestyle of a dominant class or a fraction of the dominant class (e.g. the training of the young nobleman by farming him out to a noble household – 'fosterage' – or, to a lesser extent, the making of the English gentleman in traditional Oxford).

2.3.2. Insofar as the success of any PA is a function of the degree to which the receivers recognize the PAu of the pedagogic agency and the degree to which they have mastered the cultural code used in pedagogic communication, the success of any given PA in any given social forma-

tion is a function of the system of relations between the cultural arbitrary imposed by that PA, the dominant cultural arbitrary in that social formation, and the cultural arbitrary inculcated by the earliest phase of upbringing within the groups or classes from which those undergoing the PA originate (by 2.1.2, 2.1.3, 2.2.2 and 2.3).

Gloss: It is sufficient to situate the different historical forms of PA, or the different PAs simultaneously operating in a social formation, by reference to these three principles of variation, in order to explain the likelihood of these PAs and the cultures they impose being recognized by groups or classes differently situated with respect to the pedagogic agencies and with respect to the dominant groups or classes. It goes without saying that the adequacy with which the characteristics of a PA are accounted for by reference to these three dimensions rises with the degree of integration of the different PAs of the same social formation into an objectively hierarchized system, i.e. rises in proportion as the market on which the economic and symbolic value of the product of a dominated PA is constituted, is more fully unified, so that the product of a dominated PA is that much more likely to be subjected to the principles of evaluation reproduced by the dominant PA.

2.3.2.1. In any given social formation, the differential success of the dominant PA as between the groups or classes is a function of (1) the pedagogic ethos *proper to a group or class, i.e. the system of dispositions towards that PA and the agency exerting it, defined as the product of the internalization of (a) the value which the dominant PA confers by its sanctions on the products of the different family PAs and (b) the value which, by their objective sanctions, the different social markets confer on the products of the dominant PA according to the group or class from which they come; and (2)* cultural capital, *i.e. the cultural goods transmitted by the different family PAs, whose value* qua *cultural capital varies with the distance between the cultural arbitrary imposed by the dominant PA and the cultural arbitrary inculcated by the family PA within the different groups or classes (by 2.2.2, 2.3.1.2 and 2.3.2).*

2.3.3. Insofar as it derives its PAu from a delegation of authority, PA tends to produce in those who undergo it the relation which members of a group or class have to their culture, i.e. misrecognition of the objective truth of that culture as a cultural arbitrary (ethnocentrism).

2.3.3.1. In any given social formation, the system of PAs, insofar as it is subject to the effect of domination by the dominant PA, tends to reproduce, both in the dominant and in the dominated classes, misrecognition of the truth of the legitimate culture as the dominant cultural arbitrary, whose reproduction contributes towards reproducing the power relations (by 1.3.1).

3. PEDAGOGIC WORK

3. Insofar as it is the arbitrary imposition of a cultural arbitrary presupposing PAu, i.e. a delegation of authority (by 1 and 2), which requires the pedagogic agency to reproduce the principles of the cultural arbitrary which a group or class imposes as worthy of reproduction both by its very existence and by the fact of delegating to an agency the authority needed in order to reproduce it (by 2.3 and 2.3.1), PA entails pedagogic work *(PW), a process of inculcation which must last long enough to produce a durable training, i.e. a* habitus, *the product of internalization of the principles of a cultural arbitrary capable of perpetuating itself after PA has ceased and thereby of perpetuating in practices the principles of the internalized arbitrary.*

Gloss 1: As an action which has to last a certain time in order to produce a lasting habitus, i.e. an action of imposing and inculcating an arbitrary which can be fully achieved only through PW, PA is distinguished from discontinuous and extraordinary actions of symbolic violence like those of the prophet, the intellectual 'creator' or the sorcerer. Such actions of symbolic imposition are able to bring about the profound and lasting transformation of those they reach only to the extent that they are prolonged in an action of continuous inculcation, i.e. in a process of PW (sacerdotal preaching and commentary or professorial commentary on the 'classics'). The conditions required for the performance of PW ('the educator', says Marx, 'himself needs to be educated') are such that every pedagogic agency is characterized by a longer structural duration, other things being equal, than other agencies exercising a power of symbolic violence, because it tends to reproduce, so far as its relative autonomy allows, the conditions in which the reproducers were produced, i.e. the conditions of its own reproduction: for example, the extremely slow tempo of the transformation of PA, whether in the traditionalism of family PA which, entrusted with the earliest phase of upbringing, tends to realize more fully the tendencies of all PA and is thus able, even in modern societies, to fulfil the role of a conservatory of inherited traditions; or in the inertia of educational institutions, whose essential function always leads them to self-reproduce as unchanged as possible, like traditional societies.

Gloss 2: Education, considered as the process through which a cultural arbitrary is historically reproduced through the medium of the production of the habitus productive of practices conforming with that cultural arbitrary (i.e. by the transmission of a training *[formation]* capable of durably patterning and 'informing' the receivers), is the equivalent, in the cultural order, of the transmission of genetic capital in the biological order. If the habitus is the analogue of genetic capital, then the inculcation which defines the performance of PA is the analogue of generation, in that it transmits information generative of analogous information.

3.1. Insofar as it is a prolonged process of inculcation producing a ;urable training, i.e. producers of practices conforming with the principles of the cultural arbitrary of the groups or classes which delegate to PA the PAu needed for its establishment and continuation, PW tends to reproduce the social conditions of the production of that

cultural arbitrary, i.e. the objective structures of which it is the product, through the mediation of the habitus, defined as the principle generating practices which reproduce the objective structures.

3.1.1. The specific productivity of PW is objectively measured by the degree to which it produces its essential effect of inculcation, i.e. its effect of reproduction.

3.1.1.1. The specific productivity of PW, i.e. the degree to which it manages to inculcate in the legitimate addressees the cultural arbitrary which it is mandated to reproduce, is measured by the degree to which the habitus it produces is durable, *i.e. capable of durably generating practices conforming with the principles of the inculcated arbitrary.*

Gloss: The specific effect of PA may be contrasted with the effect of political power in terms of their temporal range, in which the structural duration of the corresponding powers of imposition is expressed: PW is capable of perpetuating the arbitrary it inculcates more lastingly than political coercion (except when political power itself resorts to PW, i.e. a specific educative programme). Religious power lastingly informs practices to the extent that it is incarnated in a church performing PW directly or indirectly, i.e. through the medium of the family (Christian upbringing). In other words, the power of symbolic violence of the PA which has recourse to PW is long-term, in contrast to the authority of political power, which is always confronted with the problem of its own perpetuation (succession).

3.1.1.2. The specific productivity of PW, i.e. the degree to which it manages to inculcate in the legitimate addressees the cultural arbitrary it is mandated to reproduce, is measured by the degree to which the habitus it produces is transposable, *i.e. capable of generating practices conforming with the principles of the inculcated arbitrary in a greater number of different fields.*

Gloss: Thus, the hold of a religious power is measured by the degree to which the habitus produced by the PW of the corresponding pedagogic agencies generates practices conforming with the inculcated arbitrary in areas remote from those expressly regulated by doctrine, such as economic conduct or political choices. Similarly, the 'habit-forming force' (Panofsky) of Scholastic education may be seen in the effects it produces in the structure of the medieval cathedral or the graphical layout of manuscripts.

3.1.1.3. The specific productivity of PW, i.e. the degree to which it manages to inculcate in the legitimate addressees the cultural arbitrary it is mandated to reproduce, is measured by the degree to which the habitus it produces is exhaustive, *i.e. the completeness with which it reproduces the principles of the cultural arbitrary of a group or class in the practices it generates.*

Gloss: Although the congruence of the three measures of the reproduction effect is not logically necessary, the theory of the habitus as the principle unifying and generating practices enables us to understand why the durability, transposability and exhaustivity of a habitus in fact prove to be closely linked.

3.1.2. The delegation which establishes a PA implies, in addition to a delimitation of the content inculcated, a definition of the mode of inculcation (the legitimate mode of inculcation) and of the length of inculcation (the legitimate training period), which define the degree of completion of PW considered necessary and sufficient to produce the accomplished form of the habitus, i.e. the degree of cultural attainment (the degree of legitimate competence) by which a group or class recognizes the accomplished man.

3.1.2.1. In any given social formation, the delegation which establishes the dominant PA implies, in addition to a delimitation of the content inculcated, a dominant definition of the mode and length of inculcation which define the degree of completion of of PW considered necessary and sufficient to produce the accomplished form of the habitus, i.e. the degree of cultural attainment (the degree of legitimate competence in legitimate culture) by which not only the dominant but also the dominated classes tend to recognize the 'cultivated man' and against which the products of the dominated PAs, i.e. the different forms of the accomplished man as defined by the culture of the dominated groups or classes, come to be measured objectively.

3.1.3. Insofar as it is a prolonged process of inculcation producing a durable, transposable habitus, i.e. inculcating in all its legitimate addressees a system of (partially or totally identical) schemes of perception, thought, appreciation and action, PW contributes towards producing and reproducing the intellectual and moral integration of the group or class on whose behalf it is carried on.

Gloss: Only when it is seen that a group's integration rests on the (total or partial) identity of the habitus inculcated by PW, i.e. when the principle of the homology of practices is located in the total or partial identity of the practice-generating grammars, is it possible to escape from the naiveties of the social philosophies of consensus. Such sociologies, in reducing group integration to the possession of a common repertoire of representations, are unable, for example, to apprehend the unity and the integrative function of practices or opinions that are phenomenally different or even contradictory but produced by the same generative habitus (e.g. the style of the artistic productions of a determinate epoch and class). Moreover, the same habitus which engenders a particular practice can equally well engender the opposite when its principle is the logic of dissimilation (e.g. in apprentice intellectuals, who are inclined to play the intellectual game of self-demarcation in a particularly direct fashion, the same privileged-class habitus can generate radically opposed political or aesthetic opinions, whose deep unity is betrayed only in the modality of their declarations of position or their practices).[4]

3.1.3.1. Insofar as it is a prolonged process of inculcation producing internalization of the principles of a cultural arbitrary in the form of a durable, transposable habitus, capable of generating practices conforming with those principles outside of and beyond any express regulation or any explicit reminding of the rule, PW enables the group or class which delegates its authority to PA to produce and reproduce its intellectual and moral integration without resorting to external repression or, in particular, physical coercion.

Gloss: PW is a substitute for physical contraint: physical repression (internment in a prison or asylum) is brought in to sanction the failures of internalization of a cultural arbitrary. And it is a profitable substitute: although (and perhaps because) it is more masked, PW is in the long run at least as efficacious as physical constraint — which can continue to produce an effect once it has ceased to be applied only inasmuch as it always tends to exert an additional, symbolic, effect (which is to say, in passing, that the emperor is never naked and that only an innocently idealist conception of the intrinsic force of justice, founded on the implicit dissociation of force from the legitimacy which it necessarily engenders, could lead one to speak, like Russell and others after him, of 'naked power'). Thus PW, insofar as it secures the perpetuation of the effects of symbolic violence, tends to produce a permanent disposition to give, in every situation (e.g. in matters of fertility, economic choices or political commitment), the right response (i.e. the one laid down by cultural arbitrariness, and no other) to symbolic stimuli emanating from the agencies invested with the PAu which has made possible the PW responsible for the habitus (e.g. the effects of sacerdotal preaching or papal bulls as symbolic reactivations of the Christian upbringing).

3.2. Insofar as it is a transformative action tending to inculcate a training, a system of durable, transposable dispositions, PW, which cannot be exercised without PAu, has the effect of irreversibly confirming and consecrating PAu, i.e. the legitimacy of PA and of the cultural arbitrary·it inculcates, by masking more and more completely, through the success of the inculcation of the arbitrary, the arbitrariness of the inculcation and of the culture inculcated.

Gloss: To see a vicious circle in the presence of PAu at the beginning and end of PA is to fail to realize that, in the order of genesis (biography and the succession of the generations) the PAu commanded by every PA that is exercised breaks the pedagogic circle to which any PA without PAu would be condemned, only to lock the recipient of the PW thus made possible ever more firmly in the circle of (group or class) ethnocentrism. A paradigmatic image of this paradox is seen in the circle of baptism and confirmation: the profession of faith made at the age of reason is supposed to validate retrospectively the undertaking given at the time of baptism, which committed the infant to an education necessarily leading up this profession of faith. Thus, as it is accomplished, PW produces more and more fully the objective conditions for· misrecognition of cultural arbitrariness, i.e. the conditions for subjective experience of the cultural arbitrary as necessary in the sense of 'natural'. The man who deliberates on his culture is already cultivated and the questions of the man who thinks he is questioning the principles of his upbringing still have their roots in his upbringing. The Cartesian myth of innate reason, i.e. of a natural culture or cultivated nature pre-existing nurture, the retrospective illusion necessarily inscribed in education as an arbitrary imposition capable of imposing ignorance of its arbitrariness, is just one more magical solution of the circle of PAu: 'Since we have all been children before being men, and since it has long befallen us to be governed by our appetites and our preceptors, who were often contrary the one to another and who none of them perhaps counselled us for the best, it is nigh impossible that our judgements should be as pure or as solid as they would have been had we had full use of our reason from the moment of our birth and we never been led but by reason alone.' Thus one escapes from the circle of inevitably confirmed baptism only to offer sacrifice to the mystique of the 'second birth', whose philosphical transcript is perhaps seen in the transcendentalist phantasm of the reconquest by the sheer power of thought, of a thought leaving nothing unthought.

3.2.1. Insofar as it is a prolonged process of inculcation producing more and more complete misrecognition of the twofold arbitrariness of PA, i.e. recognition of the PAu of the pedagogic agency and recognition of the legitimacy of the product which it offers, PW produces the legitimacy of the product and, inseparably from this, the legitimate need for this produce qua legitimate product, by producing the legitimate consumer, i.e. one equipped with the social definition of the legitimate product and the disposition to consume it in the legitimate manner.

Gloss 1: Only the concept of PW can break the circle in which one is trapped when one forgets that a 'cultural need' is a cultivated need, i.e. when one severs it from the social conditions of its production. Thus, religious or cultural devotion, which engenders religious or aesthetic practices such as assiduous church-going or museum-going, is the product of the PAu of the family (and secondarily of the institution, the Church or School), which, in the process of a biography, breaks the circle of 'cultural need' by consecrating religious or cultural goods of salvation as worthy of being pursued, and by producing the need for these goods by the mere fact of imposing their consumption. Since we know that the need to frequent museums or churches is conditional on frequenting museums and churches, and that assiduous frequentation supposes the need to frequent, it is clear that breaking the circle of the first entry into a church or museum requires a predisposition towards frequentation which, short of a miraculous predestination, can only be the family disposition to cause frequenting by frequenting sufficiently to produce a lasting disposition to frequent.[5]

Genesis amnesia leads to a specific form of the Cartesian illusion in the case of the cult of art. The myth of an innate taste owing nothing to the constraints of apprenticeship because wholly given at birth transmutes the determinisms capable of producing both determined choices and ignorance of that determination into the free choices of a primal free will.

Gloss 2: If it is not seen that PW produces indissolubly both the legitimate product as such, i.e. as an object worthy of being materially or symbolically consumed (i.e. venerated, adored, respected, admired, etc.), and the propensity to consume this object materially or symbolically, one is condemned to interminable speculation as to the priority of the veneration or the venerable, the adoration or the adorable, the respect or the respectable, the admiration or the admirable, etc. that is, to oscillate between trying to deduce the dispositions towards the object from the intrinsic properties of the object and trying to reduce the properties of the object to the properties conferred on it by the dispositions of the subject. In reality, PW produces agents endowed with the adequate disposition who can apply it only to certain objects; and objects which appear to the agents produced by PW as calling forth or demanding the adequate disposition.

3.2.2. Insofar as it is a prolonged process of inculcation producing more and more complete misrecognition of the twofold arbitrariness of PA, PW tends, the more it is accomplished, to conceal more and more completely the objective truth of the habitus as the internalization of the principles of a cultural arbitrary which is more accomplished the more the work of inculcation is accomplished.

Gloss: It is clear why the social definition of excellence always tends to make reference to 'naturalness', i.e. to a modality of practice entailing a degree of accomplishment of PW capable of effacing awareness not only of the twofold arbitrariness of the PA of which it is the product, but also of all that accomplished practice owes to PW (e.g. Greek *arete,* the ease of the *honnête homme,* the *sarr* of the Kabyle man of honour, or the 'anti-academic academicism' of the Chinese mandarin).

3.2.2.1. Insofar as it is a prolonged process of inculcation producing

*more and more complete misrecognition of the twofold arbitrariness of
PA, i.e. inter alia, misrecognition of the delimitation constitutive of the
cultural arbitrary which it inculcates, PW produces more and more
complete misrecognition of the ethical and intellectual limitations
which are correlative with the internalizing of that delimitation (ethical
and logical ethnocentrism).*

Gloss: This means that the PW which produces the habitus – a system
of schemes of thought, perception, appreciation and action – produces
misrecognition of the limitations implied by this system, so that the
efficacy of the ethical and logical programming it produces is enhanced
by misrecognition of the inherent limits of this programming, a misrecognition which is a function of the degree of completion of the PW.
The agents produced by PW would not be so totally the prisoners of the
limitations which the cultural arbitrary imposes on their thought and
practice, were it not that, contained within these limits by self-discipline
and self-censorship (the more unconscious to the extent that their
principles have been internalized), they live out their thought and
practice in the illusion of freedom and universality.

*3.2.2.1.1. In any given social formation, the PW through which the
dominant PA is carried on succeeds all the better in imposing the
legitimacy of the dominant culture the more it is accomplished, i.e. the
more completely it succeeds in imposing misrecognition of the dominant arbitrary not only on the legitimate addresses of the PA but also
on the members of the dominated groups or classes (the dominant
ideology of the legitimate culture as the only authentic culture, i.e. as
universal culture).*

*3.2.2.1.2. In any given social formation, the PW through which the
dominant PA is carried on always has a function of keeping order, i.e.
of reproducing the structure of the power relations between the groups
or classes, inasmuch as, by inculcation or exclusion, it tends to impose
recognition of the legitimacy of the dominant culture on the members*

of the dominated groups or classes, and to make them internalize, to a variable extent, disciplines and censorships which best serve the material and symbolic interests of the dominant groups or classes when they take the form of self-discipline and self-censorship.

3.2.2.1.3. In any given social formation, because the PW through which the dominant PA is carried on tends to impose recognition of the legitimacy of the dominant culture on the members of the dominated groups or classes, it tends at the same time to impose on them, by inculcation or exclusion, recognition of the illegitimacy of their own cultural arbitrary.

Gloss: Contrary to an impoverished conception of the symbolic violence one class exerts on another through the medium of education (a conception paradoxically common to those who denounce an ideological domination reduced to the image of forced feeding and those who affect to deplore the imposition of culture 'not made for them' on children of 'humble origin'), a dominant PA tends not so much to inculcate the information constituting the dominant culture (if only because PW has a lower specific productivity and a shorter duration when applied to groups or classes lower down the social scale) as to inculcate the fait accompli of the legitimacy of the dominant culture. It may do so by inducing those excluded from the ranks of the legitimate addressees (whether before formal education, as in most societies, or during it) to internalize the legitimacy of their exclusion; by making those it relegates to second-order teaching recognize the inferiority of this teaching and its audience; or by inculcating, through submission to academic disciplines and adherence to cultural hierarchies, a transposable, generalized disposition with regard to social disciplines and hierarchies.

In short, in every case, the major thrust of the imposition of recognition of the dominant culture as legitimate culture and, by the same token, of the illegitimacy of the cultures of the dominated groups or classes, comes from exclusion, which perhaps has most symbolic force when it assumes the guise of self-exclusion. It is· as if the legitimate duration of the PW conceded to the dominated classes was objectively defined as the necessary and sufficient length of time for the fact of exclusion to take on its full symbolic force, i.e. appear to those undergoing it as the sanction on their cultural unworthiness, and for ignorance of the law of legitimate culture to be no excuse. One of the least noticed effects of compulsory schooling is that it succeeds in obtaining from the dominated classes a recognition of legitimate knowledge and know-how (e.g. in law, medicine, technology, entertainment or art), entailing the devaluation of the knowledge and know-how they effectively command (e.g. customary law, home medicine, craft techniques, folk art and language and all the lore handed on in the 'hedge-school of the witch and the shepherd', as Michelet puts it) and so providing a market for material and especially symbolic products of which the means of production (not least, higher education) are virtually monopolized by the dominant classes (e.g. clinical diagnosis, legal advice, the culture industry, etc.).

3.3. Insofar as PW is an irreversible process producing, in the time required for inculcation, an irreversible disposition, i.e. a disposition which cannot itself be repressed or transformed except by an irreversible process producing in turn a new irreversible disposition, primary PA (the earliest phase of upbringing), which is carried out by PW without any antecedent (primary PW), produces a primary habitus, characteristic of a group or class, which is the basis for the subsequent formation of any other habitus.

Gloss: Husserl discovers the self-evident fact of the empirical genealogy of consciousness: 'I have had the education of a German, not that of a Chinaman. But also that of a small-town dweller, in the family and school of a petty-bourgeois, not that of a great landowner, brought up in a cadet school.' And he observes that while one can always acquire a theoretic knowledge of another culture and even remake one's education along the lines of that culture (e.g. 'by trying to learn the series of courses taught at cadet school' or by 'remaking one's education Chinese-style'), this appropriation of China is not possible in the full sense, any more than 'one can appropriate the Junker type in the full sense, in its fully concrete being'.

3.3.1. The specific degree of productivity of any PW other than primary PW (secondary PW) is a function of the distance between the habitus it tends to inculcate (i.e. the cultural arbitrary it imposes) and the habitus inculcated by the previous phases of PW and ultimately by primary PW (i.e. the initial cultural arbitrary).

Gloss 1: The success of all school education, and more generally of all secondary PW, depends fundamentally on the education previously accomplished in the earliest years of life, even and especially when the educational system denies this primacy in its ideology and practice by making the school career a history with no pre-history: we know that through all the skill-learning processes of everyday life, and particularly through the acquisition of the mother tongue or the manipulation of kinship terms and relationships, logical dispositions are mastered in their practical state. These dispositions, more or less complex, more or less elaborated symbolically, depending on the group or class, predispose children unequally towards symbolic mastery of the operations implied as much in a mathematical demonstration as in decoding a work of art.

Gloss 2: Equally one sees the naivety of posing the problem of the differential efficacy of the various agencies of symbolic violence (e.g. family, school, modern media) while neglecting — like the devotees of the cult of the omnipotence of schooling or the prophets of the all-powerfulness of the mass media — the irreversibility of learning processes. Because learning is an irreversible process, the habitus acquired within the family forms the basis of the reception and assimilation of the classroom message, and the habitus acquired at school conditions the level of reception and degree of assimilation of the messages produced and diffused by the culture industry, and, more generally, of any intellectual or semi-intellectual message.

3.3.1.1. Any given mode of inculcation is characterized (in the respect considered in 3.3.1) by the position it occupies between (1) the mode of inculcation aiming to bring about the complete substitution of one habitus for another (conversion) and (2) the mode of inculcation aiming purely and simply to confirm the primary habitus (maintenance or reinforcement).

Gloss: The essential characteristics of secondary PW seeking to bring about a radical conversion *(metanoia)* may be deduced from the fact that such operations are required to organize the social conditions of their performance with a view to killing off the 'old man' and en-gendering the new habitus ex nihilo. Consider, for example, the tendency to pedagogic formalism, i.e. the flaunting of the arbitrariness of the inculcation as arbitrariness for its own sake, and more generally the imposition of rules for rules' sake, which is the main feature of the mode of inculcating proper to the PAs of conversion: e.g. exercises of piety and self-mortification (Pascal's *"abêtissez-vous"*), military drill, etc. In this respect, 'total' institutions (barracks, convents, prisons, asylums, boarding schools) unambiguously demonstrate the decul-turating and reculturating techniques required by PW seeking to produce a habitus as similar as possible to that produced in the earliest phase of life, while having to reckon with a pre-existing habitus. At the other extreme, the traditional institutions for young ladies of good family represent the paradigmatic form of all institutions which, thanks to the mechanisms of selection and self-selection, address themselves exclusively to agents endowed with a habitus as little different as possible from the one to be produced, and can therefore content themselves with ostentatiously organizing all the appearances of really effective training (e.g. the *Ecole Nationale d'Administration*). If, in all periods when the ruling classes entrust the earliest phase of their children's upbringing to agents from the lower classes, the educational institutions reserved for them have all the characteristics of the total institution, this is because they are obliged to effect nothing less than a re-education (e.g. boarding-school life in the Jesuit colleges or in the nineteenth-century German and Russian gymnasia).

3.3.1.2. Given that the primary habitus inculcated by primary PW is the basis for the subsequent formation of any other habitus, the degree of specific productivity of any phase of secondary PW is measured, in this respect, by the degree to which the system of the means required for carrying out the PW (the mode of inculcation) objectively takes account of the distance between the habitus it aims to inculcate and the habitus produced by previous PW

Gloss: Secondary PW is that much more productive when, taking into account the degree to which the addressees of the pedagogic message possess the code of the message, it creates more fully the social conditions for communication by methodically organizing exercises designed to ensure accelerated assimilation of the code of transmission and, therefore, accelerated inculcation of the habitus.

3.3.1.3. The degree of traditionalism of a mode of inculcation is measured by the degree to which it is objectively organized by reference to a limited audience of legitimate addressees, i.e. the degree to which the success of the secondary PW presupposes that the addressees be equipped with the adequate habitus (i.e. the pedagogic ethos and cultural capital proper to the groups or classes whose cultural arbitrary it reproduces).

3.3.1.3.1. Because, in any given social formation, the dominant mode of inculcation tends to correspond to the interests of the dominant classes, i.e. the legitimate addressees, the differential productivity of the dominant PW according to the groups or classes on whom it is exerted tends to be a function of the distance between the primary habitus inculcated by primary PW within the different groups or classes and the habitus inculcated by the dominant PW (i.e. the extent to which education or acculturation is re-education or deculturation, depending on the group or class).

3.3.2. Given (1) that the making explicit and the formalizing of the principles at work in a practice, i.e. symbolic mastery of that practice, must logically and chronologically follow practical mastery of those principles, i.e. that symbolic mastery is never its own foundation; and given (2) that symbolic mastery is irreducible to the practical mastery from which it proceeds and to which it nonetheless adds its own effect: it follows (a) that all secondary PW produces secondary practices irreducible to the primary practices of which it gives symbolic mastery, and (b) that the secondary mastery which it produces presupposes a previous mastery which is that much closer to simple practical mastery of practices, the earlier this secondary PW comes in the biographical order.

Gloss: The teaching of grammar in school does not, strictly speaking, inculcate a new linguistic practice-generating grammar: the child must already possess in their practical state the principles he learns to subject to logical scrutiny (e.g. conjugations, declensions, syntactic constructions); but in acquiring the theoretic codification of what he does, he acquires the capacity to do it more consciously and systematically (cf. Piaget and Vygotsky). This transformation is the analogue, in the biographical order, of the historical process by which customary law or traditional justice *(Kadi Justiz)* is transformed into rational, i.e. codified, law derived from explicit principles (cf. more generally Weber's analyses of the process of rationalization in religion, art, political theory, etc.). We have similarly seen that the success of the prophet's action of symbolic imposition is a function of the degree to which he manages to make explicit and systematize the principles which the group he addresses already holds in a practical state.

3.3.2.1. Any given mode of inculcation, i.e. the system of the means by which the internalization of a cultural arbitrary is produced, is characterized (in the respect considered in 3.3.2) by the position it occupies between (1) the mode of inculcation producing a habitus by the unconscious inculcation of principles which manifest themselves only in their practical state, within the practice that is imposed (implicit pedagogy), and (2) the mode of inculcation producing a habitus by the inculcation, methodically organized as such, of articulated and even formalized principles (explicit pedagogy).

Gloss: It would be a mistake to suppose it possible to hierarchize these two opposed modes of inculcation according to their specific productivity, since this efficiency, measured by the durability and transposability of the habitus produced, cannot be defined independently of the content inculcated and the social functions which the PW in question fulfils in a determinate social formation. Thus, implicit pedagogy is doubtless the most efficient way of transmitting traditional, undifferentiated, 'total' knowledge (the assimilation of styles or knacks), in that it requires the disciple or apprentice to identify with the physical person of the more experienced 'master' or 'companion', at the cost of a thorough self-remission which prohibits analysis of the principles of the exemplary conduct; on the other hand, an implicit pedagogy which, presupposing prior attainment, is per se ineffectual when applied to agents lacking that prerequisite, can be very 'profitable' for the dominant classes when the corresponding PA is performed in a system of PAs dominated by the dominant PA and thereby contributes to cultural reproduction, and through it, to social reproduction, by enabling the possessors of the prerequisite cultural capital to continue to monpolize that capital.

3.3.2.2. Given that all secondary PW has the essential effect of producing practices irreducible to the practices of which it gives symbolic mastery, the degree of specific productivity of any phase of secondary PW is measured in this respect by the degree to which the system of the means required for carrying out the PW (the mode of inculcation) is objectively organized with a view to ensuring, by explicit inculcation of codified formal principles, the formal transferability of the habitus.

3.3.2.3. The degrees of traditionalism of any mode of inculcation is measured by the degree to which the means required for carrying out PW are reduced to the practices which express the habitus and which tend, by the mere fact of being performed repeatedly by agents invested with PAu, to reproduce directly a habitus defined by practical transferability.

Gloss: PW is that much more traditional to the extent that (1) it is less clearly delimited as a specific, autonomous practice, and (2) is exerted by agencies whose functions are more comprehensive and more undifferentiated, i.e. the more completely it is reduced to a familiarizing process in which the master transmits unconsciously, through exemplary conduct, principles he has never mastered consciously, to a receiver who internalizes them unconsciously. In the limiting case, seen in traditional societies, the whole group and the whole environment — that is, the system of the material conditions of existence, insofar as they are endowed with the symbolic significance which gives them a power of imposition — exert an anonymous, diffuse PA without specialized agents or specified moments (e.g. the forming of the Christian habitus in the Middle Ages, through the 'catechism' of the calendar of feasts and the ordering of everyday space, or the devotional 'book' of symbolic objects).

3.3.2.3.1. In any given social formation, the primary PW to which the members of the different groups or classes are subjected rests more completely on practical transferability the more rigorously the material conditions of their existence subject them to the imperatives of practice, tending thereby to prevent the formation and development of the aptitude for symbolic mastery of practice.

Gloss: If one accepts that PW is that much closer to explicit pedagogy to the extent that it resorts to a greater degree of verbalization and classificatory conceptualization, then it can be seen that primary PW prepares that much better for secondary PW based on explicit pedagogy when exerted within a group or class whose material conditions of existence allow them to stand more completely aside from practice, in other words to 'neutralize' in imagination or reflection the vital urgencies which thrust a pragmatic disposition on the dominated classes. All the more so because the agents responsible for primary PW have themselves been very unequally prepared for symbolic mastery by secondary PW and are therefore very unequally capable of orienting primary PW towards the verbalization, formulation and conceptualization of practical mastery which are demanded by secondary PW (e.g. the limiting case of continuity between family PW and school PW in the families of teachers or intellectuals).

3.3.3. Given the delegation on which it is based, the dominant PA tends to dispense more completely with explicit inculcation of the prerequisites of its specific productivity, the more completely the legitimate addressees have mastered the dominant culture, i.e. the greater the proportion of what it is mandated to inculcate (capital and ethos) that has already been inculcated by the primary PW of the dominant groups or classes.

3.3.3.1. In a social formation in which, both in pedagogic practice and in all social practices. the dominant cultural arbitrary subordinates practical mastery to symbolic mastery of practices, the dominant PW tends to dispense with explicit inculcation of the principles. giving symbolic mastery, the more completely practical mastery of the principles giving symbolic mastery has already been inculcated in the legitimate addressees by the primary PW of the dominant groups or classes.

Gloss: Contrary to what is suggested by certain psychogenetic theories which describe intelligence development as a universal process of unilinear transformation of sensorimotor mastery into symbolic mastery, the respective primary PW of the different groups or classes produces primary systems of dispositions which differ not merely as different degrees of explicitness of the same practice but also as so many types of practical mastery unequally predisposing their bearers to acquire the particular type of symbolic mastery that is privileged by the dominant cultural arbitrary.

Thus, a practical mastery oriented towards the manipulation of things, with the correlative relation to words, is less favourable to theoretic mastery of the rules of literate verbalization than a practical mastery directed towards the manipulation of words and towards the relation to words and things which is fostered by the primacy of word manipulation.

It is precisely when its legitimate public is made up of individuals equipped by primary PW with a verbally-oriented practical mastery, that secondary PW which is mandated to inculcate above all the mastery of a language and of a relation to language can, paradoxically, content itself with an implicit pedagogy, especially as regards language, because it can count on a habitus containing, in practical form, the predisposition to use language in accordance with a literate relation to language (e.g. the structural affinity between teaching in the humanities and bourgeois primary PA). Conversely, in secondary PW which has the declared function of inculcating practical mastery of manual techniques (e.g. the teaching of technology in institutions of technical education), the mere fact of using theoretic discourse to make explicit the principles of techniques of which working-class children have practical mastery is sufficient to cast the knacks and tricks of the trade into the illegitimacy of makeshift approximation, just as 'general education' reduces their language to jargon, slang or gibberish. This is one of the most potent effects of the theoretic discourse which sets an unbridgeable gulf between the holder of the principles (e.g. the engineer) and the mere practitioner (e.g. the technician).

3.3.3.2. Given that, in the type of social formation defined in 3.3.3.1, the dominant PW which uses a traditional mode of inculcation (in the sense of 3.3.1.3 and 3.3.2.3) has a specific productivity that much lower when it is exerted on groups or classes carrying out primary PW more remote from the dominant primary PW which inculcates, inter alia, a predominantly verbal practical mastery, such PW tends in and by its very exercise to produce the delimitation of its really possible addressees, excluding the different groups or classes more rapidly the more completely they lack the capital and ethos objectively pre-supposed by its mode of inculcation.

3.3.3.3. Given that, in the type of social formation defined in 3.3.3.1, the dominant secondary PW, which uses a traditional mode of inculcation and is defined as not fully producing the conditions for its own productivity, can fulfil its eliminatory function merely by default, such PW tends to produce not only the delimitation of its really possible addressees, but also misrecognition of the mechanisms of delimitation, i.e. tends to bring about recognition of its actual addressees as the legitimate addressees and of the length of the inculcation actually undergone by the different groups or classes as the legitimate length of inculcation.

Gloss: While every dominant PA entails a delimitation of its legitimate addressees, exclusion is often carried out by mechanisms external to the agency performing the PW, whether by the more or less direct effect of economic mechanisms or by customary or juridical prescription (e.g. the numerus clausus as an authoritarian restriction of the addressees by ethnic or other criteria). A PA which eliminates certain categories of receivers merely by the effectivity of the mode of inculcation character-istic of its mode of inculcation conceals the arbitrariness of the de facto delimitation of its public better and more fully than any other, thereby imposing more subtly the legitimacy of its products and hierarchies (the sociodicy function).[6] The museum, which delimits its public and legitimates their social standing simply by the effect of its 'level of transmission', i.e. by the sheer fact of presupposing possession of the cultural code required for decoding the objects displayed, may be seen as the limiting case towards which tends all PW founded on the implicit prerequisite of possession of the conditions of its productivity. The action of the mechanisms which tend to ensure, quasi automatically — i.e. in accordance with the laws governing the relations between the different groups or classes and the dominant pedagogic agency — the exclusion of certain categories of receivers (self-elimination, deferred elimination, etc.), can moreover be masked by the fact that the social function of elimination is concealed under the overt function of selection which the pedagogic agency performs within the set of legitimate addressees (e.g. the ideological function of the examination).

3.3.3.4. Given that, in the type of social formation defined in 3.3.3.1, the dominant secondary PW which uses a traditional mode of inculcation does not explicitly inculcate the prerequisites of its specific productivity, such PW tends, by its very exercise, to produce the legitimacy of that mode of possession of the prerequisite acquirements on which the dominant classes have a monopoly because they monopolize the legitimate mode of inculcation, i.e. inculcation of the principles of the legitimate culture in their practical state through primary PW (the cultivated relation to legitimate culture as a relation of familiarity).

3.3.3.5. Given that, in the type of social formation defined in 3.3.3.1, the dominant secondary PW which uses a traditional mode of inculcation does not explicitly inculcate the prerequisites of its specific productivity, such PW presupposes, produces and inculcates, in and through its exercise, ideologies tending to justify the question-begging which is the condition of its exercise (the ideology of the 'gift' as a negation of the social conditions of the production of cultivated dispositions).

Gloss 1: A paradigmatic image of the typical effects of the ideology of 'giftedness' can be seen in an experiment by Rosenthal: two groups of experimenters who were given two batches of rats from the same stock and were told that one batch had been selected for its stupidity and the other for its intelligence, obtained significantly different progress from their respective subjects (e.g. the effects on both teachers and pupils of distributing the school population into sub-populations academically and socially hierarchized by type of establishment – classical lycées, CESs and CETs,[7] or *grandes écoles* and faculties – by section – classical or modern – and even by discipline).

Gloss 2: In the type of social formation defined in 3.3.3.1, the dominant secondary PW, characterized by a traditional mode of inculcation (in the senses of both 3.3.1.3 and 3.3.2.3), because its specific productivity varies inversely with the distance between the dominant cultural arbitrary and the cultural arbitrary of the groups or classes on which it is exerted, always tends to deprive the members of the dominated classes of the material and symbolic benefits of the accomplished education. It may be wondered whether a type of secondary PW which, conversely, took into account the distance between the pre-existent habitus and the habitus to be inculcated, and was systematically organized in accordance with the principles of an explicit pedagogy, would not have the effect of erasing the boundary which traditional PW recognizes and confirms between the legitimate addressees and the rest. Or, to put it another way, whether perfectly rational PW – i.e. PW exerted ab ovo in all domains on all the educable, taking nothing for granted at the outset, with the explicit goal of explicitly inculcating in all its pupils the practical principles of the symbolic mastery of practices which are inculcated by primary PA only within certain groups or classes, in short, a type of PW everywhere substituting for the traditional mode of inculcation the programmed transmission of the legitimate culture – would not correspond to the pedagogic interest of the dominated classes (the hypothesis of the democratization of education through the rationalization of pedagogy). But the Utopian character of an education policy based on this hypothesis becomes apparent as soon as one observes that, quite apart from the built-in inertia of every educational institution, the structure of power relations prohibits a dominant PA from resorting to a type of PW contrary to the interests of the dominant classes who delegate its PAu to it.

Furthermore, to regard such a policy as congruous with the pedagogic interest of the dominated classes entails identifying the objective interest of those classes with the sum of the individual interests of their members (e.g. as regards social mobility or cultural advancement), ignoring the fact that the controlled mobility of a limited number of individuals can help to perpetuate the structure of class relations; or, to put it another way, it entails assuming it possible to generalize to the whole class properties which socio-logically can belong to certain members of the class only inasmuch as they remain reserved for a few, hence denied to the class as a whole.

4. THE EDUCATIONAL SYSTEM

4. Every institutionalized educational system *(ES) owes the specific characteristics of its structure and functioning to the fact that, by the means proper to the institution, it has to produce and reproduce the institutional conditions whose existence and persistence (self-reproduction of the system) are necessary both to the exercise of its essential function of inculcation and to the fulfilment of its function of reproducing a cultural arbitrary which it does not produce (cultural reproduction), the reproduction of which contributes to the reproduction of the relations between the groups or classes (social reproduction).*

Gloss 1: The task is now to establish the specified form which the propositions stating in their full generality the conditions and effects of PA (1, 2 and 3) must take when that PA is exerted by an institution (ES), that is, to establish what an institution must be in order to be capable of producing the institutional conditions for the production of a habitus at the same time as misrecognition of those conditions. This question is not reducible to the essentially historical search for the social conditions of the apparition of a particular ES or even of the educational institution in general. Thus, Durkheim's effort to understand the characteristics of the structure and functioning of the French ES on the basis of the fact that it initially had to organize itself with a view to producing a Christian habitus which would as far as possible integrate the Greco-Roman heritage with the Christian faith, leads less directly to a general theory of the ES than Weber's attempt to deduce the transhistorical characteristics of every church from the functional demands which determine the structure and functioning of any institution aiming to produce a religious habitus. Only when the generic conditions of the possibility of an institutionalized PA have been formulated is one able to give full significance to the search for the social conditions necessary for the realization of these generic conditions, i.e. to understand how, in different historical situations, social processes such as urban concentration, the progress of the division of labour entailing the autonomization of intellectual tribunals or practices, the constitution of a market in symbolic goods, etc. take on a systematic meaning qua the system of the social conditions of the apparition of an ES (cf. the regressive method by which Marx constructs the social phenomena linked to the break-up of feudal society as the system of the social conditions of the apparition of the capitalist mode of production).

Gloss 2: So long as it is not forgotten that the relatively autonomous history of educational institutions has to be reinserted into the history of the corresponding social formations, certain features of the institution which first appear in conjunction with systematic transformations of the institution (e.g. paid teaching, the establishment of schools capable of organizing the training of new teachers, the standardization of educational organization over a wide area, examinations, Civil-Service status, salaried employment) may legitimately be regarded as significant thresholds in the process of the institutionalization of PW. Thus, although the educational history of Antiquity exhibits the stages

of a continuous process leading from preceptorship to the philosophy
and rhetoric schools of Imperial Rome, passing through the initiatory
education of the magi or the masters of wisdom and the independent
itinerant lecturing of the Sophists, Durkheim is justified in regarding
the medieval university as the first true ES in the West, since the advent
of juridically sanctioned validation of the results of inculcation (the
diploma), Durkheim's decisive criterion, here joins the continuity of
inculcation and the homogeneity of the mode of inculcation. It is
equally possible, from a Weberian standpoint, to consider that the
determining features of the educational institution are present with the
appearance of a corps of permanent specialists whose training, recruitment and careers are governed by a specialized organization and who
find in the institution the means of successfully asserting their claim to
a monopoly of legitimate inculcation of legitimate culture.

If it is just as possible to understand the structural characteristics
linked to institutionalization by relating them to the interests of a body
of specialists progressively gaining a monopoly as it is to understand the
latter in terms of the former, the reason is that these processes represent
two inseparable manifestations of the autonomization of a practice, i.e.
of its constitution as a specific practice. In the same way that, as Engels
observes, the apparition of law qua law, i.e. as an 'autonomous realm',
is correlative with the advances in the division of labour which lead to
the constitution of a body of professional jurists; in the same way that,
as Weber shows, the 'rationalization' of religion is correlative with the
constitution of a priesthood; and in the same way that the process
leading to the constitution of art qua art is correlative with the
constitution of a relatively autonomous intellectual and artistic field –
so the constitution of PW as such is correlative with the constitution of
the ES.

*4.1. Given that (1) an ES cannot fulfil its essential function of incul-
cating unless it produces and reproduces, by the means proper to the
institution, the conditions for PW capable of reproducing, within the
limits of the institution's means, i.e. continuously, at the least expense*

and in regular batches, a habitus as homogeneous and durable as possible in as many of the legitimate addressees as possible (including the reproducers of the institution); and given (2) that, in order to fulfil its external function of cultural and social reproduction, an ES must produce a habitus conforming as closely as possible to the principles of the cultural arbitrary which it is mandated to reproduce – the conditions for the exercise of institutionalized PW and for the institutional reproduction of such PW tend to coincide with the conditions favouring the function of reproduction, inasmuch as a permanent corps of specialized agents, equipped with the homogeneous training and standardized, standardizing instruments which are the precondition for the exercise of a specific, regulated process of PW, i.e. the work of schooling (WSg), the institutionalized form of secondary PW, is predisposed by the institutional conditions of its own reproduction to restrict its activity to the limits laid down by an institution mandated to reproduce a cultural arbitrary and not to decree it.

4.1.1. Given that it must produce the institutional conditions enabling interchangeable agents to carry on continuously, i.e. daily and over the widest possible territorial area, WSg reproducing the culture it is mandated to reproduce, the ES tends to ensure that the corps of agents recruited and trained to carry out inculcation operate within institutional conditions capable of both dispensing and preventing them from performing heterogeneous or heterodox WSg, i.e. those conditions most likely to exclude, without explicitly forbidding, any practice incompatible with the function of reproducing the intellectual and moral integration of the legitimate addressees.

Gloss: The medieval distinction between the *auctor* who produces or professes original works 'extra-ordinarily' and the *lector* who, confined to repeated, repeatable commentary on authorities, professes a message he has not himself produced, expresses the objective truth of professorial practice, which is perhaps most evident in the professorial ideology of mastery, the laboured negation of the truth of the professorial function, or in the magisterial pseudo-creation which employs all the academic tricks and dodges in the service of an academic outclassing of academic commentary.

4.1.1.1. Given that it must ensure the institutional conditions for the homogeneity and orthodoxy of the WSg the ES tends to equip the agents appointed to inculcate with a standard training and standardized, standardizing instruments.

Gloss: The teaching tools which the ES makes available to its agents (manuals, commentaries, abstracts, teachers' texts, syllabuses, set books, teaching instructions, etc.) must be seen not simply as aids to inculcation but also as instruments of control tending to safeguard the orthodoxy of SW against individual heresies.

4.1.1.2. Insofar as it must ensure the institutional conditions for the homogeneity and orthodoxy of the WSg, the ES tends to subject the information and training which it inculcates to a treatment the principle of which lies at once in the demands of the WSg and in the tendencies inherent in a corps of agents placed in these institutional conditions, i.e. tends to codify, standardize and systematize the school message (school culture as 'routinized' culture).

Gloss 1: The condemnations which prophets and creators, and, with them, all would-be prophets and creators, have levelled through the ages at professorial or priestly ritualization of the original prophecy or original work (cf. the anathemas, themselves doomed to become classic, against the 'fossilizing' or 'embalming' of the classics) draw their inspiration from the artificialist illusion that the WSg could escape bearing the mark of the institutional conditions of its exercise. All school culture is necessarily standardized and ritualized, i.e. 'routinized' by and for the routine of the WSg, i.e. by and for exercises of repetition and reconstitution which must be sufficiently stereotyped to be repeated ad infinitum under the direction of coaches *(répétiteurs)* themselves as little irreplaceable as possible (e.g. manuals summaries, synopses, religious or political breviaries and catechisms, glosses, commentaries, cribs, encyclopaedias, corpuses, selections, past examination papers, model answers, compilations of dictums, apothegms, mnemonic verses, topics, etc.). Whatever the habitus to be inculcated, conformist or innovatory, conservative or revolutionary, and whether in the religious, artistic, political or scientific fields, all WSg generates a discourse tending to make explicit and systematize the principles of that habitus in accordance with a logic which primarily obeys the requirements of the institutionalization of apprenticeship (e.g. academicism, or the 'canonization' of revolutionary writers, according to Lenin). If syncretism and eclecticism, which may be explicitly grounded in an ideology of the collection and universal reconciliation of ideas (with the corresponding conception of philosophy as *philosophia perennis*, the precondition for imaginary conversations in Hades), are one of the most characteristic features of the 'routinization' effect of all teaching, it is because the 'neutralization' and de-realization of messages and, therefore, of the conflicts between the values and ideologies competing for cultural legitimacy constitute a typically academic solution to the typically academic problem of reaching a consensus on the programme as a necessary condition for programming minds.

Gloss 2: The extent to which a given ES (or a given department of the ES) obeys the law of 'routinization' rises with the extent to which its PA is organized in relation to the function of cultural reproduction. For example, the French ES exhibits more fully than others the operating characteristics which are functionally linked to the institutionalization of PA (e.g. primacy of self-reproduction, inadequacy of research training, academic programming of the norms of research and the objects of inquiry); and within this system, literary education exhibits these characteristics to a greater extent than scientific education. This is doubtless because few ESs are less called upon by the dominant classes to do anything other than reproduce the legitimate culture as it stands and produce agents capable of manipulating it legitimately (i.e. teachers, leaders and administrators, or lawyers and doctors and, at a pinch, littérateurs, rather than researchers and scientists or even technicians).

Furthermore, the extent to which the pedagogic and, a fortiori, intellectual practices (e.g. research activities) of a category of agents obey the law of 'routinization' varies directly with the extent to which this category is defined by its position in the ES, i.e. varies inversely with the extent to which it participates in other fields of practice (for example, the scientific field or the intellectual field).

4.1.2. Given that it must reproduce through time the institutional conditions for the performance of the WSg, i.e. that it must reproduce itself as an institution (self-reproduction) in order to reproduce the culture it is mandated to reproduce (cultural and social reproduction), every ES necessarily monopolizes the production of the agents appointed to reproduce it, i.e. of the agents equipped with the durable training which enables them to perform WSg tending to reproduce the same training in new reproducers, and therefore contains a tendency towards perfect self-reproduction (inertia) which is realized within the limits of its relative autonomy.

Gloss 1: We should not see simply an effect of *hysteresis* linked to the structural duration of the cycle of pedagogic reproduction, in the tendency of every teaching body to retransmit what it has acquired by a pedagogy as similar as possible to the pedagogy of which it is the product. In reality, when they work to reproduce through their pedagogic practice the training of which they are the product, the agents of an ES, whose economic and symbolic value depends almost totally on academic sanctions, tend to ensure the reproduction of their own value by ensuring the reproduction of the market on which they have all their value. More generally, the pedagogic conservatism of the champions of the rarity of academic credentials would not receive such strong support from the groups or classes most attached to the conservation of the social order were it not that, under the guise of merely defending their market value by defending the value of their diplomas, they thereby defend the very existence of a certain symbolic market, together with its conservative functions. Dependence can take a thoroughly paradoxical form when operating through the medium of an ES, i.e. when the tendencies of the institution and the interests of the personnel can express themselves under cover of and within the limits of the institution's relative autonomy.

Gloss 2: The self-reproductive tendency is most fully realized in an ES whose pedagogy remains implicit (in the sense of 3.3.1), i.e. an ES where the agents responsible for inculcation possess pedagogic principles only in implicit form, having acquired them unconsciously through prolonged frequentation of masters who had themselves mastered them only in practical form: 'People say that the young teacher will be guided by his memories of his life at the *lycée* and as a student. Don't they see that this is to decree the perpetuity of routine? Tomorrow's teacher can only repeat the gestures of his teacher of yesterday, and since the latter was merely imitating his own teacher, it is not clear how any novelty can find its way into this unbroken chain of self-reproducing models' (Durkheim).

4.1.2.1. Given that it contains a tendency towards self-reproduction, the ES tends to reproduce the changes occurring in the cultural arbitrary that it is mandated to reproduce only after a time-lag commensurate with its relative autonomy (the cultural backwardness of school culture).

4.2. Given that it explicitly raises the question of its own legitimacy in setting up PA as such, i.e. as a specific action expressly exercised and undergone as such (school action) every ES must produce and reproduce, by the means proper to the institution, the institutional conditions for misrecognition of the symbolic violence which it exerts, i.e. recognition of its legitimacy as a pedagogic institution.

Gloss: The theory of PA brings out the paradox of the ES by juxtaposing the objective truth of every PA with the objective significance of the institutionalization of PA. In abolishing the happy unconsciousness of familial or primitive educations, actions of hidden persuasion which, better than any other form of education, impose misrecognition of their objective truth (since they tend towards the point of not even appearing as education), the ES would lay itself open to the question of its right to set up a relation of pedagogic communication and to delimit what deserves to be inculcated — were it not that the very fact of institutionalization gives it the specific means of annihilating the possibility of this question. In short, the persistence of an ES proves that it resolves by its very existence the questions raised by its existence.

Such a reflection may appear abstract or artificial when one considers an ES actually in operation, but it takes on its full meaning when one examines moments in the institutionalizing process when the questioning of the legitimacy of the PA and the masking of this question are not simultaneous. Thus, the Sophists, teachers who proclaimed their educative practice as such (e.g. Protagoras saying 'I acknowledge that I am a professional teacher — *sophistès* — an educator of men') without being able to invoke the authority of an institution, could not entirely escape the question, endlessly posed in their very teaching, which they raised by professing to teach; whence a teaching whose themes and problematics consist essentially of an apologetic reflection on teaching.

Similarly, at moments of crisis when the tacit contract of delegation legitimating the ES is threatened, the teachers, placed in a situation not unlike that of the Sophists, are called upon to resolve, each on his own behalf, the questions which the institution tended to exclude by its very functioning. The objective truth of the teacher's job, i.e. the social and institutional conditions which make it possible (PAu), is never more clearly revealed than when the crisis of the institution makes the job difficult or impossible (e.g. a teacher writes to a newspaper: 'Some parents are unaware that Sartre's *Respectable Prostitute* deals with the colour problem and imagine that the teacher — mentally deranged, drug crazed or whatever — wants to drag his class off to a brothel . . . . Others protest because the teacher has agreed to talk about the pill —

sex education is a matter for the family . . . . One teacher finds he is called a Communist for having explained Marxism to the sixth form; another learns he is suspected of religious propaganda for having thought it necessary to explain what the Bible is, or the work of Claudel . . .').

4.2.1. Insofar as it endows all its agents with a vicarious authority, i.e. school authority (SAu), the institutionalized form of PAu, by a two-step delegation reproducing within the institution the delegation of authority from which the institution benefits, the ES produces and reproduces the conditions necessary both for the exercise of an institutionalized PA and for the fulfilment of its external function of reproduction, since institutional legitimacy dispenses the agents of the institution from having endlessly to win and confirm their PAu.

Gloss 1: Resting as it does on a two-step delegation, SAu, the authority of the agent of the ES, is distinguished both from the PAu of the agents or agencies carrying on an education in a diffuse and unspecified way, and from the PAu of the prophet. Like the priest, the office-holder of a Church holding a monopoly on the legitimate manipulation of the goods of salvation, the teacher, the officer of an ES, is not required to establish his own PAu, on every occasion and at all times, since, unlike the prophet or the intellectual creator, auctores whose auctoritas is subject to the discontinuities and fluctuations of the relation between the message and the audience's expectations, he preaches to a congregation of confirmed believers, by virtue of SAu, a legitimacy by position which he is guaranteed by the institution and which is socially objectified and symbolized in the institutional procedures and rules defining his training, the diplomas which sanction it, and the legitimate conduct of the profession. (Cf. Weber: 'The priest dispenses salvation by virtue of his office. Even in cases in which personal charisma may be involved, it is the hierarchical office that confers legitimate authority upon the priest as a member of a corporate enterprise of salvation.' And Durkheim: 'The teacher, like the priest, has a recognized authority, because he is the agent of a moral body greater than himself.')

Once again the Catholic tradition offers the paradigmatic expression of the relation between the office-holder and the pedagogic office, with the dogma of infallibility, an institutional grace which is but the transfigured form of institutional PAu and explicitly described by commentators as the condition of the possibility of teaching the faith: 'In order that the Church may be able to perform the task assigned to her as guardian and interpreter of the sacred trust, it is required that she enjoy infallibility, that is, that she be assured of a special assistance from God, in virtue of which she is preserved from all error when setting forth officially a truth for the belief of the faithful. Thus the Pope is infallible when he teaches *ex cathedra* as a doctor of the Church' (Canon Bardy).

Gloss 2: Although educational institutions have almost always sprung from the laicizing of ecclesiastical institutions or the secularizing of sacred traditions (with the exception, as Weber points out, of the schools of classical Antiquity), the fact of common origin leaves unexplained the manifest similarities between the personage of the priest and that of the teacher, until one takes account of the structural and functional homology of Church and School. As happens with Durkheim (who nonetheless formulated the homology between the professorial and the sacerdotal office), the self-evidence of historical filiation tends to preclude further explanation: 'The University was made up in part of laymen who still had the clerical physiognomy, and of laicized clerics. Henceforward, alongside the ecclesiastical body there existed another body which, though separate, was partly formed in the image of the body to which it was opposed.'

4.2.1.1. Any given pedagogic agency is characterized, depending on the degree of institutionalization of its PA, i.e its degree of autonomization, by the position it occupies between (1) a system of education in which PA is not set up as a specific practice but falls to virtually all the educated members of a group or class (with only sporadic or partial

*specialization), and (2) an ES in which the PAu necessary for the
exercise of PA is explicitly delegated to and juridically reserved for a
corps of specialists, specifically recruited, trained and mandated to
carry out PW in accordance with procedures controlled and regulated
by the institution, at fixed times and in fixed places, using standardized
controlled instruments.*

*4.2.2. Insofar as it produces a SAu, an institutional authority which,
resting on a two-step delegation, seems to be based on nothing other
than the agent's personal authority, the ES produces and reproduces
the conditions for the performance of institutionalized PW since the
fact of institutionalization is capable of setting up PW as such without
either those who carry it out or those who undergo it ever ceasing to
misrecognize its objective truth, i.e. to remain unaware of the ultimate
basis of the delegated authority which makes the WSg possible.*

Gloss 1: All ideological representations of the independence of PW
with respect to the power relations constituting the social formation in
which it is carried on take on a specific form and force when, owing to
the two-step delegation, the institution stands in the way of an apprehension of the power relations which in the last analysis found the
authority of the agents appointed to carry on WSg. SAu is the source of
the illusion — which adds its force of imposition to the power relations
it expresses — that the symbolic violence exerted by an ES is unrelated
to the power relations between the groups or classes (e.g. the Jacobin
ideology of the school's 'neutrality' in class conflicts; the Humboldtian
and neo-Humboldtian ideologies of the University as the haven of
science; the ideology of *Freischwebende Intelligenz*; or the limiting case
of the Utopian vision of a 'critical university', capable of bringing
before the tribunal of pedagogic legitimacy the principles of the cultural arbitrariness from which it proceeds, a Utopia not far removed
from the illusion, cherished by certain anthropologists, that institutionalized education, unlike traditional education, constitutes a 'mechanism
of change', capable of 'creating discontinuities' and 'building a new
world' — Margaret Mead).

Inasmuch as it more fully masks the ultimate foundations of its pedagogic authority, hence of its agents' SAu, the 'liberal university' conceals the fact that there is no liberal university more effectively than a theocratic or totalitarian ES, in which the delegation of authority is objectively manifested in the fact that the same principles directly establish political authority, religious authority and pedagogic authority.

Gloss 2: The illusion of the absolute autonomy of the ES is strongest when the teaching corps is fully assimilated into the Civil Service *(fonctionnarisation)*, so that, with his salary paid by the State or the university institution, the teacher is no longer remunerated by the client, like other vendors of symbolic goods (e.g. the corporate professions), nor even by reference to the services rendered to the client, and so finds himself in the conditions most conducive to misrecognition of the objective truth of his task (e.g. the ideology of 'disinterestedness').

4.2.2.1. Insofar as it allows the authority attached to the office (SAu) to be deflected onto the person of the office-holder, i.e. insofar as it produces the conditions for the concealment and misrecognition of the institutional basis of SAu, the ES produces the conditions favouring the exercise of institutionalized WSg, since it deflects onto the institution and the groups or classes it serves, the effect of reinforcement produced by the illusion that WSg is carried on independently of its institutional conditions (the paradox of professorial charisma).

Gloss: Because sacerdotal practice can never so entirely escape stereotyping as can pedagogic practice (the manipulation of secularized goods), priestly charisma can never rest so entirely as teacherly charisma on the technique of ritual deritualization, the juggling with the syllabus that is implicitly *on* the syllabus. Nothing is more likely to enhance the authority of the institution and of the cultural arbitrary it serves than the enchanted adherence of teacher and taught to the illusion of an authority and message having no other basis or origin than the person of a teacher capable of passing off his delegated power to inculcate the cultural arbitrary as a power to decree it (e.g. scheduled improvisation as compared with the pedagogy which, in taking its stand on the argument of authority, always affords a glimpse of the authority from which the master derives his authority).

4.3. In any given social formation, the dominant ES is able to set up the dominant PW as the WSg without either those who exercise it or those who undergo it ever ceasing to misrecognize its dependence on the power relations making up the social formation in which it is carried on, because (1) by the means proper to the institution, it produces and reproduces the necessary conditions for the exercise of its internal function of inculcating, which are at the same time the sufficient conditions for the fulfilment of its external function of reproducing the legitimate culture and for its correlative contribution towards reproducing the power relations; and because (2) by the mere fact of existing and persisting as an institution, it implies the institutional conditions for misrecognition of the symbolic violence it exerts, i.e. because the institutional means available to it as a relatively autonomous institution monopolizing the legitimate use of symbolic violence are predisposed to serve additionally, hence under the guise of neutrality, the groups or classes whose cultural arbitrary it reproduces (dependence through independence).

NOTES

1. 'The word *disposition* seems particularly appropriate to express what is covered by the concept of the habitus (defined as a system of dispositions): it expresses, first, the *result of an organizing action*, with a meaning very close to that of words such as "structure"; it can also denote a manner of being, a habitual

state (especially of the body), and, in particular, a *predisposition,* tendency, *propensity* or *inclination'* (P. Bourdieu, 1972, 1, p. 247) (trans.)..

2. The word 'field' must be understood in a strong sense, as a 'field of forces' (see Translator's Note).

3. Set up at the turn of the century (in the wake of the Dreyfus affair) by a coalition of Socialist groups and Republicans, the *Universités populaires* attempted to educate the working classes in humanist culture and positivist science; the movement went into decline after about 1905 (trans).

4. See 1964, 1, Ch. III. (trans.).

5. See 1966, 1 (trans.).

6. 'Sociodicy': formed by analogy with theodicy: see Book II, Chapter 3 (trans.).

7. See glossary for these and similar terms.

Book II

KEEPING ORDER

The task of the teaching profession is thus to maintain and promote this order in people's thinking, which is just as necessary as order in the streets and in the provinces.

G. Gusdorf,

Pourquoi des professeurs?

1

CULTURAL CAPITAL AND PEDAGOGIC COMMUNICATION

> *Serpentine:* 'When I think to you, the thought, *so far as it finds corresponding ideas and suitable words in your mind,* is reflected in your mind. My thought clothes itself in words in your mind, which words you seem to hear – and naturally enough in your own language and your habitual phrases. Very probably the members of your party are hearing what I am saying to you, each with his own individual difference of vocabulary and phrasing.'
>
> *Barnstaple:* 'And that is why (...) when you soar into ideas of which we haven't even a shadow in our minds, we just hear nothing at all.'
>
> H. G. Wells,
>
> *Men Like Gods*

When we first started our research, we began with the intention of treating the pedagogic relation as a simple relation of communication and measuring its efficiency. More precisely, we sought to determine the social and scholastic factors in the success of pedagogic communication by analysing the variations in the efficiency of the communication relative to the social and scholastic characteristics of the receivers.[1] In contrast to the indices generally used to measure the output of an educational system, the informational efficiency of pedagogic communication is no doubt one of the surest indices of the specific productivity of pedagogic work, especially when, as is the case in Arts Faculties, this work tends to be reduced to the manipulation of words. Analysis of the variations in the efficiency of the action of inculcation which is performed principally in and through the relation of communication thus leads to the primary principle underlying the inequalities in the academic attainment of children from the different

71

social classes. Indeed, one can put forward the hypothesis that the specific productivity of all pedagogic work other than the pedagogic work accomplished by the family is a function of the distance between the habitus it tends to inculcate (in this context, scholarly mastery of scholarly language) and the habitus inculcated by all previous forms of pedagogic work and, ultimately, by the family (i.e. in this case, practical mastery of the mother tongue).

UNEQUAL SELECTION AND UNEQUAL SELECTEDNESS

If, as often happens, it is forgotten that the categories defined within a student population by criteria such as social origin, sex, or some characteristic of their school record have been unequally selected in the course of their previous schooling, it is impossible to account fully for all the variations which these criteria bring out.[2] For example, the scores obtained in a language test are not simply the performance of students characterized by their previous training, their social origin and their sex, or even by all these criteria considered together, but are the performance of the category which, precisely because it is endowed with the whole set of these characteristics, has not undergone elimination to the same extent as a category defined by other characteristics. In other words, it is a version of the pars pro toto fallacy to suppose that one can directly and exclusively grasp even the intersecting influence of factors such as social origin or sex within synchronic relations which, in the case of a population defined by certain past that is itself defined by the continuous action of these factors over time, take on their full significance only when reinstated in the process of the educational *career*. We have here chosen to adopt a deductive method of exposition because only a theoretical model such as one which interrelates the two systems of relations subsumed under the two concepts *linguistic capital* and *degree of selection* is capable of bringing to light the system of facts which it constructs as such by setting up a systematic relationship between them. In complete contrast to the 'pointilliste' verification which applies fragmentary experimentation to a discontinuous series of piecemeal hypotheses, the systematic verification set out below seeks to give experimentation its full power of disproof by confronting the results of theoretical calculation with the findings of empirical measurement.

Given that they have had to achieve a successful acculturation in order to meet the irreducible minimum of academic requirements as regards language, the working-class and middle-class[3] students who reach higher education have necessarily undergone more stringent selection, precisely in terms of the criterion of linguistic competence, since examiners are generally obliged, as much in the *agrégation* as in the *baccalauréat*, to lower their standards as far as knowledge and know-how are concerned, but hold fast to their requirements as regards form.[4] The influence of linguistic capital, particularly manifest in the first years of schooling when the understanding and use of language are the major points of leverage for teachers' assessments, never ceases to be felt: style is always taken into account, implicitly or explicitly, at every level of the educational system and, to a varying extent, in all university careers, even scientific ones. Moreover, language is not simply an instrument of communication: it also provides, together with a richer or poorer vocabulary, a more or less complex system of categories, so that the capacity to decipher and manipulate complex structures, whether logical or aesthetic, depends partly on the complexity of the language transmitted by the family. It follows logically that the educational mortality rate can only increase as one moves towards the classes most distant from scholarly language, but also that, in a school population constituted by selection, unequal selectedness tends to reduce progressively and even to cancel out the effects of unequal selection. And in fact, only differential selection according to social origin, and in particular the over-selection of working-class students, can provide a systematic explanation for the variations in linguistic competence relative to social origin and particularly the cancelling out or inversion of the direct relation (observable at lower levels of the school system) between the possession of cultural capital (identifiable by the father's occupation) and degree of success.

Given that the advantage of students of upper-class origin is more and more marked as one moves away from the realms of the culture directly taught and wholly administered by the School and as one passes, for example, from classical drama to avant-garde theatre or from school literature to jazz, it is clear why, in the case of behaviour like the academic use of academic language, the differences tend to be extremely attenuated or even reversed. The highly selected working-class students in fact score at least as well in this area as the less selected upper-class students and better than the middle-class students, who are equally ill-endowed with linguistic or cultural capital but less strongly selected (table 2).[5]

TABLE 1

		Linguistic capital	Degree of selection		Linguistic competence
Working classes	Paris	−	+ +	→	+
	Provinces	− −	+	→	−
Middle classes	Paris	−	+	→	0
	Provinces	− −	0	→	− −
Upper classes	Paris	+ +	− −	→	0
	Provinces	+	−	→	0

The relative degrees of selection are expressed in terms of + and −, giving an approximate indication of the various subgroups' chances of university entrance (see Appendix).

Similarly, while Parisian students, whatever their social background, score better results than provincial students, it is among students of working-class origin that the residence-related difference is most marked (91 percent as against 46 percent with a mark of 12 or over, compared with 65 and 59 percent for the upper classes), with working-class students achieving the best results in Paris, followed by middle-class and upper-class students (table 2). To understand this set of relations it must be borne in mind that on the one hand

TABLE 2

	Paris			Provinces			Whole of France		
	Working classes	Middle classes	Upper classes	Working classes	Middle classes	Upper classes	Working classes	Middle classes	Upper classes
	%	%	%	%	%	%	%	%	%
Less than 12/20*	9	31	35	54	60	41	46	55	42.5
12/20 and over	91	69	65	46	40	59	54	45	57.5

The percentages are calculated within each column; the italic figures indicate the strongest tendencies in each line, within each of the three populations (Paris, the provinces, and the whole country).

*In France most marks are given out of 20; 10 is the 'pass mark', 12 is 'fair' (trans.).

residence in Paris is associated with linguistic and cultural advantages, and on the other hand that the degree of selection associated with living in Paris cannot be defined independently of class membership, if only by virtue of the hierarchical and centralized structure of the university system and, more generally, of the power apparatuses.[6] If the importance of the linguistic capital transmitted by the different family backgrounds and the degree of selection implied by university entrance, in Paris and the provinces, for the different social categories, are defined in terms of their relative value (+, 0 or −), it can be seen that it is sufficient to combine these values in order to account for the hierarchy of results in the language exercise (cf. tables 1 and 2). This model thus gives a systematic account of the empirically observed variations, that is to say, for example, the position of working-class Parisian students (+) as compared with upper-class Parisian students (0) and as compared with provincial working-class students (−), or the relative position of middle-class students, who, both in Paris (0) and in the provinces (− −), score less well than working-class students.

It also follows from these analyses that if the proportion of working-class students entering university were significantly increased, those students' degree of relative selection would, as it declined, less and less offset the educational handicaps related to the unequal social-class distribution of linguistic and cultural capital. So we would see the reappearance of the direct correlation between academic performance and social-class background which, in higher education, is fully observed only in those areas least directly controlled by the school system, whereas in secondary education it already manifests itself in the most scholastic results.

Similarly, to understand why a test measuring very diverse language skills yields a constant superiority of the men over the women it has to be remembered that the female students' situation contrasts sharply with that of the male students in a systematic way — that is, by an apparent paradox, in different ways in the university system as a whole, in the Arts Faculties, and in each particular type of course and school career. Since we know that female students are twice as likely as male students to enrol in Arts courses (in 1962, they had a 52.8 percent chance as against 23 percent) and that, compared with the men, for whom the other faculties open their doors more widely, women Arts students, precisely because of this relegation, are less strongly selected than the male students in the same faculty, it is understandable that their performance should be weaker. Here again, the explanatory model which relates the scores of the two categories to their respective degrees of selection is capable, provided it is applied systematically, of accounting for all the facts multivariate analysis would leave unexplained, short of resorting to a fictitious and tautological explanation by 'natural inequalities between the sexes'.

Given that the female-student group is composed differently from the male-student group as regards social origin, subjects studied and previous school history (for example, 36 percent of the men have had the most classical secondary schooling as against 19.5 percent of the women), and given that these characteristics are all linked, unequally, to unequal degrees of success, one might expect straightforward multivariate analysis to reveal other effective relations behind the apparent relation between sex and test scores, by successively neutralizing the action of the different variables, i.e. by studying separately the action of the principal variable in the different sub-groups distinguished by other variables within the principal group. But how can the superiority of the male students then be explained without invoking natural inequality, since the gap cannot be imputed to the differences which separate the two categories as regards knowledge of Greek and Latin, type of secondary school, type of faculty course, and social origin?

The disparities between the men and the women run the same way in the various social-origin categories and are of roughly the same magnitude within these categories (table 5). They remain whatever the type of secondary school attended, except that the difference is slightly greater among ex-*collège* [private school] pupils, where 62 percent of the boys and 35 percent of the girls score better than 12/20, as against 70 and 54 percent in the case of former *lycée* pupils.

In order to explain both the disparity constantly observed between the male and female students in Arts faculties and its absence in the control group of lycée pupils, it is sufficient to know that the degrees of selection characteristic of the men and the women are not the same in the two cases: since the sex ratio in secondary education is very close to the sex ratio in the corresponding age groups, it can be assumed that boys and girls are there equally selected — which is not the case in Arts Faculties. If female students manifest more rarely than male students the aptitude for handling the language of ideas (which is demanded to very different degrees in the different disciplines), this is primarily because the objective mechanisms which channel girls preferentially towards the Arts Faculties and, within them, towards certain specialities (such as modern languages, art history or French) owe part of their effectivity to a social definition of the 'feminine' qualities which they help to form; in other words, to the internalization of the external necessity imposed by this definition of feminine studies. In order for a destiny, which is the objective product of the social relations defining the female condition at a given moment in time, to be transmuted into a vocation, it is necessary and sufficient that girls (and all those around them, not least their families) should be unconsciously guided by the prejudice — particularly acute and thriving in France on account of the continuity between salon culture and university culture — that there is an elective affinity between so-called 'feminine' qualities and 'literary' qualities such as sensitivity to the imponderable nuances of sentiment or a taste for the imprecise preciosities of style. Thus the apparently most deliberate or most inspired 'choices' still take into account (albeit unconsciously) the system of objective probabilities which condemns women to professions requiring a 'feminine' disposition (e.g. 'welfare' work) or which predisposes them to accept and even unconsciously demand those types of work requiring a 'feminine' relation to the job.

Even the apparent exception can be understood in terms of the model. Whereas men who have done neither Latin nor Greek, or only Latin, score better than similarly-trained women, among the classicists the women perform better than the men: 64 percent of the women, and 58.5 percent of the men, score more than the median mark (cf. table 3). This reversal of the usual difference between the sexes is explained by the fact that, since girls are less likely than boys to receive this training, those girls who do are more rigorously selected than similarly-trained boys. In the same way, because the significance of each relationship is a function of the structure in which it belongs, the most classical training (Greek and Latin) is not automatically linked to better performance: whereas the women who have done Greek and Latin score better than those who have done only Latin and those who have had a 'modern' schooling, the opposite is true of the men. Everything leads one to think that this is yet another effect of differential selection: while faculty entrance is almost as inevitable for boys as for girls when they have done Greek and Latin, boys who come from the 'modern' section and for whom Arts studies represent a less probable option are more selected than other male students.

TABLE 3

	Neither Greek nor Latin		Latin		Latin and Greek		Overall	
	Boys (%)	Girls (%)	Boys (%)	Girls (%)	Boys (%)	Girls (%)	Boys (%)	Girls (%)
Less than 12/20	34	60	39	58.5	41.5	36	38	54
12/20 and over	66	40	61	41.5	58.5	64	62	46

The percentages are calculated within each column. In each line the italic figures emphasize the stronger tendency within each of the three groups defined by their secondary schooling.

If one again defines in terms of relative value the linguistic capital attached to a given social origin and the degree of selection implied for students of each social class and each sex first by university entrance and then by entering an Arts Faculty, it is clear that one only has to combine these values in order to account for the hierarchy of the results obtained by each sub-group in a definition test (cf. tables 4 and 5). Thus for example, it follows from the model (represented in table 4) that middle-class women students must have the lowest degree of linguistic competence (− −) since, like the men of the same classes, they are as disadvantaged with respect to linguistic capital as male and female working-class students but less rigorously selected when entering higher education, and are also less selected than men from their own social class in Arts Faculties; and this is indeed the category which, with only 35 percent of its members above the median of the distribution of the whole experimental group, obtains the weakest scores in the definition exercise. In the same way, male upper-class students, who are in no way distinguished from female upper-class students with respect to linguistic capital and degree of selection at university entrance, and who in the Arts Faculties are more highly selected than the girls by virtue of the relegation of the girls to these faculties, ought to attain the highest level of success (+ +); and this is borne out by table 5, with 67 percent of them scoring more than the median for the whole group. For each sub-category the same correspondence is confirmed between the position designated by the theoretical model and the position alloted by empirical measurement.

The same theoretical model enables us to understand why the most constant and also the most powerful relations are, at the level of higher education, those which link the degrees of linguistic competence to the characteristics of the previous academic record. It is principally through the medium of the initial streamings (type of secondary school and first year − *sixième* − section) that social origin predetermines educational destiny, i.e. both the chain of subsequent school-career choices and the resulting differential chances of success or failure. It follows from this, first, that the structure of the population of selection-survivors is

TABLE 4

		Linguistic capital	Degree of selection — University entrance	Degree of selection — Arts Faculty		Linguistic competence
Working classes	Boys	−	+	+	↑	+
	Girls	−	+	−	↑	−
Middle classes	Boys	−	0	+	↑	0
	Girls	−	0	−	↑	+
Upper classes	Boys	+	−	+	↑	+
	Girls	+	−	−	↑	−

For a given social class an equal distribution of linguistic capital is assumed between the sexes. The relative degree of selection expressed in terms of + and − are the approximate reflection of the probabilities of university entrance and the conditional probabilities of entering the Arts Faculty (taking university entrance for granted) which characterize the different sub-groups.

TABLE 5

	Working classes		Middle classes		Upper classes		Overall	
	Boys (%)	Girls (%)	Boys (%)	Girls (%)	Boys (%)	Girls (%)	Boys (%)	Girls (%)
Less than 12/20	35.5	53.5	43	60.5	33	47	38	54
12/20 and above	64.5	46.5	57	39.5	67	53	62	46

constantly changing even with respect to the criterion governing elimination, which has the effect of progressively weakening the direct
relation between social origin and linguistic competence (or any other
index of scholastic success). Secondly, at every stage in their school
career, individuals of the same social class who survive in the system
exhibit less and less the career characteristics which have eliminated the
other members of their category, depending on the severity of the
selection to which their class is subject and the level of education at
which the synchronic cross-section is taken.[7] It is clear that measurement of the linguistic competences of a student population at the level
of higher education can only grasp the relation between social origin
and academic success in the form of the relation between success and
the academic characteristics which are nothing other than the *retranslation* into the specific logic of the school system of the chances
initially linked to a determinate social situation. And in fact, whereas a
significant relation between variables such as social origin or sex and
success in the language test is found only in those exercises closest to
the traditional techniques of school assessment, educational career
characteristics such as the secondary school section or indices of previous success (such as examination grades) are more strongly linked
than all other criteria to language test performance, whatever the
type of exercise.

In order to explain the relation ascertained between the type of training
received in secondary school and the aptitude for language handling, without
crediting the classical languages with the miraculous virtues ascribed to them
by the champions of the 'humanities', it is sufficient to observe that this
relation masks the whole system of relations between differential selection and
the social and scholastic factors of that selection. Given the mechanisms which
at present govern recruitment into the different sections, the choice of Greek
(when Latin has been done in sixième) is restricted to those pupils most
closely matching scholastic requirements, whether recruited from among the
few representatives of the working classes, who are already heavily over-
selected (first in being *lycéens* and then in having done Latin), or from
among the children of well-off families, who decisively consolidate their
advantage by investing their cultural capital in the sections most likely to
secure it the highest and most durable academic profitability.

There are other reasons to cast doubt on the virtues which pedagogic conservatism imputes to classical education. How can one explain, for example, why only the full classical training (Greek and Latin) is associated, whatever the exercise, with the best performance, whereas knowledge of Latin alone here seems to give no advantage as compared with the 'modern' stream. The exercises best suited to measure the capacity for mental gymnastics which the learning of Latin is supposed to develop in fact reveal no significant inequality between the 'Latinists' and the others.[8] If students who have done Latin and Greek are distinguished by their verbal ease, this is because they have selected themselves (or been selected) by reference to an image of the hierarchy of the sections of secondary education which gives pride of place to classical studies and because they have had to put up an exceptional performance in the early years of their secondary schooling in order to lay claim to entry into a section which the system reserves for its elite and which attracts to itself the teachers most likely to turn these good pupils into the very best pupils.[9] Given that the students who have done Greek and Latin have the best success rate in all the exercises in the test, that this rate is itself linked to a high rate of previous academic success, and that the students who have done classics have obtained the best rates of success in previous examinations, it may be concluded that the alumni of the classical sections, selected by and for their rhetorical ease, are the least distant from the ideally adequate student whom the teacher presupposes by the level of his discourse and which examinations demand and engender by this very demand.

If it is true that the disadvantage attached to social origin is primarily mediated by educational channelling and streaming *(orientations)* – with the degrees of differential selection they imply for the different categories of students – it is clear why the sons of senior executives should come out top in the sub-group of students who have had a modern training whereas the working-class students come top in the sub-group of Latinists because they doubtless owe the fact of having done Latin to a particularity of their family background and because, coming from a class for which this route is more improbable, they have had to manifest exceptional qualities in order to be channelled in this direction and to persist in it[10] (table 6). There remains one final difficulty, which the model again enables us to resolve: in the sub-group defined by the most classical training, the working-class students obtain results inferior to those of the upper-class students (61.5 percent as against 73.5 percent); in fact, in this sub-group, although they are over-selected to an even greater extent than in the sub-group of Latinists (a difference which appears in their results: 61.5 percent compared with 52 percent), the working-class students are competing against the fraction of privileged students who have made the most profitable academic use of their linguistic and cultural capital.

TABLE 6

	Neither Greek nor Latin			Latin			Latin and Greek			Whole group		
	Working Classes (%)	Middle Classes (%)	Upper Classes (%)	Working Classes (%)	Middle Classes (%)	Upper Classes (%)	Working Classes (%)	Middle Classes (%)	Upper Classes (%)	Working Classes (%)	Middle Classes (%)	Upper Classes (%)
Less than 12/20	52	54	39	48	58	52	38.5	55	26.5	46	55	42.5
12/20 and over	48	46	61	52	42	48	61.5	45	73.5	54	45	57.5

Similarly, the existence of considerable variations in the degree of linguistic competence between one discipline and another cannot be regarded as proof of the intrinsic, irreducible efficacy of this or that intellectual training, without ignoring the fact that the student population of a discipline is the product of a series of selections whose rigour varies as a function of the relations between the social factors determining the different academic trajectories and the system of the different types of studies objectively possible within a given educational system at a given time. For anyone tempted to attribute the superiority of the pupils in the *classes préparatoires* over those in *propédeutique*,[11] or the superiority of philosophy students over sociology students, to some inherent quality of the teaching or its recipients, one need only point out that the sons of senior executives who come out decisively on top in the group composed of students of philosophy, a discipline very highly rated in the traditional system of the humanities, have the lowest scores within the group of students of sociology, a discipline predisposed to serve as a prestigious refuge for the academically least endowed of the privileged students who therefore find themselves under-selected in comparison with fellow students from other backgrounds. And it can be seen that, to explain all the relations between academic discipline, social origin and performance (table 7), it is sufficient to posit that the relative under-selection (as compared, here, with philosophy) characterizing a subject like sociology, which, promising high intellectual prestige for minimum academic input, occupies a paradoxical place in the system of disciplines, is proportionately greater for more privileged social classes.[12]

If all the variations observed can be interpreted in terms of a single principle having different effects depending on the structure of the complete system of relations within which and through which it operates, this is because these variations express, not a sum of partial relations, but a structure in which the complete system of relations governs the meaning of each of them. Thus, in this case at least, multivariate analysis would be likely to lead to a vicious circle or to reification of abstract relations, if the structural method did not restore

TABLE 7

	Philosophy			Sociology			Non-Specialist ("Licence libre")			Overall		
	Working Classes (%)	Middle Classes (%)	Upper Classes (%)	Working Classes (%)	Middle Classes (%)	Upper Classes (%)	Working Classes (%)	Middle Classes (%)	Upper Classes (%)	Working Classes (%)	Middle Classes (%)	Upper Classes (%)
Less than 12/20	25.5	34.5	20	33.5	46	53	60	66	51	46	55	42.5
12/20 and over	74.5	65.5	80	66.5	54	47	40	34	49	54	45	57.5

to the logical classes distinguished by the criteria their full existence as social groups defined by the ensemble of the relations which unite them and by the totality of the relationships they maintain with their past, and, through the intermediary of their past, with their present situation.

The only way to escape fictitious explanations containing nothing beyond the very relationship they presume to explain (explanation in terms of the unequal distribution of natural aptitudes between the sexes, or the intrinsic virtues of a particular discipline, Latin for some, sociology for others) is to refrain from treating as substantial, isolable properties variations which must be understood as elements in a *structure* and moments in a *process*. It is essential to carry out this two-fold interrelation here, because on the one hand, the educational process of differential elimination according to social class (leading, at every moment, to a determinate distribution of competences within the various categories of survivors) is the product of the continuous action of the factors which define the positions of the different classes with regard to the school system, i.e. *cultural capital* and *class ethos*; and on the other hand, because these factors are converted and cashed, at every stage of the school career, into a particular constellation of relay factors, different in structure for each category considered (social class or sex) (cf. figure 1 at end of Book II). It is the system of factors, acting as a system, which exerts the indivisible action of a *structural causality* on behaviour and attitudes and hence on success and elimination, so that it would be absurd to try to isolate the influence of any one factor, or, a fortiori, to credit it with a uniform, univocal influence at the different moments of the process or in the different structures of factors.

It is therefore necessary to construct the theoretical model of the various possible organizations of all the factors capable of acting, if only by their absence, at the various moments of the educational career of children in the various categories, in order to be able to inquire systematically into the discontinuously observed or measured effects of the systematic action of a particular constellation of factors. For example, to understand the pattern of the *baccalauréat* results in a given section and a given subject, obtained by pupils of different sex and from different backgrounds, or more generally, to grasp the specific form and the efficacy of factors such as linguistic capital or ethos at a given level of education, each of these elements has to be related to the system in which it belongs and which represents at the moment in question the retranslation and relaying of the primary determinisms linked to social origin.

Social origin, with the initial family education and experience it entails, must therefore not be considered as a factor capable of directly determining practices, attitudes and opinions at every moment in a biography, since the constraints that are linked to social origin work only through the particular systems of factors in which they are actualized in a structure that is different each time. Thus, when one autonomizes a certain state of the structure (i.e. a certain constellation of factors acting on practices at a certain moment), by dissociating it from the complete system of its transformations (i.e. from the constructed form of the *genesis* of careers), it is impossible to discover, at the basis of all these retranslations and restructurings, the characteristics appertaining to class origin and class membership.

If there is a need for an explicit warning against such a dissociation, it is because the techniques sociologists generally use to establish and measure relations implicitly contain a philosophy that is at once analytical and instantaneist. When the sociologist fails to see that by means of a synchronic cross-section, multivariate analysis obtains a system of relations defined by conjunctural equilibrium, and that factor analysis eliminates all reference to the genesis of the ensemble of synchronic relations it is dealing with, he is liable to forget that, unlike strictly logical structures, the structures sociology deals with are the product of transformations which, unfolding in time, cannot be considered as reversible except by a logical abstraction, a sociological absurdity, since they express the successive states of a process that is aetiologically irreversible.

It is necessary to take into account the ensemble of the social characteristics which define the initial situation of children from the different classes, in order to understand the different probabilities which the various educational destinies have for them, and the significance, for individuals in a given category, of their finding themselves in a situation of greater or lesser probability for their category (e.g. in the case of a manual worker's son, the highly improbable fact of studying Latin, or the highly probable fact of having to take a job in order to continue higher education). It is therefore impossible to take any one of the characteristics defining an individual (or a category) at any one point in his career as the ultimate explanatory principle of all his characteristics. For example, when seeking to explain the relation found in higher education between academic success and paid employment which, though unequally frequent in the different social classes, can be regarded as having an equally disadvantageous effect whatever the social category, we are not entitled to conclude that by this stage social origin has ceased to exert any influence, since it is not, sociologically, a matter of indifference whether one takes as the point of departure for one's explanation the unequal likelihood of extra-curricular work among the different categories of students or the unequal likelihood of finding students from the different social backgrounds among those who have to take a job. A fortiori, we cannot reconstitute the different experiences corresponding to the situations defined by the overlapping of several criteria (e.g. the experience of the peasant's son who enters a small seminary rather than a teacher-training college or who becomes a philosophy teacher rather than a surveyor) by taking as the starting point for this reconstruction the experience defined by any single one of these criteria. Experiences which analysis is able to distinguish and specify only in terms of the intersection of logically permutable criteria cannot be integrated into the unity of a systematic biography unless they are reconstructed on the basis of the original class situation, the point from which all possible views unfold and on which no view is possible.

FROM THE LOGIC OF THE SYSTEM TO THE LOGIC OF ITS TRANSFORMATIONS

Just as we have had to go beyond a purely synchronic grasp of the relations which are established at a given level of education between the social or academic characteristics of the different groups and their degrees of success, in order to construct the diachronic model of careers and biographies, so too, in order to escape the illusion inherent in a strictly functionalist analysis of the educational system, we must re-insert the state of the system grasped by our survey into the history of its transformations. The analysis of the differential reception of the pedagogic message presented here makes it possible to explain the effects which the transformations of its public exert on pedagogic communication, and to define by extrapolation the social character-istics of the publics corresponding to the two limiting states of the traditional system — what might be called the *organic* state, in which the system deals with a public perfectly matching its implicit demands, and what might be called the *critical* state, in which, with the changing social make-up of the system's clientele, misunderstanding would even-tually become intolerable — the state actually observed corresponding to an intermediate phase.

Knowing on the one hand the relations between the social or scholastic characteristics of the different categories of receivers and the different degrees of linguistic competence, and on the other hand the evolution of the relative weight of the categories characterized by different levels of reception, we can construct a model making it possible to explain, and, to some extent, predict, the transformations of the pedagogic relationship. It is immediately clear that the transforma-tions of the system of relations between the educational system and the class structure, which are expressed, for example, in the evolution of the rates of enrolment of the various social classes, lead to a transforma-tion (in accordance with the principles which govern it) of the system of relations between the levels of reception and the categories of receivers, that is, of the educational system considered as a communication system. The capacity for reception characteristic of receivers of a given category is a function at once of that category's *linguistic capital* (which we may suppose constant for the period in question) and the *degree of selection* of the survivors in that category, as objectively measured by the rate of elimination of that category from the educational system. Analysis of the variations over time of the relative weight of the categories of receivers thus enables one to detect and explain sociologically a tendency towards a continuous fall in the *mode* of distribution of the receivers' linguistic competences, together with an increased *dispersion* of this distribution. Owing to the increased rate of enrolment of all social classes, the corrective effect of over-selection acts less and less on the reception level of the categories with the weakest linguistic heritage (as can already be seen in the case of students of middle-class origin), whereas the drop-out rate of the linguistically most favoured categories is so low that the mode of these categories tends to decline steadily while the dispersion of their reception levels increases.

Concretely, the specifically pedagogic aspect of the present crisis of the educational system, i.e. the dislocations and breakdowns which affect it as a communication system, cannot be understood without taking into account on the one hand the system of relations between the competences or attitudes of the different categories of students and their social and academic characteristics, and on the other hand the evolution of the system of relations between the school system and the social classes as objectively grasped by the statistics of the probabilities of university entrance and the conditional probabilities of entry into the various faculties. Between 1961-62 and 1965-66, a period of growth in higher education, often interpreted as a democratization of admissions, the structure of the distribution of educational opportunities relative to social class did indeed shift upwards, but it remained virtually unchanged in shape (cf. figure 2 and Appendix). In other words, the increased enrolment of 18-20 year olds was distributed among the different social classes in proportions roughly equal to those defining

FIGURE 2

The trend of educational opportunities by social class between 1961-62 and 1965-66 (probability of entry to higher education).

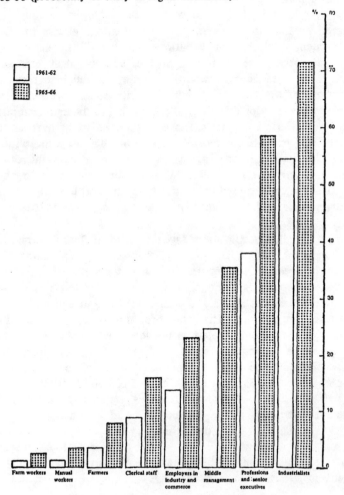

the previous distribution of opportunities.[13] To explain and understand the changes in the distribution of competences and attitudes, it is sufficient to observe that, for example, the sons of industrialists, who, in 1961-62 had a 52.8 percent chance of faculty enrolment, had a 74 percent chance in 1965-66, so that for this category, which proportionally is even more strongly represented in the *classes préparatoires* and the *grandes écoles* than in the faculties, the likelihood of higher education is around 80 percent.[14] If the principles derived from analysis of the synchronic relations are applied to this process, it can be seen that as this category advances towards quasi-total enrolment, it tends to acquire all the characteristics, in particular the competences and attitudes, associated with the academic under-selection of a category.

More generally the interrelating, for a given category, of linguistic and cultural capital (or the scholastic capital which is its transformed form at a given moment in the path through education) with the degree of relative selection the category derives from being represented in a given proportion at a given level of education and in a given type of course, would enable one to explain the differences which appear, at every moment in the history of the system, from one faculty to another and, within the same faculty, from one discipline to another, between the degrees and types of linguistic misunderstanding. Only by reference to the system of circular relations between the dominant representation of the hierarchy of disciplines and the social and scholastic characteristics of their public (which are themselves defined by the relation between the positional value of the different disciplines and the probability of the different trajectories for the different categories) can one give its true sociological meaning to the diminished value of disciplines which, like chemistry or the natural sciences in the Science Faculties or geography in Arts Faculties, admit the higher proportion of working-class students and the highest proportion of students whose secondary education was in the 'modern' sections or in second-order establishments, which are in any case the most probable routes for working-class students.

With this model it is also possible to account for the apparently paradoxical situation of a discipline like sociology, which is distinguished from the lowest-rated Arts disciplines by the social characteristics of its clientele, though it resembles them in terms of academic characteristics (cf. figure 3). If, in Paris, sociology enrols the highest proportion of upper-class students (68 percent as against 55 percent for Arts subjects as a whole), while disciplines like modern literature or geography, though close in terms of academic requirements as measured by previous performance, have the highest rates of working- or middle-class enrolment (48 and 65 percent, respectively, compared with 45 percent for Arts as a whole), the explanation is that under-selected upper-class students are able to find a substitute for their class ambitions in a subject which combines the advantages of a soft option with the glamour of fashion and which, unlike the courses leading to a teaching degree, does not sully the intellectual project with the vulgarity of vocational training.[15]

But one cannot fully account for the variations in the degree of linguistic harmony between the transmitters and the receivers without also integrating into the model of the transformations of the pedagogic relation the variations in the transmission level linked to the social and academic characteristics of the transmitters, i.e. the effects of the rapid expansion of the teaching profession and also the transformations the pedagogic message undergoes when, with the advent of disciplines like psychology and sociology, it betrays the divorce or forced marriage between the requirements of scientific discourse and the canons governing the traditional relation to language. The need for hurried recruitment, from age groups both less numerous and less schooled, of the teachers required to take more or less adequate charge of a public whose sharp expansion resulted from the conjunction, after 1965, of the general rise in enrolment rates with the increased post-war fertility rate, was bound to favour a systematic upward drift of teachers trained for a different task in the previous phase of the system. In such circumstances it might, at first sight, be supposed that the falling level of reception was automatically offset by the falling level of transmission, since the probability of acceding to higher positions in the academic hierarchy has steaily risen for a given level of university consecration. In reality, quite apart from the fact that everything inclined the teachers recruited in accordance with the traditional norms to make use of linguistic misunderstanding as a way of avoiding the pedagogic problems posed by the quantitative and qualitative transformation of their public, the newly recruited teachers, anxious to show themselves worthy of their 'high-speed promotion', doubtless found themselves more inclined to adopt the outward signs of traditional mastery than to make the effort to adjust their teaching to the real competences of their public. In an institution where the reference group remains that of the teachers most authorized to speak 'magisterially', and where the hyperbolically refined hierarchy of appelations, subtle signs of status and degrees of power, is recalled on countless occasions, the lecturers and assistant lecturers, those most directly and continuously confronted with the needs of the students, have to take greater risks in order technically to satisfy those needs. Their attempts to abandon the traditional relation to language are particularly liable to be seen as 'elementary' because the whole logic of the system tends to make them appear as so many signs of their authors' incapacity to meet the legitimate definition of the role.

Thus, analysis of the transformations of the pedagogic relation confirms that every transformation of the educational system takes place in accordance with a logic in which the structure and function proper to the system continue to be expressed. The disconcerting multiplication of practices and statements which marks the acute phase of the crisis of the University must not incline one to the illusion of creative actors or acts springing forth ex nihilo: in the apparently freest declarations of position there is still expressed the structural efficacy of the system of factors which specifies the class determinisms for a category of agents, whether students or teachers, defined by its position in the educational system. On the other hand, to invoke the direct, mechanical efficacy of immediately visible factors, such as the rapid increase in student numbers, would be to forget that the economic,

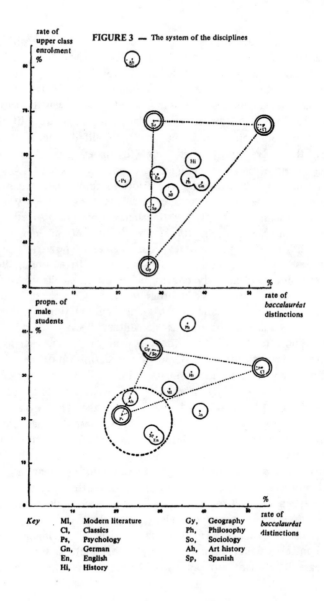

FIGURE 3 — The system of the disciplines

Key   Ml,   Modern literature   Gy,   Geography
      Cl,   Classics   Ph,   Philosophy
      Ps,   Psychology   So,   Sociology
      Gn,   German   Ah,   Art history
      En,   English   Sp,   Spanish
      Hi,   History

Whatever social or academic criteria are applied, the position of sociology remains eccentric. Since every discipline, and more generally every educational institution, can be characterized by its position in the academic hierarchy (indicated by the level of previous academic attainment, the modal age of the corresponding population, and the university status of the teachers) and by its position in a social hierarchy (indicated by the class membership and rate of feminization of the corresponding publics and the social value of the outlets), it can be seen that disciplines with a high degree of *crystallization of their positional indices* in the two hierarchies can easily be ranked in a hierarchy running from the most consecrated disciplines, such as classics in Arts Faculties, with a high proportion of privileged-class students and previously highly successful students, to disciplines such as geography, whose low status is better understood when one sees that they combine weak indices in both dimensions.

Thus the model proposed enables one to characterize all the disciplines considered, since the academic criterion and the social criterion are sufficient to distinguish non-crystallized and crystallized disciplines and to establish a hierarchy among the latter. If a final criterion – sex ratio – is then introduced, disciplines occupying the same position in the academic and social dimensions, like sociology and art history, geography and Spanish, or philosophy and German, are seen to form particular configurations, each separated by sociologically pertinent distinctions (with the exception of English and psychology). The principle of the homologous oppositions between these disciplines is to be found in the division of labour between the sexes, which consigns women to the tasks of social relations (modern languages) or society relations (art history).

To understand the phenomenon as a whole, it is necessary to think of the system of the disciplines (and more generally, the system of education) as a field structured by a centrifugal force inversely proportionate to the degree of academic success and a centripetal force proportionate to the inertia which an individual (more precisely, a category of individuals) is capable of counterposing to failure and elimination, depending on the ambitions socially defined as appropriate to his/her sex and class, i.e. depending on the modality proper to his/her sex and class ethos.

TABLE 8

Disciplines crystallized in the two hierarchies (academic and social)

| | High | | Middle | | | Low | | | | Disciplines not crystallized | |
	Classics	History	Philosophy	German	Modern Literature	English	Psychology	Spanish	Geography	Sociology	Art history
Academic hierarchy (rate of distinctions)	+	0	0	0	0	–	–	–	–	–	–
Social hierarchy (proportion of upper classes)	+	+	0	0	0	0	0	–	–	+	+
Proportion of male students	+	+	+	–	0	–	–	–	+	+	–

In order to situate each discipline in the three hierarchies considered here, the following conventions have been adopted: (1) for the rate of *baccalauréat* distinctions, (–) 20-30%, (0) 30-40%, (+) 40-50% and above; (2) for the proportion of students from the upper classes, (–) 35-50%, (0) 50-60%, (+) 60-70% and above; (3) for the proportion of male students, (–) 15-25%, (0) 25-30%, (+) 30-40% and above.

TABLE 9

	Classics	History	Philosophy	German	Modern Literature	English	Psychology	Spanish	Geography	Sociology	Art history	Statistical reference values (%)
Rate of distinctions (%)	37	37	36	39	32	29	21	28	27	28	23	53
Percentage of upper classes	60	55	54	52	56	55	49	35		68	82	67
Percentage of male students	31	41	22	27	16	17	17	37	38	25		32

demographic or political events which pose the educational system question alien to its logic can only affect it in accordance with its logic:[16] at the same time as it destructures or restructures itself under their influence, it subjects them to a conversion conferring a specific form and weight on their efficacy. A situation of nascent crisis is an opportunity to discern the hidden presuppositions of a traditional system and the mechanisms capable of perpetuating it when the prerequisites of its functioning are no longer completely fulfilled. It is when the perfect attunement between the educational system and its chosen public begins to break down that the 'pre-established harmony' which upheld the system so perfectly as to exclude all inquiry into its basis is revealed. The misunderstanding which pervades pedagogic communication remains tolerable only so long as the school system is able to eliminate those who do not meet its implicit requirements and manages to obtain from the others the complicity it needs in order to function. Because we are dealing with an institution which can fulfil its essential function of inculcation only so long as a minimum of adequacy is maintained between the pedagogic message and the receivers' capacity to decode it, it is necessary to grasp the specifically pedagogic effects of the expansion of the public and scale of the institution, in order to discover, at the moment of the crisis arising from the breaking of that equilibrium, that the contents transmitted and the institutionalized modes of transmission were objectively adapted to a public defined at least as much by its social recruitment as by its small number. An educational system based on a traditional type of pedagogy can fulfil its function of inculcation only so long as it addresses itself to students equipped with the linguistic and cultural capital — and the capacity to invest it profitably — which the system presupposes and consecrates without ever expressly demanding it and without methodically transmitting it. It follows that, for such a system, the real test is not so much the number as the social quality of its public.[17] To the extent that it disappoints the unforeseen and untimely expectations of the categories of students who no longer bring into the institution the means of meeting its expectations, the educational system betrays the fact that it tacitly demanded a public which could be satisfied with the institution because it satisfied the institution's demands from the out-set: perhaps the Sorbonne has only ever been fully satisfactory for those who had no need of its services, like the *normaliens* of the *belle époque* who still fulfilled its secret law when elegantly denying it their seal of approval. In addressing a public ideally defined by the capacity – which they do not give – to receive what they do give, teachers unconsciously express the objective truth of a system which, in its heyday, enjoyed a public made to measure and which, in the phase of nascent disequilibrium, still provides its teachers with the technical and ideological means of concealing from themselves the growing distance between their real public and their putative public. When, by the loftiness of their discourse, they presuppose a public whose capacities for reception are distributed in a J-curve, i.e. in which the greatest number of listeners correspond to the speaker's maximum demands, teachers betray their nostalgia for the pedagogic paradise of traditional education where they could dispense with any pedagogic scruple what-ever.[18]

To refuse to credit the growth of the public with an action working mechanically and directly, i.e. independently of the structure of the educational system, does not mean granting this system the privilege of an absolute autonomy which would enable it to encounter only those problems engendered by the logic of its functioning and its transforma-tions. In other words, by virtue of its power of retranslation (correlative with its relative autonomy), the educational system cannot feel the effects of morphological changes and the social changes to which they correspond, except in the form of pedagogic difficulties, even if its agents are unable to pose for themselves in specifically pedagogic terms the pedagogic problems that are objectively posed for the system. It is in fact sociological analysis which formulates the difficulties arising from numerical growth as pedagogic problems, in treating the pedagogic relation as a relation of communication whose form and efficiency are a function of the correspondence between socially conditioned trans-mission levels and reception levels. Thus, it is in the discrepancy between the educational system's implicit demands and the reality of its public that one can read both the conservative function of traditional pedagogy — i.e. non-pedagogy — and the principles of an explicit pedagogy which may be objectively demanded by the system without being automatically demanded in teachers' practice, because it expresses the contradiction of the system and contradicts its fundamental principles.[19]

Thus, empiricist interpretation of the relations observed which, under the appearance of fidelity to the real, would have limited itself to the apparent object, i.e. to a student population defined independently of its relation to the population eliminated, would have denied itself the possibility of systematically explaining the empirical variations. In order to escape the trap which the educational system sets in offering for observation only a population of survivors, we have had to extract from this preconstructed object the true object of research, i.e. the principles by which the school system selects a population whose pertinent properties, as it moves through the system, are increasingly the effect of the system's own action of training, channelling and eliminating. Analysis of the social and academic characteristics of the receivers of a pedagogic message is therefore meaningful only if it leads to the construction of the system of relations between, on one side, the school system conceived as an institution for the reproduction of legitimate culture, determining inter alia the legitimate mode of imposition and inculcation of academic culture, and, on the other side, the social classes, characterized, with respect to the efficiency of pedagogic communication, by unequal distances from academic culture and different dispositions to recognize and acquire it. There would be no end to an enumeration of the impeccable and irreproachable omissions to which the sociology of education is condemned when it studies separately the school population and the organization of the institution or its system of values, as if it were dealing with two substantial realities whose characteristics pre-existed their interrelation, committing itself by these unconscious autonomizations to fall back in the last resort on an explanation in terms of simple entities such the pupils' cultural 'aspirations' or parental 'motivation'. Only by constructing the system of relations between the educational system and the structure of the relations between the social classes can one genuinely escape these reifying abstractions and produce relational concepts, such as probability of enrolment, disposition towards school, distance from academic culture, or degree of selection, which integrate into the unity of an explanatory theory properties linked to class membership (such as ethos and cultural capital) and pertinent properties of school organization, such as, for example, the hierarchy of values implied by the hierarchy of establishments, sections, disciplines, diplomas or practices. Doubtless this interrelation is still only partial: insofar as it deals only with the pertinent features of class membership defined in its synchronic and diachronic relations with the school system treated *only* as a system of communication, this theoretical construction tends to treat the relations between the educational system and the social classes as simple relations of communication. But this methodological abstraction is also the precondition for grasping the most specific and best hidden aspects of those relations. It is through the particular manner in which it performs its technical function of communication that a given school system additionally fulfils its social function of conservation and its ideological function of legitimation.

NOTES

1. A presentation of the instruments and main results of the inquiry on which the analyses which follow are based, can be found in P. Bourdieu, J.-C. Passeron and M. de Saint-Martin, 1965, 2. Seeking to grasp the variations in the aptitudes of the different categories of Arts students for the comprehension and use of language, we made use of different types of exercises so as to explore at once the different domains of linguistic competence, from the most scholastic to the most 'free', and the different levels of linguistic behaviour, from the compre-

hension of words in context to the most active form of word manipulation, that demanded by the formulation of definitions.

2. The fallacy of ignoring the properties which a population produced by a series of selections owes to this process would be less frequent if it did not express one of the most deep-rooted tendencies of spontaneous epistemology, namely the propensity towards a realist, static representation of the categories of analysis, and if it did not, moreover, find encouragement and ratification in mechanical use of multivariate analysis, which freezes a given state of a system of relations. To put an end to some of the objections aroused by those of our analyses which are based on systematically taking into account the effect of relative selection, we would doubtless have to go to the trouble of dismantling, in accordance with the analytical requirements of the methodological canon, the logical springs of the illusion which would merit a place in the catalogue of methodological errors under the typically methodological name of the 'multivariate fallacy'. If we abstain from the grim delights of that academic exercise, it is because a refutation which, even by way of a pastiche, adopted the outward signs of the methodological panoply would set yet another seal of approval on the dissociation of practice from reflection on practice which defines the methodological temptation; above all we refrain because sociology offers tasks less sterile than the full-scale denunciation of errors which would be less resistent to logical refutation if they were less necessary sociologically.

3. The names of the social classes have been translated as follows: *classes supérieures*, upper classes; *classes moyennes*, middle classes; *classes populaires*, working classes [trans.].

4. As examiners never tire of saying, 'the essential thing is that it should be well written'. Referring to the *Ecole Normale Supérieure* entrance examination, Celestin Bouglé wrote: 'It is clearly understood that, even in the history dissertation, which presupposes a certain amount of factual knowledge, the examiners must above all assess the qualities of composition and exposition' (*Humanisme, sociologie, philosophie, Remarques sur la conception française de la culture générale*, Travaux de l'Ecole normale supérieure, Hermann et Cie, 1938, p. 21). The *aggrégation* and CAPES examiners' reports abound in such affirmations.

5. By contrast with the working classes, for whom over-selection is still the rule, craftsmen and private traders have benefited more from the broadening of the social base of university admissions (their representation rising from 3.8 percent in 1939 to 12.5 percent in 1959). This is doubtless an effect of the relative improvement in their standard of living, and is connected with the extension to that category of the middle-class attitude to education. So it is not surprising that, being severely selected but coming from backgrounds culturally no less disadvantaged, students from these categories should come off worst in all the tests: 40.5 percent of them score more than 12/20 in the definition test,

compared to 57 percent for the sons of senior executives, who score better results than students in all categories when they come from lycées and score the weakest results when they come from private secondary collèges, the sons of craftsmen and tradesmen remain in bottom place whether they have been to State or private schools.

6. Multivariate analysis shows that when allowance is made for the action of the other positive factors, the Parisian students still perform better than the provincials, and do so in each of the sub-groups. In Paris 79 percent of the students who have had the most classical secondary schooling, 67 percent of those who have come through the 'modern' section and 65 percent of those who have done Latin, score more than 12 in the definition test, as against 54, 45.5 and 42 percent, respectively, for the provincial students. It is also found that men and women alike, philosophers and sociologists alike, ex-lycée students and ex-collège [private school] students alike, all score better results in Paris than in the provinces.

7. The characteristics associated with elimination or survival in the system are not randomly distributed amongst individuals of the same class, but are themselves liable to be linked to social or cultural criteria differentiating sub-groups within a class. For example, student sons of manual workers are distinguished by a large number of secondary characteristics (social ones, such as the mother's educational level or the grandfather's occupation, and scholastic ones, such as their secondary school section) from female students in their age group belonging to the same social class. More precisely, the higher the educational level they reach, or, at a given level, the higher they are situated in the hierarchy of disciplines or establishments, the greater the number of these compensatory characteristics they exhibit. By the same token, at a given level of attainment, girls always exhibit more of these compensatory characteristics than boys from the same social class.

8. Another indication that knowledge of Greek and Latin does not in itself give any academic advantage is the fact that ex-lycée pupils, proportionately fewer of whom have done Greek and Latin than ex-private school pupils (25.8 percent as against 31 percent), nonetheless attain higher scores. Moreover, the group of ex-lycéens who have done neither Greek nor Latin perform better than those students who have done Greek and Latin but in private schools.

9. The pre-eminence of the classical sections was, not so long ago, still such that one could scarcely speak of 'guidance' *[orientation]* since the successive choices at the various crossroads of the school career were determined quasi-automatically by the degree of success measured according to a single, undisputed scale of values and since entry into the 'modern' section was perceived by everyone, including those concerned, as a relegation and a failure.

10. Whatever their secondary training, middle-class students regularly have the

weakest results (more than half of the test group scoring less than 12 in all cases).

11. *Propédeutique:* (1948-66) an intermediate one-year course between secondary schooling and the faculties; for the *classes préparatoires,* see Glossary (trans.).

12. The 'theories' sociologists invoke to explain the variations in student political attitudes according to their discipline would perhaps less often ignore the system of diachronic and synchronic relations concealed by membership in a discipline if the links between an intellectual training and political practice did not tend to appear immediately, especially to intellectuals and teachers who have a vested interest in believing and propagating belief in the omnipotence of ideas, as *the* explanatory relation par excellence. Few analyses of student movements written by sociologists and sociology teachers fail to attribute the 'revolutionary' dispositions of sociology students to the beneficent or malignant power of sociology teaching.

13. A similar pattern of development of educational opportunity, combining increased enrolment of all social classes with stability of the structure of disparities between the classes, can be observed in most European countries (Britain, Denmark, Netherlands, Sweden) and even in the USA (see OECD, *Development of Secondary Education: Trends and Implications,* 1969, pp. 78-80).

14. See below (Chapter 3) for a description of the mechanisms of deferred elimination which, despite increased working-class participation in secondary education, tend to perpetuate the gaps between the classes at the level of higher education.

15. If the language test (in which the 'sociologists' obtain systematically weaker results than the 'philosophers') were not sufficient proof that, at least in Paris, sociology is the privileged arena for the easiest form of upper-class student dilettantism, a reading of the statistics makes clear the paradoxical position this discipline occupies within the Arts Faculties. Thus, while in terms of the academic capital it requires, sociology is opposed to philosophy as modern literature is opposed to classics, its intake is socially higher than that of philosophy (68 percent upper-class students, as against 55 percent), whereas classics has a socially higher intake than modern literature, which, together with geography, is the most probable destination for working-class students from the 'modern' sections of secondary education (67 percent compared with 52 percent).

16. Explanation of the crisis in terms of the mechanical effects of morphological determinisms is doubtless so frequent only because it reactivates the metaphorical schemes of spontaneous sociology, such as the scheme which conceives the relation between an institution and its public as a relation between container and contained, with 'mass pressure' causing the structures to 'crack', especially when 'worm-eaten'.

17. While it is necessary to treat the educational system as a communication

system in order to grasp the specific logic of the traditional pedagogic relation and, therefore, of its breakdown, the model constructed by means of the methodological autonomization of the educational system must not be credited with the power to explain the totality of the social aspects of the crisis of the system, in particular everything that affects its function of reproducing the structure of relations between the social classes.

18. Once the variations in the structure of the distribution of competences are taken into account, the question of the optimizing of the pedagogic relationship can no longer be evaded. A public whose competences are distributed in a bell-shaped curve calls for pedagogic choices of different types depending on whether the transformations which affect it over the course of time are expressed in a displacement of the mode or a variation of the dispersion. A lowering of the mode requires the transmitter simply to lower the level of transmission, whether by a controlled increase in redundancy or by a systematic effort to deliver the code of the message in full within the message, through definition or exemplification. On the other hand, increased dispersion of competences tends, beyond a certain threshold, to pose problems which cannot be resolved simply by adjusting the transmission level, as is shown by the situation in certain scientific disciplines, where the growing dispersion of reception levels cannot so easily be masked by an agreement to misunderstand as it can in Arts Faculties.

19. This product of an analysis of the school system which the system's own evolution makes possible, i.e. a pedagogy explicitly aiming to secure the optimum adjustment between transmission level and reception level (each defined by both mode and dispersion), owes nothing to any ethical adhesion to a trans-historical, trans-cultural ideal of educational justice or any belief in a universal idea of rationality. If the implementation of the principles of this pedagogy cannot be taken for granted, this is because it would imply the institutionalization of a continuous testing of reception by both teachers and taught; and, more generally, because it would require all the social characteristics of the communication to be taken into account, in particular the unconscious presuppositions which teachers and taught owe to their social background and academic training. It would, for example, be a mistake to attribute virtues or vices to this or that technique of transmission or assessment (lectures or non-directive teaching, the dissertation or the multiple-choice test), since it is only in the complete system of relations between the content of the message, its place in the learning process, the functions of the training, the external demands bearing on the communication (urgency or leisure), and the morphological, social and academic characteristics of the public or the teaching corps, that the specifically pedagogic productivity of a technique can be defined.

2

THE LITERATE TRADITION
AND SOCIAL CONSERVATION

Our magistrates have understood this mystery. Their scarlet robes, the ermine in which they swaddle themselves, the palaces where they preside, all this august apparel was most necessary; and if doctors had no cassocks and scholars no four-cornered caps, no spreading, four-pieced robes, they would never have fooled the world, which cannot resist such authentic display. Only men of war have not disguised themselves in this way, because their role is indeed more essential: they establish themselves by force, the others with airs and graces.

Pascal,

Pensées

The *skeptron* is passed to the orator before he begins his speech so that he may speak with authority (. . .). It is an attribute of the person who brings a message, a sacred personage whose mission is to transmit the message of authority.

E. Benveniste,

Indo-European Language and Society

In highlighting the extent of the wastage of information which occurs in teacher-student communication, our intention of treating the pedagogic relation as a simple communicative relation so as to measure its informational efficiency brings out a contradiction forcing us to challenge the inquiry that has given rise to it.[1] Could the informative efficiency of pedagogic communication be so low if the pedagogic relation were reducible to a simple relation of communication? To put it another way, what are the particular conditions such that the relation of pedagogic communication can perpetuate itself even when the information transmitted tends towards zero? The logical contradiction brought out by our research must make us wonder whether the very intention of submitting pedagogic communication to the test of measurement is not ruled out by the whole logic of the system to which it is applied. We are led to ask, in other words, what are the institutional means and social conditions which enable the pedagogic relation to perpetuate itself, in the happy unconsciousness of those engaged in it, even when it so utterly fails to achieve its apparently most specific end – in short, to seek to determine that which sociologically defines a relation of pedagogic communication, as opposed to a relation of communication defined in formal terms.

PEDAGOGIC AUTHORITY AND
THE AUTHORITY OF LANGUAGE

The confident use that teachers make of the university idiom is no more fortuitous than students' tolerance of semantic fog. The conditions which make linguistic misunderstanding possible and tolerable are inscribed in the very institution: quite apart from the fact that ill-known or unknown words always appear in stereotyped configurations capable of inducing a sense of familiarity, magisterial language[2] derives its full significance from the situation in which the relation of pedagogic communication is accomplished, with its social space, its ritual, its temporal rhythms; in short, the whole system of visible or invisible constraints which constitute pedagogic action as the action of imposing and inculcating a legitimate culture.[3] In designating and consecrating every agent appointed to inculcate as worthy to transmit that which he transmits, the institution confers on professorial discourse a *status authority* tending to rule out the question of the informative efficiency of the communication.

To reduce the pedagogic relation to a purely communicative relation would make it impossible to account for the specific characteristics it owes to the authority of the pedagogic institution. The mere fact of transmitting a message within a relation of pedagogic communication implies and imposes a social definition (and the more institutionalized the relation, the more explicit and codified the definition) of what merits transmission, the code in which the message is to be transmitted, the persons entitled to transmit it or, better, impose its reception, the persons worthy of receiving it and consequently obliged to receive it and, finally, the mode of imposition and inculcation of the message which confers on the information transmitted its legitimacy and thereby its full meaning. The lecturer finds in the particularities of the space which the traditional institution arranges for him (the platform, the professorial chair at the focal point on which all gazes converge) material and symbolic conditions which enable him to keep the students at a respectful distance and would oblige him to do so even if he did not wish to. Elevated and enclosed in the space which crowns him orator, separated from his audience, if numbers permit, by a few empty rows which materially mark the distance the laity fearfully keep before the *mana* of the Word and which at all events are only ever occupied by the most seasoned zealots, pious ministers of the magisterial utterance, the professor, remote and intangible, shrouded in vague and terrifying rumour, is condemned to theatrical monologue and virtuoso exhibition by a necessity of position far more coercive than the most imperious regulations. The professorial chair commandeers, willy-nilly, the intonation, the diction, the delivery, the oratorical gestures of its occupant, so that the student who presents an exposé ex cathedra is seen to inherit the professor's oratorical manner. Such a context governs teachers' and students' behaviour so rigorously that efforts to set up a dialogue immediately turn into fiction or farce. The lecturer can call for participation or objection without fear of it really happening: questions to the audience are often purely rhetorical; the answers, serving chiefly to express the part the faithful take in the service, are generally no more than *responses*.[4]

Of all the distancing techniques with which the institution equips its officers, magisterial discourse is the most efficacious and the most

subtle: unlike the distances inscribed in space or guaranteed by regulation, the distance words create seems to owe nothing to the institution.
Magisterial language, a status attribute which owes most of its effects to
the institution, since it can never be dissociated from the relation of
academic authority in which it is manifested, is able to appear as an
intrinsic quality of the person when it merely diverts an advantage of
office onto the office-holder. The traditional professor may have abandoned his ermine and his gown, he may even choose to descend from
his dais and mingle with the crowd, but he cannot abdicate his ultimate
protection, the professorial use of a professorial language. There is
nothing on which he cannot speak, be it incest or the class struggle,
because his position, his person, his role imply the 'neutralization' of
his utterances; and also because language can ultimately cease to be an
instrument of communication and serve instead as an instrument of
incantation whose principal function is to attest and impose the pedagogic authority of the communication and the content communicated.

Such a use of language presupposes that measurement of the informative efficiency of the communication be discouraged. Indeed,
everything takes place as if exposés and dissertations, the only means of
feedback the institution offers to students and teachers, had the latent
function of preventing precise measurement of comprehension and
hence of the echolalia which palliates misunderstanding. Thus the ex
cathedra lecture and the dissertation make up a functional couple, as
the professorial solo and the lonely prowess of the examinee, or the
harangue *de omni re scibili* which testifies to mastery and the wordy
generalities of the dissertation. If dissertational rhetoric gives the
teacher the impression that his words have not been too badly understood, this is because the dissertation authorizes a discourse and a
relation to discourse which prohibit clear-cut choices and induce the
marker to pass a judgement as prudent as its object. Teachers never tire
of repeating how difficult it is to mark the 'mass' of 'mediocre' scripts
which offer no purchase for clear-cut judgements and have to be read
and re-read in laborious board-meetings before scraping a hairsbreadth
acquittal tinged with contempt: 'Give her a pass mark' or 'Let him

through'. Agrégation examiners' reports tirelessly deplore as a natural disaster the effect which the very principle of the exercises and the traditional criteria of marking necessarily produce: 'There are few very bad scripts; but even fewer good ones; the rest, no less than 76 percent, are bogged down between 6 and 11/20'.[5] The language of these reports inexhaustibly stigmatizes the congenital 'mediocrity' of the 'great mass of candidates', the 'greyness' of the 'dull', 'insipid' or 'flat' scripts from which there 'fortunately stand out' the few 'distinguished' or 'brilliant' scripts which 'justify the existence of the examination'.[6] Analysis of dissertational rhetoric enables us to perceive the anomic forms of a garbled feedback whose simplifications, decontextualizations and re-interpretations belong less to the logic of cultural apprenticeship than to the logic of acculturation as observed, for example, by linguists in their analysis of 'creolized' languages. The allusive, elliptical discourse which characterizes the modal dissertation presupposes the complicity in and by misunderstanding which defines the pedagogic relationship in its traditional form. Transmitting in a language which is little or not at all understood, the professor logically ought not to understand what his students send back to him. However, just as the status legitimacy of the priest, as Weber remarks, causes the responsibility for failure to fall neither on the god nor on the priest but solely on the conduct of the faithful, so the teacher who, without acknowledging it and without drawing all the inferences, suspects he is less than perfectly understood, can, so long as his status authority is not contested, blame his students when he does not understand their utterances.

The whole logic of an academic institution based on pedagogic work of the traditional type and ultimately guaranteeing the 'infallibility' of the 'master', finds expression in the professorial ideology of student incapacity, a mixture of tyrannical stringency and disillusioned indul-gence which inclines the teacher to regard all communication failures, however unforeseen, as integral to a relationship which inherently implies poor reception of the best messages by the worst receivers.[7] If the student fails to be what he ought to be, which is none other than his 'being-for-the-teacher', then all the faults — whether of error or ill-will — are on his side. 'On the lips of the candidates', as the agrégation reports put it, the most brilliant theories are reduced to the state of logical monstrosities, as if the students, incapable of understanding what they are taught, had no other role than to illustrate the futility of the efforts which the teacher squanders and will, despite everything, continue to squander on them, out of a sense of professional duty but with a disenchanted lucidity which only adds to his merit.[8] Like evil in the theodicies, the existence of 'bad students', periodically recalled to mind, prevents any feeling of this being the best of all possible educational worlds while furnishing a justification for pedagogic morals which can claim to be the best possible, since by making pedagogic failure appear inevitable it provides the one unimpeachable excuse for it.

Thus the illusion of being understood and the illusion of understanding can reinforce each other by serving as each other's alibi because they have their foundations in the institution. All the conditioning received in their previous training and all the social conditions of the relation of pedagogic communication cause students to be objectively condemned to enter the game of fictitious communication, even if this entails adherence to the academic world-view which casts them into unworthiness. As in the Kula cycle, where the armshells always go round in one direction and the necklaces in the other,[9] all the wit and wisdom go from teachers to students and all the dullness and crudity from students to teachers. Students are the less inclined to interrupt the professorial monologue when they do not understand it, because status resignation to approximate understanding is both the product and the condition of their adaptation to the university system: since they are supposed to understand, since they must have understood, they cannot accede to the idea that they have a right to understand and must therefore be content to lower their standards of understanding. Like the priest who actually serves the institution when, as the holder of power over the oracles delegated to him by the institution, he manages to preserve the representation of his infallibility by making the failure of the practices of salvation redound on the faithful, so the teacher protects the institution when he tends to shun and prevent the assessment of a failure which is not so much his as the institution's, and which he can exorcize, through the stereotyped rhetoric of collective guilt, only by sharpening the thirst for salvation.

In short, students and teachers have a duty – to themselves and to each other – to over-estimate the quantity of information which really circulates in pedagogic communication, because this is their duty to the institution. In recognizing them as legitimate transmitters or receivers of the pedagogic message, the University imposes on them obligations towards the institution which are the exact counterpart of their institutional worthiness as attested by their presence in the institution.[10] And, in choosing (not usually by conscious calculation) the line of conduct that is academically most economical or profitable, teachers and students are simply obeying the laws of the educational universe, considered as a system of sanctions. Not only could the teacher not adopt a new language and relation to language without effecting a dissociation of the contents communicated and the manner of communicating them which he cannot conceive of because they were indissociably linked in the manner in which he himself received and assimilated them; but also he could not measure exactly the students' understanding of his language without destroying the fiction which enables him to teach with the least effort, i.e. as he was taught. And if he did want to draw all the pedagogic inferences from his discovery, he would be liable to appear even to his students as an elementary school teacher who had strayed into higher education.[11] As for the student, it is necessary and sufficient for him to follow his bent in the use of language to which his whole training predisposes him, for example in writing a dissertation, in order to enjoy all the safeguards secured by keeping the teacher at arm's length with the pseudo-generalities and prudent approximations which are 'not even wrong' and will win him, as the phrase goes, 'a mark between 9 and 11',[12] in short, to avoid having to reveal, in the clearest code possible, the exact level of his understanding and knowledge, which would condemn him to pay the price of clarity.[13]   Students can always concoct, at least for the teacher's purposes, a semblance of sustained discourse in which no palpable absurdity ever shows through, since the dissertational genre authorizes the use of a second-order, second-hand *ars combinatoria* which, applied to a finite batch of semantic atoms, can only produce strings of words mechanically linked. Summoned to defend themselves with words in a combat in which all words are not allowed, often their only course is the rhetoric of despair, a regression towards the prophylactic or propitiatory magic of a language in which the grandiloquence of magisterial discourse is reduced to the passwords or sacramental phrases of a ritual murmur; the poor-man's relativism, imaginary exemplifications, and hybrid notions, hovering between the abstract and the concrete, the verifiable and the unverifiable, are so many defensive tactics which minimize the risks by throwing a smokescreen of vagueness over the possibility of truth or error. Desperate imitation of magisterial ease, when the social conditions of its acquisition have disappeared, leads to the caricature of mastery in which, as in nativistic movements, regulated variations have given way to mechanical or anarchic deformations.

LANGUAGE AND RELATION TO LANGUAGE

But how could such a system of education continue to exist, did it not, through the traditional form of communication which it sets up, continue to serve the classes or groups from whom it derives its authority, even when it seems so utterly to fail the demands inherent in the performance of its essential function of inculcation? Would the freedom the system allows to the agents appointed to inculcate be so great if it were not conceded in return for the class functions which the university never ceases to fulfil even when its pedagogic efficiency tends towards zero? From Renan to Durkheim, it has often been remarked how much an education so concerned to transmit a style, that is, a type of relation to language and culture, owes to the humanist tradition inherited from the Jesuit colleges — an academic, Christian reinterpretation of the social demands of an aristocracy, which leads distinguished detachment from the professional task to be seen as the accomplished form of the accomplishment of every distinguished profession. But one cannot account for the pre-eminent value the French system sets on literary aptitude and, more precisely, on the capacity for turning all experience, not least literary experience, into literary discourse; in short, everything that goes to make up the French way of living the literary — and sometimes even the scientific — life like a Parisian life, unless one sees that this intellectual tradition nowadays still fulfils a social function in the functioning of the educational system and in the equilibrium of its relations with the intellectual field and the different social classes.

University French has never been anyone's mother tongue, even for the children of the privileged classes, but this timeless amalgam of former states of the history of the language is very unequally removed from the languages actually spoken by the different social classes. Doubtless there would be something arbitrary, as has been pointed out, in 'distinguishing a determinate number of French parlances, for the various levels of society intermingle. Nonetheless, there exist at the two extremities of the scale two well-defined modes of speech: *bourgeois parlance* and *common parlance*.'[14] With its high proportion of lexical and syntactic borrowings from Latin — which, imported, used and imposed exclusively by literate groups, have escaped assimilatory restructuring and reinterpretation — constantly checked and braked in its evolution by the standardizing, stabilizing intervention of scholarly or fashionable legitimating agencies, the bourgeois language can be adequately handled only by those who, thanks to the School, have been able to convert their practical mastery, acquired by familiarization within the family group, into a second-degree aptitude for the quasi-scholarly handling of language. Given that the informative efficiency of pedagogic communication is always a function of the receivers' linguistic competence (defined as their variably complete mastery of the code of university language), the unequal social-class distribution of *educationally profitable linguistic capital* constitutes one of the best-hidden mediations through which the relationship (grasped by our tests) between social origin and scholastic achievement is set up, although its weight as a factor varies according to the constellation of factors in which it belongs and, consequently, according to the type and level of education concerned. The social value of the different linguistic codes available in a given society at a given time (i.e. their economic and symbolic profitability) always depends on the distance separating them from the linguistic norm the school manages to impose in defining the socially recognized criteria of linguistic 'correctness'. More precisely, the academic market value of each individual's linguistic capital is a function of the distance between the type of symbolic mastery demanded by the School and the practical mastery he owes to his initial class upbringing (primary PW).[1 5]

But no one acquires a language without thereby acquiring a *relation to language.* In cultural matters the manner of acquiring perpetuates itself in what is acquired, in the form of a certain manner of using the acquirement, the mode of acquisition itself expressing the objective relations between the social characteristics of the acquirer and the social quality of what is acquired. So it is in the relation to language that one finds the principle underlying the most visible differences between bourgeois language and working-class language. What has often been described as the tendency of bourgeois language to abstraction, formalism, intellectualism and euphemistic moderation, should be seen primarily as the expression of a socially constituted disposition towards language, i.e. towards the interlocutor and even the object of conversation. The distinguished distance, prudent ease and contrived naturalness which are the foundations of every code of society manners, are opposed to the expressiveness or expressionism of working-class language; which manifests itself in the tendency to move from particular case to particular case, from illustration to parable, or to shun the bombast of fine words and the turgidity of grand emotions, through banter, rudeness and ribaldry, manners of being and doing characteristic of classes who are never fully given the social conditions

for the severance between objective denotation and subjective conno-
tation, between the things seen and all they owe to the viewpoint from
which they are seen.[16]

So it is simultaneously in the distance between the practical mastery
of language transmitted by domestic pedagogic work and the symbolic
mastery demanded by the school, and in the social conditions of the
more or less complete acquisition of this verbal mastery, that one finds
the principle underlying the variations in the relation to academic
language — a relation which, reverential or casual, tense or detached,
stilted or easy, heavy-handed or well-tempered, ostentatious or
measured, is one of the surest distinctive signs of the speaker's social
position. The disposition to express feelings and judgements in words,
which is greater the higher the level in the social hierarchy, is only one
dimension of the disposition, demanded more and more the higher the
level in the educational hierarchy and the hierarchy of occupations, to
manifest, even in one's practice, the capacity to stand aloof from one's
practice and from the rule governing that practice. Contrary to appearances, nothing is more opposed to literary ellipsis or metaphor, which
almost always presupposes the context of a literate tradition, than the
practical metaphors and 'ellipsis by *deixis*', as Bally calls it, which
enable working-class speech to supply all or part of the verbal information by implicit (or gestural) reference to the situation and 'circumstances' (in Prieto's sense). Rhetorical devices, expressive effects,
nuances of pronunciation, melody of intonation, registers of diction or
forms of phraseology by no means solely express the conscious choices
of a speaker preoccupied with the originality of his expression (as a
summary reading of the opposition between *langue* and *parole* qua
execution might suggest): all these stylistic features always betray, in
the very utterance, a relation to language which is common to a whole
category of speakers because it is the product of the social conditions
of the acquisition and use of language. Thus the avoidance of the
everyday expression and the search for the rare turn of phrase which
characterize the relation to language that professional practitioners of
writing and difference through writing maintain with language, are only

the extreme form of the literary disposition towards language which is proper to the privileged classes, who are inclined to make the choice of language and the manner of its use a means of excluding the vulgar and thereby affirming their distinction.

Like everything pertaining to the *modality of behaviour,* the relation to language tends to elude the sort of experimental measurement practised in empirical research that is often as routine-bound in the production of its questionnaires as in interpreting its results. But it is not impossible to find indices of the modality of linguistic behaviour in the objective characteristics of the linguistic competence measured by a vocabulary test.[17] Thus, for example, an index of differing relations to language may be seen in the fact that Sorbonne students – or students of privileged-class origin and a fortiori privileged-class Sorbonne students – are proportionately more numerous in hazarding a definition of a non-existent word deliberately inserted into a vocabulary test *(gérophagie).* When one adds that the students with the most 'brilliant' academic records (classical training, baccalauréat distinctions, etc.) are more ready to define the trick word, and that it is the category privileged in each of the respects previously mentioned who produce the largest number of imperturbably prolix definitions of this anthropological-sounding term, it may be concluded that ease in the handling of language can run to off-handedness when combined with the self-assurance given by membership of a privileged category.[18]

Similarly, methodical observation of the linguistic and gestural behaviour of candidates in an oral examination enables us to bring to light some of the social signs by which professorial judgement is unconsciously guided, and among which we must count the indices of the modality of the use of language (grammar, accent, tone, delivery, etc.), itself linked to the modality of the relation to the teacher and the situation which is manifested in bearing, gesture, dress, make-up and mimicry.[19] The analysis required for the purposes of experimentation reveals that nothing, certainly not the appreciation of even the most technical knowledge and know-how, goes uncontaminated by the system of convergent or, more precisely, redundant impressions bearing on one total disposition, that is, on the system of *manners* character-istic of a social position.[20] Thus, in contrast to the ease that is called 'forced', particularly frequent among those middle- or working-class students who strive, by rapid delivery and not without many false notes, to conform to the norms of university verbalizing, the ease that is called 'natural' affirms the well-mastered mastery of language in the casualness of the delivery, the evenness of the tone and the stylistic under-statement that betoken the art of concealing art, the supreme manner of suggesting, by the tempering applied to the temptation of speaking too well, the potential excellence of one's speech. If the laboured relation to language is unconsciously catalogued as the poor man's ease, or, what amounts to the same thing, the ostentation of the nouveau riche, this is because it lets its presentational function show through too clearly not to be suspected of self-interested vulgarity in the eyes of academics attached to the prestigious fiction of an exchange which, even in an examination, remains an end in itself.

The opposition between these two types of relation to language stems from the opposition between the two modes of acquiring verbal mastery, the exclusively scholastic acquisition which condemns the acquirer to a 'scholastic' relation to scholastic language and the mode of acquisition through insensible familiarization, which alone can fully produce the practical mastery of language and culture that authorizes cultivated allusion and cultured complicity.[21] There is a world of difference between the experience of school that is prepared for by a childhood spent in a family circle where words define the reality of things, and the experience of unreality given to working-class children by the scholastic acquisition of a language which tends to make unreal the things it speaks of because it makes up their whole reality: the 'pure', 'correct' — i.e. 'corrected' — language of the classroom is opposed to the language the teacher's marginal notes stigmatize as 'vulgar' or 'common', and even more to the anti-language of the boarding school, where children from rural areas, confronted with the simultaneous experience of forced acculturation and insidious counter-acculturation, can only choose between duplication and acceptance of exclusion.

There is perhaps no better indication of the objective functions of the French educational system than the well-nigh absolute pre-ponderance it gives to oral transmission and the manipulation of words, at the expense of other techniques of inculcation or assimilation. The disproportion between the space accorded to lecture halls and the space devoted to practical-work rooms or reading rooms, or the extreme difficulty of obtaining access to the tools of self-teaching, whether books or machines, betrays the disproportion between learning by hearsay and learning from documentary evidence through orderly dis-cussion, practice, experiment, reading or production of work.[22] More precisely, the primacy of oral transmission must not conceal the fact that communication is conducted through a spoken word dominated by the written word, as is shown by the great value set on the rules of written expression and literate stylistics, which tend to be imposed on all utterances regulated and sanctioned by the university institution, whether in the lecture or in the candidates' oral productions. In an academic universe in which the ideal is to 'talk like a book', the only fully legitimate speech is one which presupposes at every point the whole context of legitimate culture and no other context.[23]

The hierarchy of pedagogic tasks, as manifested objectively in the organization of the institution and the ideology of its agents, is no less revelatory. Of all the obligations of professorship, transmission by literate word of mouth is the only one felt as an unconditional im-perative; and so it takes pride of place over the tasks of organizing and assessing the students' work, such as the marking of scripts, commonly held to be the dull obverse of the act of teaching and left to assistant lecturers, except when it is an occasion to exercise the sovereign power of the examining board of one of the great national *concours.* The titles designating the different university ranks are evidence that the higher one rises in the hierarchy the more one is legitimated to speak the legitimate language of the institution: the *assistant* will only ever give 'practicals' even if he does nothing but talk; the *chargé d'enseignement* gives 'teaching' *(enseignement)* and the *maître de conférences,* who does just the same thing, gives 'lectures' *(conférences),* but only the professor delivers allegedly magisterial courses *(cours magistraux).*[24] This stratified system of 'terms of reference' hides, under the guise of a technical division of tasks, a hierarchy of degrees of excellence in the performance of a single function, still held, ideally, to be indivisible, even if hard times and operational requirements oblige the exclusive holders of tenure to distribute that function among an ever growing army of auxiliaries.[25]

The relation to language and knowledge implied in the primacy of words and the well-read manipulation of words constitutes, for the teaching corps, the most economical way, that is, the one most consonant with their previous training, of adapting themselves to the institutional conditions in which they work, and particularly to the morphology of the pedagogic space and the social structure of their public:

> Twice a week the professor had to appear for an hour before a random audience often made up, for two successive lectures, of quite different individuals. He had to speak without concerning himself with his pupils' special needs, without having inquired what they know and do not know (. . .) Long scientific deductions requiring the listener to have followed a whole series of arguments had to be eliminated (. . .) Open to all, turned into the arena of a sort of competition to attract and hold the public, what can university courses be in such circumstances? Brilliant expositions, 'recitations' in the manner of the orators of declining Rome (. . .) The swing-door opening and shutting throughout the performance, the perpetual coming and going, the listeners' air of having nothing better to do, the professor's tone, rarely didactic, sometimes declamatory, his skill at hunting out sonorous commonplaces which convey nothing new but which infallibly spark off signs of assent — it all seems remote and improbable.[26]

More generally, it is impossible to understand the style peculiar to French academic and intellectual life unless it is seen that a mode of inculcation which tends to reduce pedagogic action to a verbal incantation or an exemplary exhibition is particularly appropriate to the interests of a body of professors directly subjected, especially nowadays, to the models of the intellectual field and called upon to affirm themselves as intellectuals in their pedagogic practice itself. Doubtless

there is nothing to prevent the ex cathedra lecture from serving functions different from or even opposed to those it has in a traditional
pedagogy, as when, for example, in an initiatory phase, it enables the
preliminaries of pedagogic communication and work to be transmitted
in the most economical way, or, in research teaching, is used to present
a theoretical synthesis or a problematic, or when it is recorded for use
as a simple technical support for repeated exercises. However, by virtue
of the weight it carries in the system of the means of inculcation, and
by virtue of the relation to language and knowledge it calls for, the
French-style professorial lecture, a well-tempered balance between com-
pilation without heaviness and creation without excess, authorizes and
produces, even in its most desperate imitations, a double-dealing with
the norms it purports to accept: the demands of didactic clarity
dispense it from the meticulousness of erudite references, the appearances of erudition dispense it from original research, and the appearance of creative improvisation can in any case dispense it from both
clarity and erudition. It can be seen that the institutional conditions of
pedagogic communication authorize and favour a professorial charisma
(if the oxymoron will pass) capable of imposing the academic summas
which, for the space of a university reign or dynasty, oust all the works
they claim to conserve and supersede.[27]

It is also clear why so many actual or would-be intellectuals manifest
their conformity to the dominant model of the relation to language and
culture even in those aspects of their behaviour seemingly least marked
by their education. It is only an apparent paradox that 'extra-curricular'
culture should contain the truth of school culture, or more precisely
that it should be in the least academic utterances of the intellectuals
most free of academic constraints that one finds the clearest expression
of the complacent attitude to culture which is encouraged and recognized by a university bound by its contract of delegation to
shoulder the depreciation of everything which savours of the academic.
If Parisian-style culture fades away the moment one tries to assess it by
means of a test of knowledge, this is because it owes its insubstantial
structure to the conditions in which it is acquired, whether through

brief encounters with authors, their works and those who talk about both, or through weekly consultation of the gazettes of the intellectual demi-monde; above all it is because the relation to culture acquired in such conditions is appropriate for use in areas abandoned to distinguished conversation or bohemian argument and consigned to the classificatory grimaces of salon conversation or the all-embracing taxonomies which in the twinkling of an eye confound left and right in art or philosophy with left and right in politics. But it would be naive to suppose that the function of social distinction performed by the cultivated relation to culture is exclusively and eternally attached to 'general culture' in its 'humanistic' form. The glamour of econometrics, computer science, operational research or the latest thing in structuralism can serve, no less well than knowledge of the classics or the ancient languages in another epoch, as an elegant ornament or an instrument of social success: consider the technocrats who hawk from conference to conference knowledge acquired at conferences; the essayists who draw from a diagonal reading of the most general pages of the least specialized works of specialists matter for general disquisitions on the inherent limits of the specialization of specialists; or the dandies of scientificity, past masters in the art of the chic allusion which instantly places the speaker in the outposts of the avant-garde sciences which bear no stain of the plebeian sin of positivism.

CONVERSATION AND CONSERVATION

But to suppose that practices and ideologies whose possibility and probability are objectively inscribed in the structure of the relation of pedagogic communication and in the social and institutional conditions of its conduct can be explained solely by reference to the interests of the teaching corps or, still more naively, by the pursuit of prestige or gratifications of self-esteem, would be to forget that, in order to fulfil its social function of legitimating the dominant culture, an educational system must obtain the recognition of the authority of its action, even if this has to take the form of recognition of the authority of the masters appointed to inculcate that culture. Reference to the limiting case of an educational system having no other technical function beyond its social function of legitimating the culture and relation to culture of the dominant classes enables us to bring to light some of the tendencies of the French system, which is able to communicate so little while giving such prominence to the spoken word, only because it always tends to give primacy to the social function of culture (scientific as well as literary culture) over the technical function of competence. If magisterial discourse were to owe its audience entirely to the authority of the institution, it would at least impose the authority of the institution which makes it possible and the legitimacy of its de facto addressees. 'What is left when you have forgotten everything else' is a relation to culture defined by the right to forget which is implied by the fact of having known or, rather, of being socially recognized as having learnt. What indeed is left from long frequentation of ancient texts or protracted dealings with classic authors, apart from the right to hear phrases from the pink pages of the dictionary without a blush[28] and, at a higher degree of academic consecration, the ease and familiarity characteristic of the 'relations as between a famous father and his sons or nephews' with which Giraudoux complacently credits *normaliens,* those 'intimates of the great ethics, the great aesthetics and the great authors'?

In conceding the teacher the right and the power to deflect the authority of the institution onto his own person, the educational system secures the surest means of getting the office-holder to put all the resources and zeal of the person into the service of the institution and through it the institution's social function. Whether or not he wants to or is even aware of it, the teacher must define himself by reference to the social definition of a practice which, in its traditional form, cannot forego some dramatic action. Although it presupposes pedagogic authority in order to take place, pedagogic action must, by an apparent paradox, obtain the recognition of its authority in and through the performance of the work of inculcation. Being required to exalt the quality of his office and the culture he communicates by the quality of his personal manner of communicating it, the teacher must be equipped by the institution with the symbolic attributes of the authority of his mission (not least the livery of the Word which is to the teacher what the white overall or jacket is to the cook, the hairdresser, the waiter or the nurse), so as to be able to afford the elegance of ostentatiously renouncing the most visible protections of the institution, while accentuating those aspects of his task which, like the gestures of the surgeon, the soloist or the acrobat, are predisposed to manifest symbolically the unique quality of the performer and the performance. The most typically charismatic feats, such as verbal acrobatics, hermetic allusion, disconcerting references or peremptory obscurity, as well as the technical tricks which serve as their support or substitute, such as the concealment of sources, the insertion of studied jokes or the avoidance of compromising formulations, owe their symbolic efficacy to the context of authority the institution sets up for them. And if the institution tolerates and so strongly encourages disrespect for the accessories and even the institutional rules, this is because pedagogic action must always transmit not only a content but also the affirmation of the value of that content, and there is no better way of doing so than by diverting onto the thing communicated the glamour which the irreplaceable manner of communicating it secures for the interchangeable author of the communication.

But ultimately, to authorize the games with the institutional rule which, like the liberties taken with the syllabus that implicitly are on the syllabus, contribute better than crude, immediate imposition of the rule towards imposing unconscious recognition of the rule, is to inculcate, through a relation to the teacher, a relation to the academic institution and, through this, a relation to language and culture which is none other than that of the dominant classes. Thus the ruse of academic reason, by which the institution leads the teacher to serve it by disposing him to make use of it, ultimately serves a function of social conservation which academic reason cannot recognize. If the freedom the educational system allows the teacher is the best guarantee that he will serve the system, the freedom allowed to the educational system is the best guarantee that it will serve the perpetuation of the relations prevailing between the classes, because the possibility of this redirection of ends is inscribed in the very logic of a system which never better fulfils its social function than when it seems to be exclusively pursuing its own ends.

To establish in another way that the relation to language and culture, that infinite sum of infinitesimal differences in manners of doing and saying which seems to be the most perfect expression of the autonomy of the school system and the academic tradition, sums up in one respect the ensemble of the relations between this system and the structure of class relations, one only has to imagine all the prerequisites which would be objectively implied in setting up a different relation to language in all school practices.[29] Thus it is impossible to imagine a teacher able to maintain with his own discourse, his pupils' discourse and his pupils' relation to his own discourse. a relation stripped all of indulgences and freed from all the traditional complicities, without at the same time crediting him with the capacity to subordinate his whole pedagogic practice to the imperatives of a perfectly explicit pedagogy which could actually implement the principles logically implied in affirmation of the autonomy of the specifically scholastic mode of acquisition. There is indeed every difference in the world between a teaching oriented by the express intention of minimizing code mistakes by continuously and methodically stating the code, and the forms of teaching which are able to dispense with expressly teaching the transmission code because they speak by tacit agreement to a public prepared by insensible familiarization to understand their tacit meanings. Pedagogic work expressly guided by the methodical pursuit of maximum efficiency would thus tend consciously to reduce the gap between the level of transmission and the level of reception — whether by raising the reception level by giving, together with the message, the code for deciphering it, in a mode of expression (verbal, graphic or gestural) whose code the receiver is already familiar with; or by temporarily lowering the transmission level in accordance with a programme of controlled progress, in which each message serves to prepare for reception of the message at the next level of transmission and so produces a steady rise in the level of reception by giving the receivers the means of acquiring complete possession of the code through repetition and practice.[30]

Maximizing the productivity of pedagogic work would ultimately imply not only recognition of the gap between the linguistic competences of transmitter and receiver but also knowledge of the social conditions of the production and reproduction of that gap, that is, knowledge both of the modes of acquisition of the different class languages and of the scholastic mechanisms which consecrate and so help to perpetuate inter-class linguistic differences. It is immediately clear that, short of relying on the accidents or miracles of individual conversions, such practice can be expected only from teachers objectively constrained to satisfy a specifically and exclusively pedagogic demand; to put it another way, it would require a pedagogic action directed towards the inculcation of a different relation to language and culture, i.e. subordinated to the objective interests of a quite different public, and teachers recruited and trained to satisfy the requirements of posts that were differentiated technically — and not merely hierarchically — and thus capable of preventing the play of circular alibis that is authorized by the traditional cumulation of the tasks of teaching, research and even management.[31] In short, only a school system serving another system of external functions and, correlatively, another state of the balance of power between the classes, could make such pedagogic action possible.

If the French educational system perpetuates and consecrates a cultural privilege founded on a monopoly of the conditions of acquisition of the relation to culture that the privileged classes tend to recognize and impose as legitimate precisely to the extent they monopolize it, this is because the relation to culture it recognizes is fully mastered only when the culture it inculcates has been acquired by familiarization; it is also because the mode of inculcation that the system sets up remains, despite its relative autonomy, continuous with the mode of inculcation of legitimate culture for which the social conditions are only ever given to families whose culture is the culture of the dominant classes. It can be seen, first, that in not explicitly giving what it demands, the system demands uniformly of all its students that they should have what it does not give, i.e. the relation to language and culture exclusively produced by a particular mode of inculcation. Secondly, it is clear that, in perpetuating a mode of inculcation differing as little as possible from the family mode, it gives training and information which can be fully received only by those who have had the training it does not give. Thus the dependence of the traditional system on the dominant classes is to be seen in the primacy it gives to the relation to culture over culture and, among the possible types of relation to culture, to the one it can never fully produce: the school system betrays the final truth of its dependence on class relations when it disparages the over-scholastic manners of those who owe their manners to it, thereby disavowing its own manner of producing manners and confessing by the same token its incapacity to affirm the autonomy of a specifically scholastic mode of production.

Just as traditional economic conduct is defined as an objectively economic practice which cannot declare itself as such and consequently cannot explicitly pose itself the question of its perfect adequacy to its objective ends,[32] so traditional pedagogic work may be defined as a *pedagogy in itself*, i.e. as a pedagogic practice which is unaware of or refuses rational calculation of the means best suited to achieve the functions it objectively asserts by its very existence. The academic depreciation of the academic manner, of which the French university provides countless examples and which is paralleled both in the debate set up by the ancient Greek schools on the possibility of teaching excellence and in the Confucian cult of amateurism, is so universal only because it manifests the contradiction inherent in academic institutions which can neither repudiate their pedagogic function without denying themselves as schools nor recognize it completely without denying themselves as traditional schools. The 'academic anti-academicism' of

ch the hierarchies remain fluid. In accordance with the eternal scheme
always confirmed because it produces what confirms it, only 'a few
ividuals' ever emerge from 'the whole batch , *rari nantes in gurgite*
agrégation reports might put it: 'The exercise was satisfactory in that
light talent or the absence of talent' (*Agrégation féminine de lettres*
9, p. 23). Not that traditional humanities teaching has a monopoly
of thought: 'Apart from a few exceptional candidates of striking
dazzling personality, the examination leaves an impression of
iners' observations on the work of the candidates for the Ecole
inistration, *Epreuves et statistiques du concours de 1967*, Paris.
nale, 1968, p. 9) (see also 1975, 10).
model pupils who would like to have no pupils except future
are predisposed by their whole training and all their educational
the game of the institution. In addressing himself to the
ought to be, the teacher infallibly discourages the student's
d the right to be only what he is: the teacher respects, by the
e fictitious student whom a few 'gifted pupils', objects of all
authorize him to regard as real.
as its fashion, in which, as in a clumsy caricature, one
image of the advice or teaching of some master or other'
de lettres, 1950, p. 10). 'Looking through the batch of
than in anger, one finds . . .'. To account for the destruc-
t inflicts on everything he touches, professorial discourse
hors of barbarism and those of natural disaster: the
havoc', 'tortures', 'corrupts', 'devastates' language or
icate text was ill-treated and savaged' (*Agrégation
es*, 1964, p. 22).
Argonauts of the Western Pacific, London, RKP,

ic relations between transmitters and receivers only
sis, the structure of objective relations defining the
nonetheless capable of adding their own force to
critical states of the system, when, within certain
fictitiously the appearances of a communication
no longer fulfilled. Thus the adhesion of teachers
ological, hence ethical, vision of the pedagogic
ir complicity in misunderstanding and in the
rstanding, are evidence that the representations
ations, experienced as interpersonal relations,
spect to those objective conditions, since, up
onceal the transformations of the structure of

the Ming and Ch'ing periods stands in the same relation to the formal
conventions, devices, restrictions and prescriptions which define the
tradition of scholarly painting as professorial exaltation of creative
inspiration to the routine didactics of literature professors, pious
ministers of genius who are as far from practising what they preach as
they are from preaching what they practise.[33] But the apparent contradiction between the reality of literate traditions or traditional
schools and the ideology of the 'gift', which is perhaps most stridently
affirmed in the most routine-bound school systems, must not conceal
the fact that the scholastic cult of the non-scholastic relation to culture
— even school culture — is predisposed to assume a conservative
function, since, even in its omissions, schooling of the traditional type
automatically serves the pedagogic interests of the classes which need
the school in order to give scholastic legitimation to a relation to
culture which they never owe to it in full.

In bringing to light the relations which prevail, in the most diverse
historical situations, between the culture of the dominant classes and
traditional pedagogy, or more precisely, the relations of structural and
functional affinity between the value systems of any privileged class
(inclined to stylize a culture reduced to a code of manners) and
traditional school systems devoted to reproducing the legitimate
manner of using the legitimate culture, historical comparison enables us
to understand those aspects of the French system in which this recurrent combination of elements is expressed. To explain the specific form
this combination has taken in the French academic and intellectual
tradition, one would no doubt have to go back to the work of the
Society of Jesus which, in secularizing Christian ethics, succeeded in
converting the theology of grace into a worldly, 'society' ideology of
good grace. But the persistence of this historical form has no explanatory value unless it is in turn explained by the persistence of its
functions: the continuity of pedagogic customs within the continuous
history of the education system has been made possible by the continuity of the services rendered by a School which, despite the changes
in the social structure, has always managed to occupy homologous

positions in the system of relations which link it to the dominant classes.[34] Thus, the constellation of attitudes which was codified in the seventeenth-century ethic of the *honnête homme* — and is not so far removed from the ethic of the 'literary gentleman' in the Confucian tradition — owes to the historical permanence of its function the ease with which it has been able to perpetuate itself, at the cost of a few reinterpretations, despite the changing of the content of school curricula and the changing of the classes placed in the dominant position. Consider, for example, the primacy of manner and style; the value attached to naturalness and lightness, conceived as the antithesis of pedantry, didacticism or effort; the cult of the 'gift' and the disparagement of apprenticeship, the modern reformulation of the ideology of 'birth' and contempt for study; the disdain for specialization, trades and techniques, the bourgeois transposition of contempt for business; the pre-eminence conferred on the art of pleasing, that is, the art of adapting oneself to the diversity of social encounters and conversations; the attention devoted to nuances and imponderables, perpetuating the aristocratic tradition of 'refinement' and expressed in the subordination of scientific to literary culture, and of literary culture to artistic culture, still more conducive to the indefinite niceties of the games of distinction; in short, all the ways, declared or tacit, of reducing culture to the relation to culture, in other words, of setting against the vulgarity of what can be acquired or achieved a manner of possessing an acquirement whose whole value derives from the fact that there is but one way of acquiring it.

NOTES

1. The first part of this chapter takes up certain analyses which have been published elsewhere (P. Bourdieu, J.-C. Passeron and M. de Saint-Martin, 1965, 2)

but which, because they were not suppor
authority as the social condition of the p
communication, could lend themselves
the most radical refusal of purely ps
action, and to challenge the naivety c
of the agents, this is because a sea
allowed it to be supposed that th
their ideology, would still be ob
in and by its functioning, prod
conditions of the possibility of

2. *le langage magistral:*
but also that of the ex cath

3. The relation of sy
characteristic of a domin
arbitrariness in the eyes
crisis when the whole
challenge. There is a c
most educational in
liturgy, suppression
tion, use of the
participation by

4. If univ
because it sy
traditional f
spatial orga
more real
other re
prevent
retaine
which

c

objective relations which made them possible.

11. Unless this unlikely and incongruous endeavour earned him the equally spurious prestige of non-conformism, in which case the institution would still have put him in the wrong.

12. I.e. a bare pass with 10/20 (trans.).

13. It sometimes happens, in the *classes préparatoires* for example, that the rules defining the traditional relation to language are made explicit in the maxims of academic prudence which testify to the fact that 'higher rhetoric' and 'the rhetoric of despair' ultimately presuppose the same relation to language. Every candidate knows, for example, that it would be the height of naivety 'to write nothing just because you know nothing' and that 'you don't need to know much to scrape a pass in History', provided you know how to use a chronology without exposing egregious lacunae. To be sure, this crafty prudence has its risks, as shown by the story of the candidate who, having read in the chronology *Krach boursier à Vienne* (Vienna stockmarket crash), wrote about the Viennese stockbroker Krach *(Krach boursier à Vienne)*. When teachers joke about such gems, they forget that these misfirings of the system contain the truth of the system. If one remembers that the 'university elite' was trained in this way, and if one considers the ethical implications of such exercises, then a whole aspect of *homo academicus* and his intellectual productions is illuminated.

14. J. Damourette and E. Pichon, *Des mots à la pensée, Essai de grammaire de la langue française*, Paris, Collection des linguistes contemporains, 1931, T.I, p. 50.

15. It can be seen, for example, that the syntactic complexity of the language used is taken into account not only in explicit evaluation of the qualities of form which language exercises — composition, dissertation, etc. — are supposed to measure, but also in every evaluation of intellectual operations (mathematical demonstration as well as the decoding of a work of art) that entail the handling of complex schemes, an accomplishment unequally accessible to individuals equipped with a practical mastery of language unequally predisposing them towards the most accomplished form of symbolic mastery.

16. The description of the opposition between bourgeois language and working-class language could be taken further with the aid of the remarkable analyses Basil Bernstein and his school have devoted to the differences between the 'formal language' of the 'middle classes' and the 'public language' of the working class. However, in failing to formulate the implicit assumptions of the theoretical tradition to which his analyses belong (whether the Sapir-Whorf anthropological tradition or the philosophical tradition which runs from Kant to Cassirer through Humboldt), Bernstein tends to reduce to intrinsic characteristics of the language, such as degree of syntactic complexity, differences whose unifying, generative principle lies in the different types of relation to language,

themselves embedded in different systems of attitudes towards the world and other people. Though the modus operandi can be grasped most objectively in the opus operatum, the productive habitus (i.e. in this case, the relation to language) must not be reduced to its product (here, a certain structure of discourse): to do so would mean seeking in the language the determining principle of speakers' attitudes, in short, taking the linguistic product for the producer of the attitudes that produce it. The *realism of the structure* inherent in such a sociology of language tends to exclude from the field of research the question of the social conditions of production of the attitude system governing, inter alia, the structuration of language. To make just one example, the distinctive features of the language of the lower middle classes [*les classes moyennes*], such as faulty hyper-correctness and proliferation of the signs of grammatical control, are indices among others of a relation to language characterized by anxious reference to the legitimate norm of academic correctness. The uneasiness about the right manner – whether table manners or language manners – which petty-bourgeois speech betrays is expressed even more clearly in the avid search for the means of acquiring the sociability techniques of the class to which they aspire – etiquette handbooks and guides to usage. This relation to language can be seen to be an integral part of a system of attitudes to culture which rests on the pure will to respect a cultural code more recognized than known, and on a meticulous respect for rules, a cultural willingness which, in the last analysis, expresses the objective characteristics of the condition and position of the middle strata in the structure of class relations (see also 1975, 7).

17. To ignore the distinction between behaviour and modality of behaviour inevitably leads one purely and simply to treat as identical practices or opinions that are separated only by their modalities – in politics, for example, the different ways (linked to social origin) of being and declaring oneself 'left wing' which make all the difference between the leftist and the thwarted rightist, or in art, the different ways of appreciating or admiring the same work which would be revealed in the whole constellation of works conjointly admired or in the manner of the utterance in which admiration is declared. Everything that is referred to as culture is at stake in the 'trifling' nuances which separate cultivated allusion from scholastic commentary or, more subtly, the different significations of acquiescence by interjection and mimicry. Those who would see in this only an inconsequential *distinguo* should bear in mind that the modality of a 'commitment' reveals, more tellingly than the manifest content of opinions, the likelihood of its being acted upon, because it directly expresses the habitus as the conduct-generating principle and so provides a more reliable basis for forecasting, especially in the long term.

18. Among the remarks made on the term gérophagie it is easy to distinguish two phraseologies betokening two relations to language (M = male, F = female, P = Paris, p = provinces, Wo = working class, Mi = middle class, Up = upper class): 'I

don't know the definition' (M p Wo). 'Means nothing to me' (F p Mi). 'Gero (perhaps old?); phagy: act of eating; so someone who eats old people? (subject to correction)' (M p Mi). 'The etymology seems to indicate the fact of eating the old' (F p Mi). These responses, expressing either lucidity or scholastic prudence, or more precisely the desire to 'do one's best' to make use of one's knowledge within the bounds of scholastic prudence, contrast with another phraseology, peremptory, arrogant, off-hand or recherché: 'The etymology is as follows (. . .) Gerophagy is therefore the custom of eating the aged among certain non-Promethean clansmen' (M P Up). 'If *gero* comes from *geras*, an old man, then gerophagy designates a form of anthropophagy preferentially oriented towards the older elements of population X' (F P Up). 'Formed from the aorist of –, to eat; the consumption of old people, a practice encountered among certain primitive tribes' (F P Mi). 'The eating of *gero* as in the eating of *anthropo*' (M P Up).

19. Initial methodical observation reveals, for example, that the positive or negative signs of verbal or postural ease (oratorical action, bodily manifestations of embarrassment or anxiety such as trembling of the hands or blushing, way of speaking, whether improvising or reading notes, manners characterizing the relation to the examiner, such as the search for approval or well-bred detachment, etc.) appear to be strongly linked to one another as well as to social origin. Whatever its limitations, this experiment at least has the effect, because it entails the unusual standpoint of analytical observation, of bringing to light certain social factors of assessment, and also the devious paths they have to take in order to act in spite of the censorship on taking them expressly into account. Thus the embarrassment or clumsiness of working-class students or the insistent willingness of middle-class students can play their part in the examiners' deliberations only in the guise of 'psychological' qualities such as 'timidity' or 'nervousness'. Only experimental measurement of these indices, by which the appreciation of the candidates' worth is unconsciously governed, would make it possible to draw out the social implications of the categories of university perception which are expressed in the terminology of professorial jurisprudence – examiners' reports, marginal comments on scripts, termly reports etc. (cf. 1975, 10).

20. It is this system of manners, working as a mass of infinitesimal indices of indissolubly intellectual 'qualities', that supplies the cues for social perception of the 'spirit' proper to this or that training. 'In the seminary', said Stendhal, 'there is a way of eating a boiled egg which announces the progress made in the religious life.' The edifying literature of the alumni's associations strives through incantatory, sometimes desperate prose, to evoke this phenomenon: 'The H.E.C. spirit is a whole way of thinking, a cast of mind (. . .) a certain way of conducting oneself in life.' And one could quote countless examples of solemn disquisitions or sententious chatter on the style of the *normalien* or the virtues of the

polytechnicien [see Glossary].

21. It is significant that to distinguish genuine bilingualism from scholarly, i.e. scholastic, bilingualism, some linguists will resort to the criterion of ease, 'the native-like control of two languages', as Bloomfield puts it (L. Bloomfield, *Language*, 1933, rpt. London, Allan & Unwin, 1956, p. 56).

22. An indication of the influence of oral transmission on school learning may be seen in the fact that the lecture-course tends, to an unequal extent, depending on the category of students (by the general law of attitude variation according to sex, residence and social origin), to take the place of every other mode of acquisition, especially books, as is shown by the value attached to lecture notes, which are read and reread, swapped and borrowed.

23. It is not difficult to show that French university language obeys the implicit rules of written discourse more fully than does the scholarly language of other educational traditions. Three-point composition, the organization of each part of the statement (particularly the professorial lecture, often given straight to the publishers) in accordance with a plan which implies reference to the whole at all times, has as its model, and often its precondition, written discourse, with the second thoughts and revisions (successive drafts) it permits. Not to mention the inhibition of the products of French education towards the use of foreign languages, which they would rather not speak at all than not speak them as they ought to be written.

24. As for the primary school teacher, he prosaically 'does the class' ['il fait la classe'], i.e. his job. It is not surprising that students whose social origin predisposes them to distinguished casualness betray in so much of their conduct aristocratic contempt for subaltern tasks (a reflection of the university opposition between the perfectly accomplished intellectual act and the laborious processes of pedagogic work), since the academic institution objectively relegates to the lowest place in its hierarchy the methodical inculcation of the material and intellectual techniques of intellectual work and the technical relation to these techniques.

25. The recruitment policy which has led to a great increase, since about 1960, in the number of junior, untenured faculty staff, while the rules defining access to the rank of full professor remained unchanged, would not have been so readily accepted if the traditional institution had not produced the conditions for that policy and the agents most disposed to go along with it: the university power-holders profited from an expansion on the cheap which extended the scope of their authority without endangering it; those who paid the price for the economies thus made found in the traditional model of promotion by seniority grounds for identifying in advance, qua potential successors, with the inaccessible master (witness their resigned and sometimes militant submission to the self-mortification of the interminable *thèse d'état*); and, more profoundly, each side found in a university organization which, like the medieval corporation, knew no

other division of labour than hierarchical distinction between the degrees of a scale of dignity, an incitement to regard as natural or inevitable the indefinite lengthening of a career of indefinitely multiplied stages.

26. E. Renan, *Questions contemporaines*, Paris, Calman-Lévy, 1868, pp. 90-91. It is very generally observed that the higher a profession ranks in the hierarchy of occupations, the more the socially approved definition of accomplished exercise of the profession implies a detached distance from the task in hand, i.e. from the minimum (and subaltern) definition of the task. But teachers also have to reckon, especially in higher education, with an image of the accomplished exercise of their profession which has the objectivity of an institution and which can only fully be accounted for by a social history of the position of the intellectual fraction within the dominant classes and the position of university teachers within that fraction (i.e. in the intellectual field). But a complete analysis of the functions of these practices and ideologies would, above all, have to take into account the very real services they render this or that category of teachers in a given state of the educational system. Thus conduct which, like the flaunted refusal to check student attendance or demand the punctual submission of assignments, offers a means of achieving with less effort the image of a quality teacher for quality students, enables teachers who, especially in subordinate positions, are condemned to permanent juggling of research with teaching, to reduce their work-load and so find a practical solution to the situation which the most over-crowded faculties and disciplines create for them.

27. Kant, whose historical position predisposed him to perceive the first signs of the Romantic revolt against Enlightenment rationalism, particularly against its confidence in the powers of education, well describes the effects of the *institutional charisma* authorized by the ideology of inspiration and creative genius:

> But a breed of so-called men of genius (apes of genius, rather) has insinuated itself under that sign: speaking the language of minds exceptionally favoured by nature, they declare painstaking learning and research to be mere bungling, and claim to have grasped the spirit of all science in an instant but to dispense it concentrated in strong doses. This breed of men, like the race of quacks and mountebanks, is very deleterious to progress in scientific and moral culture when, from the chair of wisdom, it dogmatizes on religion, politics or ethics in incontrovertible tones, like an adept or potentate, and so contrives to mask the poverty of its mind. What is one to do against them, except laugh, and continue patiently on one's way, with diligence, order and clarity, without glancing back at those tricksters?

> (I. Kant, *Anthropologie in pragmatischer Hinsicht* (1798), *Sämmtliche Werke*, Leipzig, Voss, 1868, Bd. VII, p. 544.)

28. The reference is to the (pink) pages in the *Dictionnaire Larousse*, which

list 'Latin and other foreign expressions' [trans.].

   29. This imaginary variation presupposes that, in another historical context, culture could be dissociated from relation to culture, i.e. from the mode of acquisition by familiarization which bourgeois ideology posits as constitutive of the *nature of culture* by refusing to recognize as cultured any relation to culture other than the 'natural' one. Far from justifying the populist temptation of purely and simply canonizing popular culture by academic recognition, discovery of the pre-established harmony between the relation to culture recognized by the school and the relation to culture monopolized by the dominant classes requires one, when all the inferences are drawn, to completely reformulate the question of the relationship between academic culture and the culture of the dominant classes, since the school consecrates the dominant culture at least as much by the relation to culture it presupposes and consecrates, as by the content of the culture it transmits.

   30. Action directed towards the express goal of a higher level of reception is to be distinguished from the pure and simple lowering of the transmission level which generally characterizes the enterprise of popularization, and still more from the demagogic concessions of instruction (or any other form of cultural diffusion) which seeks to dispense with pedagogic work by fixing the transmission once and for all on a given state of the reception level. If one accepts that an educational system always has to reckon with a social definition of the competence technically demandable, i.e. to ensure at all events the inculcation of an incompressible minimum of information and training, then it is clear that it is impossible to lower indefinitely the quantity of information transmitted in order to minimize its wastage, as happens in some non-directive teaching which boasts a high rate of assimilation but at the cost of a considerable lowering of the quantity of information assimilated. Pedagogic work is more productive, both absolutely and relatively, the more completely it satisfies two contradictory demands, neither of which can be completely sacrificed: first, the maximizing of the absolute quantity of information received, which may lead it to minimize redundance and seek conciseness and density (not to be confused with the ellipsis by omission and unspoken assumption found in traditional teaching); and secondly, the minimizing of loss, which may involve, among other techniques, the increasing of redundance in the form of conscious, calculated repetition (not to be confused with traditional redundance in the form of musical variation on a few themes).

   31. Without actually bringing about such a radical restructuring, the transformations of educational technology (audiovisual devices, programmed learning, etc.) tend to trigger a systematic set of transformations of the educational system. It would of course be a mistake to regard changes in the technological base of pedagogic communication as automatically determining; this would amount to

ignoring the dependence of the technical means on the system of the technical and social functions of the educational system (e.g. the sole effect of closed-circuit television can be to accentuate ad absurdum the traditional characteristics of the professorial lecture). However, to the extent that it affects the pedagogic relation in its most specific aspect, i.e. the instruments of communication, transformation of the technology of pedagogic action is liable to affect the social definition of the pedagogic relation, particularly the relative importance of the act of transmission and the work of assimilation, since, with the possibility of recording in advance a message which can be endlessly retransmitted, teaching is freed from the constraints of place and time and tends to be centred less on the transmitters and more on the receivers, who can make use of it when it suits them. Thus the intrinsic effect of recording is likely to bring about a strengthening of control over the act of transmission and a transformation of the system of reciprocal demands, with students tending, for example, to write off the traditional teacher's most cherished effects, such as his jokes or anecdotes, as 'useless', while teachers are forced into stricter self-censorship by the disappearance of the safeguards previously given by the irreversible flight of speech.

32. See 1977, 1, for an analysis of the misrecognition which founds archaic economic conduct (trans.).

33. J. R. Levenson, *Confucian China and its Modern Fate*, London, RKP, 1958, Vol. I, *passim*, esp. p. 31. Cf. also E. Balazs, 'Les aspects significatifs de la société chinoise', *Asiatische Studien*, VI (1952), pp. 79-87.

34. The mode of inculcation and mode of imposition characteristic of a determinate educational system can never be entirely dissociated from the specific characteristics which the culture it is mandated to reproduce owes to its social functions in a determinate type of structure of class relations. Thus, as Calverton points out, whereas in France it is a *grande bourgeoisie* still partly faithful to the cultural ideal of the aristocracy that has given its specific form to the dominant culture and to the institutions mandated to reproduce it, in the US from the very beginning it is the petty bourgoisie that has marked the cultural and academic traditions (V. F. Calverton, *The Liberation of American Literature*, New York, Charles Scribner's Sons, 1932, p. xv). Similarly, it is in a systematic comparison of the relative positions of the bourgeoisie and aristocracy in France and Germany in different periods that one would doubtless find the principle underlying the differences between the educational systems of the two countries, particularly as regards their relationship with the dominant representation of the cultivated man.

3

EXCLUSION AND SELECTION

The examination is nothing but the bureaucratic baptism of knowledge, the official recognition of the transubstantiation of profane
knowledge into sacred knowledge.

Marx

Critique of Hegel's Doctrine of the State

To explain the importance of the role the French educational system
assigns to the examination, it is first necessary to break with the
explanations offered by spontaneous sociology, which imputes the
most salient features of the system to the unexplained legacy of a
national tradition or the inexplicable action of the congenital conservatism of academics. But the question is not at an end when, by
recourse to the comparative method and to history, one has accounted
for the characteristics and internal functions of the examination within
a particular system of education: it is only by making a second break,
this time with the illusion of the neutrality and independence of the
school system with respect to the structure of class relations, that it
becomes possible to question research into examinations so as to
discover what examinations hide and what research into examinations
only helps to hide by distracting inquiry from the elimination which
takes place without examination.

THE EXAMINATION WITHIN
THE STRUCTURE AND HISTORY
OF THE EDUCATIONAL SYSTEM

It is all too obvious that, at least in present-day France, examinations dominate university life, that is to say, not only the representations and practices of the agents but also the organization and functioning of the institution. Commentators have often enough described the anxiety engendered by the total, harsh and partly unpredictable verdicts of the traditional tests, or the dislocated rhythm inherent in a system of organizing school work which, in its most anomic forms, tends to acknowledge no other incentive than the imminence of an absolute deadline. In fact the examination is not only the clearest expression of academic values and of the educational system's implicit choices: in imposing as worthy of university sanction a social definition of knowledge and the way to show it, it provides one of the most efficacious tools for the enterprise of inculcating the dominant culture and the value of that culture. As much as or more than through the constraints of curriculum and syllabus, the acquisition of legitimate culture and the legitimate relation to culture is regulated by the customary law which is constituted in the jurisprudence of examinations and which owes its main characteristics to the situation in which it is formulated.[1]

Thus, for example, the French-style dissertation defines and diffuses rules of writing and composition whose authority extends into the most diverse areas, since one can find the stamp of these school manu-facturing devices in products as different as an administrative report, a doctoral thesis or a literary essay. To get a complete idea of the characteristics of this mode of written communication, which pre-supposes the examiner as the sole reader, one would only have to compare it with the *disputatio,* a debate between peers, conducted in the presence of the masters and a whole audience, through which the medieval university inculcated a method of thought applicable to any form of intellectual and even artistic production; or the *pa-ku-wen,* the 'eight legged-essay' which constituted the decisive test in the competitions of the Ming and early Ch'ing periods and was the school of formal refinement for poet and learned painter, or with the British university essay, whose rules are not so different from those of the literary genre of the same name and in which the subject must be approached with wit and a light touch, unlike the French-style dissertation which must start with an introduction setting out the problem 'with brio and brilliance', but in a style free from all familiarity or personal comment. It would be seen that the different types of academic test, which are always, at the same time, institutionalized models of communication, provide the prototype for the pedagogic message and, more generally, for any message of a certain intellectual ambition (lectures, reports, political speeches, press conferences, etc.).[2] Thus, the schemes of expression and thought which are too hastily put down to national character' or 'schools of thought' may well derive from the models organized by a training directed towards a particular type of academic test:[3] for example the forms of mind associated with the French grandes écoles can be related to the forms of the entrance competitions and, more precisely, to the models of composition, style and even articulation, delivery or diction, which define in each case the accomplished form of presentation or elocution. More generally, it is clear that, as Renan showed, a selection procedure such as the *concours* reinforces the primacy which the whole tradition of the French University gives to qualities of form:

> It is most regrettable that the concours should be the only means of entering the teaching profession and that practical skill, combined with adequate knowledge, cannot give access to it. Those men most experienced in educating, who bring to their difficult task not brilliant faculties but a solid mind with a little slowness and timidity, will in public examinations always be placed after young men who know how to amuse their audience and their judges and who, though their glib tongues will get them out of trouble, have neither patience nor firmness enough to teach well.[4]

If it is true that examinations always express, inculcate and consecrate the values linked to a certain organization of the educational system, a certain structure of the intellectual field and, through these mediations, the dominant culture, it is clear why questions as insignificant at first sight as the number of baccalauréat sessions per year, the breadth of the syllabuses or the marking procedures should give rise to passionate polemics, not to mention the indignant resistance encountered by any challenging of institutions which crystallize as many values as the agrégation, the dissertation, the teaching of Latin, or the grandes écoles.

When one sets out to describe the most marked effects of the preponderance of examinations in intellectual practices and institutional organization, the French system offers the most perfect examples and, because it constitutes a limiting case, raises with particular force the question of the (internal and external) factors that can explain the historical or national variations in the functional weight of the examination within the educational system. Consequently, there is no alternative to using the comparative method when one wants to separate out what derives from external demands and what derives from the way they are responded to, or what, in the case of a given system, derives from the generic tendencies every educational system owes to its essential function of inculcation, to the particular traditions of a university history, and to its social functions, which are never completely reducible to the technical function of communication and producing skills.

If it is true that, as Durkheim observed, the advent of the examination — unknown to Antiquity, which saw only independent or even competing schools and teachers -- presupposes the existence of a university institution, i.e. an organized corps of professional teachers providing for its own perpetuation;[5] and if it is also true, as Weber argued, that a system of hierarchized examinations consecrating a specific skill and giving access to specialized careers appeared, in modern Europe, only in conjunction with the growing demand from bureaucratic organizations for hierarchized, interchangeable individuals to correspond to the hierarchy of posts offered;[6] and if it is true that a system of examinations ensuring formal equality for all before identical tests (the pure form of which is the national concours) and guaranteeing identically qualified individuals equal chances of entering the profession satisfies the petty-bourgeois ideal of formal equity — then there seem to be grounds for seeing no more than a particular manifestation of a general tendency of modern societies in the proliferation of examinations, the broadening of their social range and the growth of their functional weight within the educational system. But this analysis accounts only for the most general aspects of educational history (explaining, for example, why social upgrading independent of educational level tends to decline as a society becomes more industrialized and bureaucratized[7]) and fails to grasp that which the functioning and function of examinations owe, in their specific form, to the inherent logic of the educational system. By virtue of the particular inertia which characterizes it, especially when invested with the traditional function of conserving and transmitting a culture inherited from the past and when provided with specific means of self-reproduction, the school system is able to subject external demands to a systematic *retranslation* (systematic because effected in accordance with the principles which define it as a system). This is where the prerequisite stated by Durkheim takes on its full significance: Weber, who, in his sociology of religion, makes allowance for the tendencies proper to the sacerdotal corps, fails to take account (probably because he considers the educational system from an external point of view, i.e. from the point of view of the requirements of a bureaucratic organization) of what an educational system owes to the transhistorical and historical characteristics of a body of professional educators. Everything in fact suggests that the force of tradition weighs particularly heavily in an institution which, as Durkheim remarked, is more directly dependent on its own past because of the particular form of its relative autonomy.

To be convinced that the French system which, of all the educational systems of Europe, gives the greatest weight to examinations, defines itself less than it appears to in relation to the demands of economy, it is sufficient to observe that, in a system like that of classical China, which aimed primarily to train the functionaries of a prebendal bureaucracy, most of the features of the French system of selection could be paralleled.[8] If the Confucian tradition managed to impose its literary ideal so completely, it did so because no educational system has ever been more totally identified with its function of selection than the mandarin system, which was more concerned with organizing and codifying its competitions than with setting up schools and training teachers. And perhaps also because the hierarchy of academic achievement has never more rigorously determined the other social hierarchies than in a society where the official 'remained throughout his life under the control of the school':[9] the three major degrees (in which, as Weber points out, French translators immediately saw the equivalent of the *baccalauréat, licence* and *doctorat*)

> were considerably augmented by intermediary, repetitive and preliminary examinations (. . .) For the first degree alone there were ten types of examinations. The question usually put to a stranger of unknown rank was how many examinations he had passed. Thus, in spite of the ancestor cult, how many ancestors one had was not decisive for social rank. The very reverse held: it depended upon one's official rank whether one was allowed to have an ancestral temple (or a mere table of ancestors, which was the case with illiterates). How many ancestors one was permitted to mention was determined by official rank. Even the rank of a city god in the Pantheon depended upon the rank of the city's mandarin.[10]

Thus systems as different as those of modern France and classical China owe their common orientations to the fact that both treat a demand for *social selection* (in one case the demand of a traditional bureaucracy, in the other that of a capitalist economy) as an opportunity for fully expressing the peculiarly professorial tendency to maximize the social value of the human qualities and vocational qualifications which those systems produce, assess and consecrate.[11]

But for a full explanation of how the French system has been able to take advantage, more successfully than any other system, of the opportunities which the demand for social and technical selection characteristic of modern societies gave it in order to realize the potentialities of its own logic, we must also take into account the particular past of the educational institution, whose relative autonomy is objectively expressed in its capacity at each moment in history to retranslate and reinterpret external demands in terms of the norms inherited from a relatively autonomous history. If, unlike the mandarin system, the French system is not able to enforce recognition of the hierarchy of academic values as the official principle of every social hierarchy and every hierarchy of values, it nonetheless succeeds in competing with the other principles of hierarchization, especially when its action of inculcating the value of academic hierarchies is exerted on categories socially disposed to recognize the institution's pedagogic authority. Although the adherence individuals give to school hierarchies and to the scholastic cult of hierarchy is always related to the rank the School gives them in its hierarchies, it depends primarily, on the one hand, on the value system they owe to their social class of origin (the value accorded to the School within this system being, itself, a function of the degree to which that class's interests are linked to the School) and, on the other hand, on the degree to which their market value and social position depend on educational guarantees. This is why the school system is most successful in imposing recognition of the value of itself and its classifications when its action is applied to social classes or class fractions who are unable to counterpose to it any rival principle of hierarchy. This is one of the mechanisms which enable the academic institution to attract students from the middle classes or the intellectual fraction of the big bourgeoisie into the teaching profession, diverting them from aspiring to rise in other hierarchies, e.g of money or power, and thus from cashing their academic credentials into economic and social profit like students from the big bourgeoisie of business or power, who are better placed to relativize academic judgements.[12]

Thus, protest against the material and social conditions of teachers, or bitter, self-righteous denunciation of the compromises and corruptions of unscrupulous politicians and businessmen, doubtless expresses, in the mode of moral indignation, the revolt of the subordinate and middle-rank executives of education against a society incapable of fully honouring its debts towards the School, i.e. towards those who owe everything to the School, including the conviction that the School ought to be the principle of every economic and social hierarchy. Among the senior executives of the University, the Jacobin Utopia of a social order in which everyone would be rewarded according to merit, i.e. according to his School rank, cohabits with the aristocratic pretension to recognize no other values than those of the institution which alone fully recognizes their value and the pedagogocratic ambition of subjecting all acts of civil and political life to the moral magisterium of the University.[13]

It can be seen how the French system has been able to find in the external demand for mass-produced, guaranteed, interchangeable 'products' the opportunity to perpetuate — while making it serve another social function related to the interests and ideals of other social classes — the tradition of competition for competition's sake, inherited from the eighteenth-century Jesuit colleges which made emulation the favoured tool of an education designed for aristocratic youth.[14] The French University always tends to go beyond the technical function of the competitive examination and to solemnly draw up, within the quota of candidates it is asked to elect, hierarchies based on the imponderables of derisory quarter points. Derisory no doubt, but decisive: consider the weight the academic world attaches in its assessments — often fraught with professional consequences — to the rank attained in the entrance examinations taken in late adolescence, or even to the title of 'cacique' or 'major', first in a hierarchy itself situated in a hierarchy of hierarchies, that of the grandes écoles and the major concours. Max Weber observed that if one set aside the Confucian tradition of the literary gentleman, the technical definition of the official posts of the imperial administration did not explain how the mandarin examinations were able give such prominence to poetry; similarly, in order to understand how a simple demand for vocational selection, imposed by the need to choose the most suitable persons to fill a limited number of specialized posts, could have served as a pretext for the typically French religion of classification, it is necessary to relate academic culture to the social universe in which it was formed, that is to say, to the protected, self-enclosed microcosm in which, through the methodical, enveloping organization of competition and the establishment of scholastic hierarchies which were as prevalent in play as in work, the Jesuits fashioned a *homo hierarchicus*, transposing the aristocratic cult of 'glory' into the order of social success, literary prowess and scholastic triumph.

But explanation in terms of survival explains nothing unless one explains why the survival survives by establishing the functions it performs in the present functioning of the educational system and by showing the historical conditions authorizing or favouring the manifestation of the generic tendencies the system owes to its essential function. When seeking to explain the French system's very special capacity to decree and impose hierarchies, even beyond the specifically academic spheres of activity and sometimes against the most patent demands it is supposed to answer, one cannot fail to observe that in its teaching and examining it still today gives pride of place to the self-perpetuation and self-protection of the teaching corps, functions which were served in a more open fashion by the examinations of the medieval University, all defined in terms of entry into the corps or into the course of study giving access to it, the baccalauréat (a lower form of the *inceptio*), the *licentia docendi*, and the *maîtrise*, marked by the *inceptio*, a ceremony of induction into the corporation with the rank of *maître*.[15] It is sufficient to observe that most countries' university systems have broken more fully with the medieval tradition than have the French system and some others, e.g. those of Austria, Spain or Italy, which similarly underwent the educational influence of the Jesuits, in order to grasp the role played by the eighteenth-century colleges. Endowed by the Jesuits with particularly effective means of imposing the academic cult of hierarchy and inculcating an autarkic culture cut off from life, the French educational system was able to develop its generic tendency towards autonomization to the point of subordinating its whole functioning to the demands of self-perpetuation.[16] This tendency towards autonomization found the social conditions for its full realization in that it fell in with the interests of the petty bourgeoisie and the intellectual fractions of the bourgeoisie, who found in the Jacobin ideology of formal equality of opportunity new strength for their exacerbated impatience with all forms of 'favouritism' and 'nepotism'; and also in that it was able to take advantage of the centralized structure of the State bureaucracy which, in calling forth a proliferation of national, externally marked, anonymous examinations and competititions, gave the school institution the perfect opportunity to secure recognition of its monopoly in the production and imposition of a unitary hierarchy or, at least, hierarchies reducible to the same principle.[17]

In the French system, the concours is the fully realized form of the examination (which university practice always tends to treat as a competition) and the competition for the recruitment of secondary school teachers, the agrégation, constitutes, together with those advance recruitment competitions, the *Concours Général* and the *Ecole Normale Supérieure* entrance examination, the archetypal triad in which the University acknowledges its authentic self and of which all other competitions and examinations are but variously distant emanations and more or less deformed copies.[18] The ambition of the teaching corps to impose universal recognition of university credentials, and in particular the absolute supremacy of that supreme credential, the agrégation, is most clearly seen in the action of the pressure groups of which the *Société des agrégés* is merely the least clandestine expression, and which have succeeded in securing a de facto recognition of this strictly scholastic title out of all proportion to its de jure definition. The vocational profitability of the titles of *agrégé* and ex-student of the ENS is manifested in the very many cases in which they are used as unofficial criteria for co-option: 15 percent of the holders of Arts Faculty professorships or *maître de conférences* posts (not to mention the *assistants* and *maîtres-assistants*, making up 48 percent of the university staff) do not have the doctorat, the degree theoretically required, whereas they are virtually all agrégés and 23 percent of them are *normaliens*. If homo academicus par excellence is the *normalien-agrégé-docteur*, i.e. the actual or potential Sorbonne professor, this is because he combines all the titles defining the rarity which the University produces, promotes and protects. Nor is it an accident that in the agrégation, as if carried away by its tendency to reinterpret external demand, the University institution can even go so far as to deny the very content of that demand: not uncommonly the agrégation jury, faced with the eternal threat of 'declining standards', sets the imperative of 'quality' over the necessity, felt as a profane interference, of filling all the vacant posts, and sets up, so to speak, through comparison with previous years, a competition between competitions that will yield the yardstick, or rather, the essence of the agrégé — even if this means refusing the means, elsewhere demanded, of perpetuating the real University, in the name of the exigencies of the self-perpetuation of the ideal University.[19]

To understand fully the functional significance of the agrégation, one would have to reinstate this institution in the system of transformations which examinations, or more precisely the system they constitute, have undergone: if it is true that, in an academic system dominated by the imperative of self-perpetuation, the degree par excellence corresponds to the examination which gives access qua master to the order of teaching most representative of the profession, i.e. secondary education, it follows that, in each historical conjuncture, it is the examination best placed to symbolize that function which holds, both in reality and in ideology, the positional value of examination par excellence, that is to say, successively in the history of the University, the doctorat, the licence and now the agrégation, which, despite the apparent preeminence of the doctorat, owes to its relationship with secondary education and its character as a recruitment competition not only its ideological force but also its weight in the organization of careers and more generally in the functioning of the University.[20] Everything takes place as if the school system had made use of the new possibilities offered by each new state of the system of examinations, resulting from the duplication of an existing examination, in order to express the same objective meaning.

To regard the present state of the University as the contingent outcome of a succession of disparate, discontinuous events in which only retrospective illusion could create the impression of a pre-established harmony between the system and the legacy of history, would be to ignore what is implied in the relative autonomy of the educational system. The evolution of the school system depends not only on the strength of external constraints but also on the coherence of its structures, that is, both the resistance it can counterpose to events and its power to select and reinterpret accidents and influences in accordance with a logic whose general principles are laid down as soon as the function of inculcating a culture inherited from the past is taken in hand by a specialized institution served by a body of specialists. Thus the history of a relatively autonomous system presents itself as the history of the systematizations to which the system subjects the constraints and innovations it encounters, in accordance with the norms which define it as a system.[21]

EXAMINATION AND UNEXAMINED EXCLUSION

We have had to grant the educational system the autonomy it asserts and manages to maintain in the face of external demands, in order to understand the characteristics of its functioning that it derives from its essential function. But were we to take its declarations of independence too literally, we should be in danger of losing sight of its external functions and particularly the social functions which academic selection and hierarchization always additionally perform, even when they seem to be exclusively obeying the logic, and even the pathology, proper to the educational system. Thus, for example, the apparently purely academic cult of hierarchy always contributes to the defence and legitimation of social hierarchies, because academic hierarchies, whether of degrees and diplomas or establishments and disciplines, always owe something to the social hierarchies which they tend to re-produce (in both senses). So it has to be asked whether the freedom the educational system is given to enforce its own standards and its own hierarchies, at the expense for example of the most evident demands of the economic system, is not the quid pro quo of the hidden services it renders to certain classes by concealing social selection under the guise of technical selection and legitimating the reproduction of the social hierarchies by transmuting them into academic hierarchies.

Indeed, one begins to suspect that the functions of the examination are not reducible to the services it performs for the institution, still less to the satisfactions it gives the teaching staff, as soon as one observes that most of those excluded from studying at the various levels of education eliminate themselves before being examined, and that the proportion of those whose elimination is thus masked by the selection overtly carried out differs according to social class. In every country, the inequalities between the classes are incomparably greater when measured by the *probabilities of candidature* (calculated on the basis of the proportion of children in each social class who reach a given educational level, after equivalent previous achievement) than when measured by the *probabilities of passing*.[22] Thus, previous performances being equal, pupils of working-class origin are more likely to 'eliminate themselves' from secondary education by declining to enter it than to eliminate themselves once they have entered, and a fortiori more likely not to enter than to be eliminated from it by the explicit sanction of examination failure.[23] Moreover, those who do not eliminate themselves at the moment of moving from one stage to another are more likely to enter those branches (establishments or sections) from which there is least chance of entering the next level of education; so that when the examination seems to eliminate them, it most often merely ratifies that other form of advance self-elimination which relegation to a second-order branch, a deferred elimination, in fact amounts to.

The opposition between the 'passed' and the 'failed' is the source of a false perspective on the educational system as a selecting agency. Based on a candidate's experience (actual or potential, direct or mediate, past or present), this opposition between the two sub-sets separated by selection in the examination from within the set of candidates hides the relation between this set and its complement (i.e. the set of non-candidates), thereby ruling out any inquiry into the hidden criteria of the election of those from whom the examination ostensibly makes its selection. A good deal of research on the educational system as an agency of continuous selection (drop-out) simply takes over this opposition from spontaneous sociology when it takes for its object the relation between those entering a stage of schooling and those successfully completing it, neglecting to examine the relation between those who leave one stage and those who enter the next one. To apprehend the latter relation it is sufficient to look at the whole process of selection from the point of view which, if the system did not impose its own point of view on them, would be that of the social classes condemned to immediate or deferred self-elimination. What makes this reversal of the problematic difficult is that it requires something more and other than a simple logical conversion: if the question of examination failure rates holds the limelight (consider the reactions to a change in the baccalauréat pass rate), it does so because those who have the means to pose this question belong to the social classes for whom the risk of elimination can only come from the examination.

There are several ways of missing the sociological significance of the differential educational mortality rate of the different social classes. Technocratic research, which is only interested in the problem inasmuch as the abandonment of a course by a proportion of the pupils who enter it has a manifest economic cost, immediately reduces it to a false problem of exploiting 'abandoned reserves of intelligence'; such research can even grasp the numerical relation between those completing each stage and those entering the next, and see the weight and social range of the self-elimination of the disadvantaged classes, without going beyond negative explanation in terms of 'lack of motivation'. In the absence of analysis of what the resigned withdrawal of the members of the working classes from the School owes to the functioning and functions of the educational system as an agency of selection, elimination and concealment of elimination under selection, all that technocratic research is able to see in the statistics of educational opportunity which highlight the unequal representation of the different social classes in the different stages and types of education, is the manifestation of an isolated relationship between scholastic performance, taken at face value, and the series of advantages or disadvantages deriving from social origin. In short, if one fails to take as one's explanatory principle the system of relations between the structure of class relations and the school system, one is condemned to the ideological options which subtend the seemingly most neutral scientific choices. Thus some writers reduce educational inequalities to social inequalities, ignoring the specific form they take in the logic of the educational system, while others tend to treat the School as an empire within an empire, whether, like the docimologists,[24] they reduce the problem of equality before the examination to that of normalizing the distribution of marks or equalizing their variance, or whether, like some social psychologists, they identify the 'democratization' of education with the 'democratization' of the teacher-pupil relation, or whether, like so many hasty critics, they reduce the conservative function of the University to the conservatism of academics.

Seeking to explain why the fraction of the school population which eliminates itself before entering the secondary stage or during that stage is not randomly distributed among the different social classes, one is condemned to an explanation in terms of characteristics which remain individual, even when imputed equally to all individuals in a category, so long as one fails to see that they befall the social class *as such* only in and through its relation to the school system. Even when it seems to be imposed by the strength of a 'vocation' or the discovery of inability, each individual act of choice by which a child excludes himself from access to a stage of education or resigns himself to relegation to a devalorized type of course takes account of the ensemble of the objective relations (which pre-existed this choice and will outlast it) between his social class and the educational system, since a scholastic future is of greater or lesser probability for a given individual only insofar as it constitutes the objective and collective future of his class or category. This is why the structure of the objective chances of social upgrading according to class of origin and, more precisely, the structure of the chances of upgrading through education, conditions agents' dispositions towards education and towards upgrading through education – dispositions which in turn play a determining role in defining the likelihood of entering education, adhering to its norms and succeeding in it, hence the likelihood of social upgrading.[25] Thus, the objective probability of entering this or that stage of education that is attached to a class is not just an expression of the unequal representation of the different classes in the stage of education considered, a simple mathematical device merely enabling one to evaluate the magnitude of the inequalities more precisely or more eloquently; rather, it is a theoretical construction providing one of the most powerful principles of explanation of these inequalities. The subjective expectation which leads an individual to drop out depends directly on the conditions determining the objective chances of success proper to his category, so that it must be counted among the mechanisms which contribute to the actualization of objective probabilities.[26] The concept of subjective expectation, conceived as the product of the internalization of objective conditions through a process governed by the whole system of objective relations within which it takes place, has the theoretical function of designating the intersection of the different systems of relations – those linking the educational system to the class structure and also those set up between the system of these objective relations and the system of dispositions (ethos) which characterizes each social agent (individual or group), inasmuch as when agents make up their minds, they always, albeit unwittingly, make reference to the system of the objective relations which make up their situation. Explanation in terms of the relationship between subjective expectation and objective probability, i.e. in terms of the system of the relations between two systems of relations, is able to account, on the basis of the same principle, not only for the educational mortality of the working classes or the survival of a fraction of those classes, together with the particular modality of the survivors' attitude towards the system, but also for the variation in the attitudes of pupils from the different social classes towards work or success, depending on the degree of probability and improbability of their continuing into a given stage of education. Similarly, if the rate of working-class enrolment varies, from region to region, with the rate of enrolment of the other classes, and if urban residence, with the consequent social heterogeneity of acquaintance groups, is associated with a higher rate of working-class enrolment, this is because the subjective expectation of these classes is never independent of the objective probability characteristic of the acquaintance group (allowing for the reference groups or aspiration groups it contains), a fact which helps to increase the educational chances of the working classes, at least insofar as the gap between the objective probabilities attached to the reference or aspiration group and the objective class probabilities is not such as to discourage any identification or even reinforce the acceptance of exclusion ('That's not for the likes of us').[27]

Thus, to give a full account of the selection process which takes place either within the educational system or by reference to the system, we must take into account not only the explicit judgements of the academic tribunal, but also the convictions by default or suspended sentences which the working classes inflict on themselves by eliminating themselves from the outset or by condemning themselves to eventual elimination when they enter the branches which carry the poorest chances of escaping a negative verdict on examination. By an apparent paradox, university science courses, in which success seems at first sight to depend less directly on the possession of inherited cultural capital and which constitute the inevitable culmination of the sections admitting the highest proportion of working-class children on entry to secondary education, do not have a significantly more democratic intake than other types of faculty course.[28] In reality, not only is the relation to language and culture continuously taken into account throughout secondary education and even (doubtless to a lesser extent and at any rate less overtly) in higher education, not only are logical and symbolic mastery of abstract operations and, more precisely, mastery of the laws of transformation of complex structures, a function of the type of practical mastery of language and the type of language acquired in the home — but the organization and functioning of the school system continuously and through multiple codes retranslate inequalities in social level into inequalities in academic level. Given that, at every stage, the educational system establishes among the disciplines or subjects a de facto hierarchy which runs, in Science Faculties for example, from pure mathematics to the natural sciences (or, in Arts Faculties, from literature and philosophy to geography), i.e. from those intellectual activities perceived as the most abstract to the most concrete; given that this hierarchy is retranslated, at the level of school organization, into the hierarchy of types of secondary school (from the lycée down to the *Collège d'Enseignement Technique,* through the *Collège d'Enseignement Général* and the *Collège d'Enseignement Secondaire*) and the hierarchy of sections (from classical to technical); given that this hierarchy of schools and sections is closely connected, through the mediation of the correspondence between the hierarchy of degrees and the hierarchy of schools, with the hierarchy of the teachers' social origins; and given, finally, that the different branches and different schools attract pupils of different social classes very unequally, in accordance with their previous academic success and the class-differentiated social definitions of the types of course and types of schools — it can be seen why the different types of curriculum give very unequal chances of entering higher education. It follows that working-class children pay the price of their access to secondary education by relegation into institutions and school careers which entice them with the false pretences of apparent homogeneity only to ensnare them in a truncated educational destiny.[29]

Thus, the combination of the educational chances of the different classes and the chances of subsequent success attached to the different sections and types of schools constitutes a mechanism of deferred selection which transmutes a social inequality into a specifically educational inequality, i.e. an inequality of 'level' or success, concealing and academically consecrating an inequality of chances of access to the highest levels of education.[30]

It may be objected that democratization of secondary education intake tends to reduce the role of self-elimination since the probability of working-class children entering secondary education has significantly increased over the last few years. But one has to set against this the statistics of admission to higher education according to school or section of origin, which indicate a social and educational opposition between the 'noble' sections of the 'noble' secondary establishments and second-order secondary education, perpetuating in a better concealed form the old cleavage between the lycée and extended primary education.[31] Furthermore, in reducing the role of self-elimination at the end of primary schooling, in favour of deferred elimination or elimination by examination alone, the educational system fulfils its conservative function yet more successfully, if it is true that, to perform this function, it must disguise chances of entry as chances of success. Those who invoke 'the interest of society' to deplore the economic cost of 'educational wastage' contradict themselves in failing to take into account the profit accruing from it, namely the advantage the social order derives from spacing out and so concealing the elimination of the working classes.

It is clear why, in order to carry out in full this function of social conservation, the school system must present the 'moment of truth' of the examination as its own objective reality: the elimination, subject solely to the norms of educational equity, which it undertakes and conducts with formal irreproachability, conceals the performance of the function of the school system by masking, behind the opposition between the passed and the failed, the relation between the candidates and those whom the system has de facto excluded from the ranks of the candidates, and so concealing the links between the school system and the structure of class relations. Like the spontaneous sociology which understands the system as the system asks to be understood, a number of would-be scientific analyses, which allow the same autonomization to be foisted upon them and adopt the very logic of the examination, consider only those who are in the system at a given moment, excluding those who have been excluded from it. But the relationship of each of those remaining in the system to his whole social class of origin dominates and informs his relationship to the system: his behaviour, aptitudes, and dispositions towards school bear the stamp of his whole academic past, because they owe their characteristics to the degree of probability or improbability of his still being within the system, at that stage and in that branch. Thus, mechanical use of multivariate analysis might lead one to deny the influence of social origin on academic success, at least in higher education, on the grounds, for example, that the primary relation between social origin and success disappears when each of the two categories of students defined by a 'classical' or 'modern' secondary training is considered separately.[32]

But that would be to ignore the specific logic by which social advantages and disadvantages are progressively retranslated, through successive selections, into educational advantages or disadvantages and, more concretely, it would be to neglect the specifically educational characteristics, such as type of school, section entered in sixième, etc. which relay the influence of social origin. One only has to compare the examination success rate of students combining the most improbable characteristics for their class of origin, e.g. working-class students from a big Paris lycée having done Greek and Latin and having the best previous results (if indeed this is not a blank category), with the success rate of students endowed with the same educational characteristics but belonging to a social class for which these characteristics are the most probable ones (students from the Parisian bourgeoisie, for example), to observe the disappearance or even reversal of the relation which prevails in most cases between position in the social hierarchy and academic success.[33] But this finding remains meaningless and even a source of absurdities until the relation ascertained is reinstated in the complete system of the relations and of their transformations in the course of the successive selections which have led to the *compounding of improbabilities* which bestows its exceptional success on a group characterized by a cumulation of successive over-selections.

Analysis — even multivariate analysis — of the relations observed at a given point in time between the characteristics of categories of a student body which is the product of a series of selections taking into account these same characteristics or, to put it another way, is the product of a series of 'draws' biased with respect to the variables considered (primarily social origin, sex and place of residence) grasps only misleading relations unless one is careful to reintroduce not only the unequal degrees of selectedness capable of hiding the inequalities of selection, but also the differential dispositions which differential selections produce in those selected.

A purely synchronic approach inevitably sees a set of absolute probabilities, redefined ex nihilo at each stage of education, in what is in fact a series of conditional probabilities throughout which the initial probability (of which perhaps the best indicator at present is the probability of entering secondary education in this or that section according to social origin) has been progressively specified and limited.

By the same token, such an approach is unable to give a full account of the dispositions characteristic of the different categories of students. 'Attitudes' such as bourgeois students' dilettantism, self-assurance and, irreverent ease, or working-class students' tense application and educational realism can only be understood as a function of the probability or improbability of occupying the position occupied which defines the objective structure of the subjective experience of the 'wonderboy' or the 'inheritor'.[34] In short, what offers itself to be grasped, at every point on the curve, is the slope of the curve; in other words, the whole curve.[35] If it is true that the relation an individual maintains with the School and with the culture it transmits is more or less 'effortless', 'brilliant', 'natural', 'laboured', 'tense' or 'dramatic', according to the probability of his survival in the system, and if it is also the case that in their verdicts the School and 'society' take as much account of the relation to culture as of culture, then it is clear how much remains unintelligible until one goes to the principle underlying the production of the most durable academic and social differences, the *habitus* – the generative, unifying principle of conducts and opinions which is also their explanatory principle, since at every moment of an educational or intellectual biography it tends to reproduce the system of objective conditions of which it is the product.

Thus an analysis of the functions of the examination which seeks to break with spontaneous sociology, i.e. with the misleading images the educational system tends to offer of its own functioning and functions, must lead one to discard purely docimological inquiry, which continues to serve the hidden functions of the examination, in favour of the systematic study of the mechanisms of elimination as a privileged locus in which to apprehend the relations between the functioning of the educational system and the perpetuation of the structure of class relations. Nothing is better designed than the examination to inspire universal recognition of the legitimacy of academic verdicts and of the social hierarchies they legitimate, since it leads the self-eliminated to count themselves among those who fail, while enabling those elected from among a small number of eligible candidates to see in their election the proof of a merit or 'gift' which would have caused them to be preferred to all comers in any circumstances. Only when the examination is seen to have the function of concealing the elimination which takes place without examination, can it be fully understood why so many features of its operation as an overt selecting procedure still obey the logic governing the elimination which it conceals.

When one knows how much examiners' judgements owe to implicit norms which retranslate and specify the values of the dominant classes in terms of the logic proper to the educational system, it is clear that candidates are handicapped in proportion to the distance between these values and those of their class of origin.[36] Class bias is strongest in those tests which throw the examiner onto the implicit, diffuse criteria of the traditional art of grading, such as the dissertation or the oral, an occasion for passing total judgements, armed with the unconscious criteria of social perception on total persons, whose moral and intellectual qualities are grasped through the infinitesimals of style or manners, accent or elocution, posture or mimicry, even clothing and cosmetics; not to mention orals like those of the *École Nationale d'Administration* or the literature agrégation, where the examiners almost explicitly insist on the right to implicit criteria, whether bourgeois ease and distinction or university tone and breeding.[37] Proust remarks that 'on the telephone you discover the inflections of a voice which you could not distinguish until it was dissociated from the face in which you objectified its expression'. In the same way, only experimental decomposition of the examiner's syncretic judgement can reveal all that a judgement formulated in the context of an examination owes to the system of social marks which constitutes the objective basis of the examiner's sense of the candidate's 'presence' or 'insignificance'.

But it should not be supposed that formal rationalization of the criteria and techniques of judgement would suffice to free the examination from its social functions: that is what the docimologists seem to ignore when, fascinated by the two-fold inconsistency of examiners unable to agree with one other because they are unable to agree with themselves on the criteria of judgement, they forget that different judges could, theoretically, agree on judgements that were identically biased because based on the same implicit criteria, if they had in common all the social and academic characteristics determining their grading. In drawing attention to the haven of irrationality which examinations represent, the docimologists bring to light the discrepancy between the ideology of equity and the reality of selection processes but, failing to inquire into the social functions of such 'irrational' procedures, they are liable to make further contributions to the exercise of these functions by diffusing the belief that a rationalization of grading would suffice to harness examinations to the service of the declared functions of the School and the examination.[38]

Thus, in order for the examination to fulfil to perfection its function of legitimating the cultural heritage and, through it, the established order, it would be sufficient for the Jacobin confidence that so many French academics have in national, anonymous competition to be extended to measurement techniques which have in their favour all the outward signs of scientificity and neutrality. Nothing would better serve this function of *sociodicy*[39] than formally irreproachable tests which could claim to measure, at a given point in time, the subjects' aptitude to occupy vocational posts, while forgetting that this aptitude, however early it is tested, is the product of a socially qualified teaching and learning, and that the most predictive measurements are precisely the least neutral ones socially. In fact, nothing less than the neo-Paretian Utopia of a society protected against the 'circulation of the elites' and the 'revolt of the masses' can be read between the lines of some descriptions which present tests as the privileged tool and guarantee of American democracy qua meritocracy:

> One conceivable consequence of a greater reliance on tested ability as a criterion for the assignment of educational or occupational status is a more rigid class structure based on ability. The contribution of inheritance to ability and the extensive use of objective selection tests may accentuate the position of the individual born to parents of low ability. The fact that individuals tend to choose marriage partners from the same social stratum makes it likely that over time it will become more, rather than less, difficult for an individual to improve his social position over that of his parents.[40]

And when these utopists describe the 'demoralizing' effects such a system of selection would inevitably have on the members of the 'lower classes', who, like the 'deltas' in *Brave New World*, would be obliged to acknowledge that they are the lowest of the low and happy to be so, perhaps the only reason why they over-estimate the capacity of tests to grasp natural abilities is that they under-estimate the ability of the School to accredit the natural character of abilities or inabilities.

TECHNICAL SELECTION AND SOCIAL SELECTION

Thus it may be that an educational system is more capable of concealing its *social function* of legitimating class differences behind its *technical function* of producing qualifications, the less able it is to ignore the incompressible demands of the labour market. Doubtless modern societies are more and more successful in getting the School to produce, and guarantee as such, more and more skilled individuals, i.e. agents better and better qualified for the demands of the economy; but this restriction of the autonomy imparted to the educational system is no doubt more apparent than real, insofar as the raising of the minimum level of technical qualification required for occupational purposes does not, ipso facto, entail a reduction of the gap between the technical qualification guaranteed by the examination and the social quality which it bestows by what might be called its *certification effect.*

A system of education consistent with the norms of technocratic ideology can, at least as successfully as a traditional system, confer on the academic scarcity which it produces or decrees by means of the diploma a social scarcity relatively independent of the skills demanded by the post to which the diploma gives legitimate access: it is this alone which explains why so many professional posts can be occupied, on different terms and with unequal remuneration, by individuals who (assuming the hypothesis most favourable to the reliability of the diploma) differ only in the degree to which they have been consecrated by school and university. Every organization has its 'stand-ins', condemned to a subordinate position by their lack of academic qualifications although their technical competence makes them indispensable, and everyone is familiar with the competition which exists between categories separated in the administrative hierarchy by their educational label although they perform the same technical tasks (such as engineers from different schools or the numerous categories of secondary teachers). If the principle of 'equal pay for equal work' can serve to justify hierarchies which, if it were taken literally, it would seem to contradict, this is because the value of a professional production is always socially perceived as related to the value of the producer and the latter in turn is seen as a function of the academic value of his qualifications. In short, the diploma tends to prevent the relation between the diploma and occupational status from being related to the more uncertain relation between capacity and status; if this connection were made, it would raise the question of the relation between capacity and the diploma and so lead to a questioning of the reliability of the diploma, i.e. of everything that is legitimated by recognition of the reliability of diplomas. Modern bureaucracies are in fact defending the very principles on which their organization and hierarchies are based when they appear to contradict their most visible interests in failing to test the technical content of their agents' academic qualifications, because they could not submit individuals certified by the diploma to tests liable to endanger them, without also endangering the legitimacy of the diploma and of all the hierarchies it legitimates. Equally it is to the necessity of masking the gap between the technical skills actually guaranteed by the diploma and the social profitability of its certification effect that the ideology of 'general culture' corresponds, its primary function perhaps being to make it impossible, de facto and de jure, for the 'cultivated man' ever to be called upon to supply technical proof of his culture. It is understandable that the classes who objectively monopolize a relation to culture defined as indefinable (because it can be objectively defined only by this de facto monopoly) are predisposed to extract the maximum profit from the certification effect and have every interest in defending the ideology of disinterested culture which legitimates this effect by dissimulating it.[41] By the same token, one sees the social functions of the ostentatious squandering of teaching and learning which defines the mode of acquisition of those aptitudes worthy of belonging to general culture, whether it be the acquisition of the classical languages, conceived as a necessarily slow initiation into the ethical and logical virtues of 'humanism' or complacent drilling in every sort of formalism, literary, aesthetic, logical or mathematical.

If every selecting operation always has the indissolubly two-fold effect of regulating technical qualifications by reference to the demands of the labour market and of creating social grades by reference to the structure of class relations which the educational system helps to perpetuate, if, in short, the School has both a technical function of producing and attesting capacities and a social function of conserving power and privileges, it can be seen that modern societies furnish the educational system with vastly increased opportunities to exercise its power of transmuting social advantages into academic advantages, themselves convertible into social advantages, because they allow it to present academic, hence implicitly social, requirements as technical prerequisites for the exercise of an occupation.[42] Thus, when Max Weber associated rationalization of selection and recruitment procedures with the development of the great modern bureaucracies and their ever growing demand for experts trained for specific tasks, he overestimated the autonomy of the technical functions of both the educational system and the bureaucratic system relative to their social functions. In reality, the top ranks of the French Civil Service have perhaps never before so totally recognized and consecrated the most general and even the most diffuse dispositions, at any rate those most resistent to rational formulation and codification, and never before so completely subordinated specialists, experts and technicians to the specialists-on-general-matters graduating from the most prestigious grandes écoles.[43]

In ever more completely delegating the power of selection to the academic institution, the privileged classes are able to appear to be surrendering to a perfectly neutral authority the power of transmitting power from one generation to another, and thus to be renouncing the arbitrary privilege of the hereditary transmission of privileges. But through its formally irreproachable verdicts, which always objectively serve the dominant classes since they never sacrifice the technical interests of those classes except to the advantage of their social interests, the School is better able than ever, at all events in the only way conceivable in a society wedded to democratic ideologies, to contribute to the reproduction of the established order, since it succeeds better than ever in concealing the function it performs. The mobility of individuals, far from being incompatible with reproduction of the structure of class relations, can help to conserve that structure, by guaranteeing social stability through the controlled selection of a limited number of individuals — modified in and for individual upgrading — and so giving credibility to the ideology of social mobility whose most accomplished expression is the school ideology of "*l'Ecole libératrice*", the school as a liberating force.[44]

NOTES

1. Examiners' reports on the concours for the agrégation or entry to the grandes écoles therefore constitute exemplary documents for anyone seeking the criteria by which the teaching corps trains and selects those it considers worthy of perpetuating it: these sermons for the academic seminary set out the grounds for verdicts betraying, in their murky clarity, the values which guide the examiners' choices and on which the candidates' training has to be patterned.

2. The effects of scholastic programming can be found in the most unexpected areas: when the French Public Opinion Institute (IFOP) asks its interviewees to say 'whether the progress of modern science in the field of atomic energy will do humanity more harm than good or more good than harm', what is the opinion poll but a national examination resurrecting a question put a thousand times in a thousand scarcely different forms to school-leaving certificate, baccalauréat or Concours Général candidates, 'the moral value of scientific progress'? And do not the alternatives offered in the precoding of the replies (more good than harm; more harm than good; as much good as harm) evoke the reach-me-down dialectic of three-point dissertations in which, after a laborious forcing of arguments for and against, a triumphant synthesis climbs onto the fence and faces both ways?

3. A more extended analysis of the *function of intellectual and moral integration* which every educational system fulfils by inculcating common forms of expression which are also common principles of organization of thought, can be found in P. Bourdieu, 1967, 2.

4. E. Renan, 'L'instruction publique en France jugée par les Allemands', *Questions contemporaines,* p. 266.

5. E. Durkheim, *L'évolution pédagogique en France,* Paris, Alcan, 1938, p. 161.

6. *From Max Weber: Essays in Sociology,* trans., ed. and introd. H. H. Gerth and C. Wright Mills, London, Kegan Paul, 1947, pp. 240 ff.

7. In the US, for example, statistics show a continuous increase in the proportion of members of the ruling categories who are graduates, and graduates of the best universities, a tendency which has become more marked in recent years. W. L. Warner and J. C. Abegglen (*Big Business Leaders in America,* New York, Harper & Brothers, 1955, pp. 47-55) have shown that 'in 1928, 32% of the big business leaders were college graduates; in 1952, 57%' (p. 47). In France, a survey of a representative sample of personalities who had achieved fame in the most diverse fields showed that 85 percent of them were graduates, a further 10 percent having completed secondary education (A. Girard, *La réussite sociale en France, ses caracteristiques, ses lois, ses effets,* Paris, Institut Nationale d'Études

Démographiques, P.U.F., 1961, pp. 233-59). A recent survey of the leaders of large industrial organizations established that 89 percent of French managing directors are graduates, as against 85 percent for the Belgians, 78 percent for the Germans and Italians, 55 percent for the Dutch and 40 percent for the British ('Portrait-robot du P.D.G. européen', *L'expansion*, Nov. 1969, pp. 133-43). Research is needed to see whether, in most French careers particularly those in administration, the growth and codification of the advantages attached to degrees and diplomas have led to a decline in internal promotion, i.e. an increasing rarity of senior executives promoted from the ranks and trained 'on the job'; the opposition between the 'back door' and the 'front door', which roughly corresponds, in an administrative organization, to the opposition between the petty bourgeoisie and the bourgeoisie, may well have been intensified as a result.

8. Confucian education tended to impose the traditional ideal of the 'literary man': 'Puns, euphemisms, allusions to classical quotations, and a refined and purely literary intellectuality were considered the conversational ideal of the genteel man. All politics of the day were excluded from such conversation. It may appear strange to us that this sublimated "salon" cultivation [*"Salon"-Bildung*], tied to the classics, should enable a man to administer large territories. And in fact, one did not manage the administration with mere poetry even in China. But the Chinese prebendary official proved his status quality, that is, his charisma, through the canonical correctness of his literary forms. Therefore, considerable weight was placed on these forms in official communications' (M. Weber, 'The Chinese Literati', in *From Max Weber: Essays in Sociology*, p. 437).

9. Ibid., p. 434.

10. Ibid., p. 423.

11. Because the State gave it the means to enforce the overt supremacy of its specific hierarchies, the mandarin system constitutes a privileged case: here the School manifested in a codified law and a proclaimed ideology a tendency towards the autonomization of academic values which is elsewhere expressed only in a customary law and through multiple reinterpretations and rationalizations. Even the function of scholastic legitimation of hereditary cultural privileges took in this case a juridical form: this system, which claimed to accord the right to office solely on the basis of personal merit, attested by examination, explicitly reserved a privileged right of candidature for the sons of high-ranking officials.

12. It is in this light that one should interpret the statistics of entry to schools such as the École Normale Supérieure or the École Nationale d'Administration by the candidates' social category of origin and previous academic success. Our survey of the students of all the grandes écoles shows, inter alia, that while the ENS and the ENA both, and to much the same degree, have a much less democratic intake than the faculties, since only 5.8 and 2.9 percent, respectively, of their students are working-class (as against, for example, 22.7 percent in the

Arts Faculties and 17.1 percent in the Law Faculties), on closer analysis the –
preponderant – category of privileged-class students (66.8 percent at the ENS and
72.8 percent at the ENA) exhibit characteristic differences: sons of teachers make
up 18.4 percent of the ENS intake, as against 9 percent at the ENA; sons of Civil
Servants make up 10 percent at the ENA, compared with 4.5 percent at the
ENS . . ... Moreover, the academic records of the students at the two schools
testify that the University is more successful in orienting pupils towards the
studies which most epitomize it (e.g. the ENS), the more clear-cut their previous
academic success has been (as measured by the number of baccalauréat distinctions) – for a more extended analysis, see P. Bourdieu et al., *Le système des
grandes écoles et la reproduction des classes dominantes,* in preparation.

13. Although it suggests only some of the relations linking the characteristics
of teachers' practice and ideology to their social origin, class membership and
position in the academic institution and the intellectual field, this analysis, like
the one presented below (Chapter 4, pp. 200-03), should suffice to warn the
reader against the temptation of taking the earlier descriptions of French teachers'
professional practice for analyses of essences (Chapter 2).

14. See E. Durkheim, *L'évolution pédagogique,* II, pp. 69-117, followed up
by G. Snyders, *La pédagogie en France au XVIIe et au XVIIIe siècles,* Paris,
P.U.F., 1965.

15. The resistance to any attempt to dissociate the certificate sanctioning
completion of one stage of schooling from the right to enter the next stems, as
can be seen in the polemics over the baccalauréat, from a conception of the
school career as a unilinear trajectory culminating, in its accomplished form, in
the agrégation. Indignant refusal to award 'cheap' certificates, which has recently
tended to draw on the technocratic language of adapting the University to the
employment market, can readily ally itself with the traditionalist ideology which
would extend the criteria of the specifically academic guarantee to every certificate of proficiency, in order to safeguard the means of creating and controlling
the conditions of academic 'rarity'. The pre-eminence of the royal road is such
that all academic careers, and a number of professional careers which do not
follow it all the way through, can only be defined in terms of lack. Such a system
is thus particularly prone to produce 'failures', condemned by the University
which has condemned them to maintain an ambivalent relation to it.

16. The teaching of the Jesuits should doubtless be seen as the source of most
of the systematic differences which distinguish the intellectual 'temperament' of
the Catholic countries marked by its influence from that of the Protestant
countries. As Renan points out, 'the French University has too much imitated the
Jesuits, with their insipid harangues and Latin verses; it recalls too much the
rhetors of declining Rome. The great French fault of perorating, the tendency to
make everything degenerate into declamation, is kept up by the stubborn in-

sistence by a part of the University on disdaining the content of knowledge and valuing only style and talent' (E. Renan, *Questions contemporaines*, p. 79). Those who directly attribute the dominant characteristics of a nation's intellectual production to the values of the dominant religion, e.g. an interest in the experimental sciences or philological scholarship to Protestantism, or the taste for belles-lettres to Catholicism, omit to analyse the specifically pedagogic effect of the retranslation performed by a determinate type of school organization. When Renan sees in the 'pseudo-humanist' teaching of the Jesuits, and in the 'literary mind' it encourages, one of the fundamental features of the mode of thought and expression of French intelléctuals, he brings out the consequences for French intellectual life of the revocation of the Edict of Nantes, which halted the scientific movement that had got under way in the first half of the seventeenth century and 'put an end to historical criticsm': 'With the literary mind alone encouraged, there ensued a certain frivolity. Holland and Germany, partly thanks to our exiles, built up a near monopoly of scholarship. It was decided then that France would be above all a nation of men of wit, a nation writing well, talking wonderfully, but inferior in knowledge of things and exposed to all the blunders that are only avoided with breadth of knowledge and maturity of judgement' (ibid.).

17. In the field of education, too, the centralizing action of the Revolution and the Empire continued and completed a tendency which had already begun under the Monarchy. Beside the Concours Général, which, set up in the eighteenth century, extended onto a national scale the competition taking place in each Jesuit college and consecrated the humanist ideal of belles-lettres, the agrégation, re-established by decree in 1808, was first organized in 1776, in a form and with a significance very close to those it has today. If such facts and more generally everything relating to the educational system's own history are almost always ignored, this is because they would belie the common representation which, reducing university centralization to an aspect of bureaucratic centralization, would have it that the French system owes its most significant characteristics to Napoleonic centralization.

If one forgets all that the educational system owes to its essential function of inculcation, one fails to recognize the specifically pedagogic foundations and functions of standardization of the message and of the instruments of its transmission (a pedagogic homogenization which is to be found in the administratively most decentralized systems, such as, for example, the British system). More subtly, one is prevented from grasping the specifically pedagogic function and effect of carefully cultivated distance from the university bureaucracy, which are an integral part of all pedagogic practice, particularly of French-style traditional pedagogy. Thus, for example, the flaunted, factitious liberties taken with the official syllabuses, or the ostentatious disavowal of the administration and its rules, and more generally all the tricks which consist in deriving charismatic effects from contempt for the non-teaching staff, are authorized and favoured by the institution only because they help to affirm and impose the pedagogic authority required for the performance of inculcation, as well as giving teachers an economical way of illustrating the cultivated relation to culture.

18. 'I remember I once said to the future General de Charry, when I gave him back an exercise: "That's a script worthy of the agrégation" ' (R. Blanchard, *Je découvre l'Université* Paris, Fayard, 1963, p. 135).

19. The concern to maintain and manifest the absolute autonomy of academic hierarchies is expressed through innumerable indices, whether in the tendency to attribute an absolute value to the marks awarded (with the use of decimals, taken to absurd lengths) or in the constant tendency to compare marks, averages, the best scripts and the worst, from one year to another. For example: in the *Rapport de l'agrégation de grammaire féminine* for 1959, after a table of the number of posts offered, the number of candidates eligible [to take the oral, having passed the written examination] and the number of candidates finally admitted, from 1955 to 1959 (in which it is seen that the number of successful candidates is almost always only half as great as the number of posts available), and the average marks, worked out to two decimal places, of the last eligible and first and last successful candidates, one reads (p. 3):

> This year's vintage was not exactly uplifting (. . .) The 1959 competition did not fail to bring in some scripts savouring of knowledge or culture; but the figures themselves bespeak a falling-off which can only be regarded with alarm (. . .) The averages of the last eligible and last admitted have never been so low since 1955 (. . .). The lengthening of the lists (of candidates admitted), forced on us by the present unfortunate circumstances, appeared to us to be justified solely in terms of the recruiting crisis which mainland France is not alone in suffering (. . .). There is reason to fear that the inexorable law of supply and demand will bring about a decline in standards so grave as to jeopardize the very spirit of secondary education.

Countless similar texts could be quoted, in which every word is laden with the whole university ideology.

20. This 'national peculiarity' was highlighted by Durkheim: by the forms of organization it imposed and the spirit it diffused, secondary education has from the very beginning 'more or less absorbed the other levels of education and taken up almost all the space' (Durkheim, *L'évolution pédagogique*, I, pp. 23-24, 137, and passim).

21. This analysis of the French system does not pretend to do more than bring to light a particular structure of internal and external factors which is

capable of explaining, in the particular case, the weight and modalities of the examination. Further research would have to show how, in other national histories of the university system, different configurations of factors define different tendencies or equilibriums.

22. Although academic performance and rate of sixième entry are closely dependent on social class, the overall inequality in sixième entry rates derives more from inequality of sixième entry at equal levels of performance than from inequality of academic performance (see P. Clerc, 'Nouvelles données sur l'orientation scolaire au moment de l'entrée en sixième' (II), *Population*, Oct.-Dec., 1964, p. 871). Similarly, statistics on the transition from one stage of education to the next in relation to social origin and academic performance show that in the US and Great Britain it is not, strictly speaking, the School that is responsible for elimination (see R. J. Havighurst and B. L. Neugarten, *Society and Education*, Boston, Allyn and Bacon, 2nd edn, 1962, pp. 230-35).

23. See R. Ruiter, *The Past and Future Inflow of Students into the Upper Levels of Education in the Netherlands*, OECD, DSA/EIP/63; J. Floud, 'Social Class Factors in Educational Achievement', in *Ability and Educational Opportunity*, ed. A. H. Halsey, OECD, 1961; T. Husen, 'Educational Structure and the Development of Ability', ibid., table (p. 125) showing the percentage of non-applicants to pre-university school in Sweden, by school marks and social origin.

24. Docimology: the science of examinations (trans.).

25. In the terms used here, subjective expectation and objective probability are contrasted as the standpoint of the agent and the standpoint of science, which constructs objective regularities by means of methodical observation. By our recourse to this sociological distinction (which has nothing in common with the distinction some statisticians make between a priori and a posteriori probabilities), we seek to indicate here that objective regularities are internalized in the form of subjective expectations and that the latter are expressed in objective behaviours which contribute towards the realization of objective probabilities. Hence, depending on the point of view adopted – that of explaining practices in terms of structures or that of forecasting the reproduction of structures in terms of practices – we are led to privilege in this dialectic either the first relation or the second.

26. For an analysis of the process of internalization through which the chances objectively contained in conditions of existence are transmuted into subjective expectations or despondency, and, more generally, of the mechanisms referred to above, see P. Bourdieu, 1966, 2; 1974, 1.

27. To be persuaded that this apparently abstract schema covers the most concrete experiences, one can read in *Elmstown's Youth* an educational biography which shows how membership of a peer group can, to a certain extent at least, falsify assessment of the chances linked to class membership (see A. E.

Hollingshead, *Elmstown's Youth*, New York, John Wiley & Sons, 1949, pp. 169-71).

28. See M. de Saint-Martin, 1968, 2: 1971, 2.

29. In France in 1961-62, manual workers sons made up 20.3 percent of the sixième intake into the lycées (a term covering schools of very different standards) and 38.5 percent of the intake of the Collèges d'Enseignement Générale, whereas the sons of senior executives and members of the professions (also strongly represented in private schools) made up 14.9 percent of the lycée intake and only 2.1 percent of the CEG intake (see *Informations statistiques*, Paris, Ministère de l'Education Nationale, Jan. 1964). Elimination from both lycée and CEG before completion of the course accentuates the under-representation of the working classes; furthermore, the difference of standard between the two types of school is such that, for those who might wish to continue their studies beyond the *brevet* [certificate of secondary technical education], access and adaptation to a *classe de seconde* [fifth form] in a lycée, an institution differing in its teaching staff, mentality and social intake, are both unlikely and difficult to accomplish.

30. The specific influence of the subjective expectation linked to the objective probability of success which is attached to a particular curriculum or type of school can be seen in the 'demoralizing' effect of entering a devalorized curriculum or type of school: it has been observed in Britain that children who scored equally well at age 11 had better scores at age 15 if they went to grammar schools, whatever their social origin, and worse if they went to secondary modern schools (Robbins Report, Appendix I, Pt II, p. 50 – Great Britain: Committee on Higher Education, *Higher Education Report of the Committee Appointed by the Prime Minister under the Chairmanship of Lord Robbins*, 1961-63, London, HMSO, 1963).

31. There have been many descriptions of how the diversification of its institutions of higher education enables the American school system to 'cool out' those who, failing to meet the standards of 'real schooling', are quietly directed towards 'dumping grounds' which the institution and its agents are able to present as leading to 'alternative achievements' (B. R. Clark, 'The "Cooling-Out" Function in Higher Education', in *Education, Economy and Society*, eds. J. Floud and C. A. Anderson, New York, Free Press, 1961). In the same way, the French University is tending more and more to use the implicit, interlocking hierarchies which underpin the whole educational system to secure the 'progressive withdrawal' of the students it relegates into channels for 'rejects'.

32. On the 'multivariate fallacy' see above, Chapter 1, p. 103, note 2.

33. A study of the social and educational characteristics of Concours Général prizewinners supplies an exemplary illustration of these analyses. See P. Bourdieu and M. de Saint Martin, 1970, 1.

34. The 'wonderboy' (*le miraculé*) – i.e. the working-class child who succeeds 'against all the odds'; cf., perhaps, in Britain, the 'scholarship boy'. For 'the inheritor', cf. Bourdieu & Passeron, 1964, 1, (trans.).

35. Clearly one should not credit the subjects with an absolute lucidity as to the truth of their experience: their practices can be adjusted to their position in the system without being directly governed by anything other than the reinterpretation, offered by the system, of the objective conditions of their presence in the system. Thus, while the educational attitudes of the 'miraculously' successful working-class pupil appear as objectively (but indirectly) governed by his objective class chances, his conscious representations and his discourse may have as their guiding principle the magical image of the permanent miracle, merited by an effort of the will.

36. By way of a limiting case, the competitive examinations in medicine starkly reveal features observed elsewhere – the primacy given to the function of selection, conceived as class co-option; the role of rhetoric (not only verbal but also gestural and, so to speak, postural); the artificial creation of castes irreversibly separated by different educational backgrounds (see H. Jamous, *Contribution à une sociologie de la décision*, Paris, CSE, 1967, pp. 86-103).

37. A host of examples could be cited to show how examiners transform the most technical tests into an ethical ordeal: 'I see the examination, especially the viva, as bearing on extremely complex qualities. When taste, probity and modesty are appreciated all at once, what you have is one personality seeking to understand another' (C. Bouglé, *3rd Conference on Examinations*, pp. 32-44). 'A competition such as ours is not merely a technical challenge; it is also a test of morality, of intellectual probity' (*Agrégation de grammaire. masculine*, 1957, p. 14). 'The text having been thoroughly understood and the translation prepared by analysis, in order to transform it into Greek it is then necessary to bring into play at once moral qualities and technical knowledge. The moral qualities, which may include courage, enthusiasm and so on, are concentrated in the virtue of probity. There are duties towards the text. One must submit oneself to it and not cheat' (*Agrégation de grammaire masculine*, 1963, p. 20-21). There is no end to the repertoire of adjectives used to account for technical faults in the language of moral depravity: 'smug complacency', 'dishonesty', 'culpable negligence', 'cowardliness', 'intellectual laziness', 'crafty prudence', 'unacceptable impudence', 'shameless nullity', etc.

38. Just as, failing to take account of the social characteristics of the examiners and the examinees, the docimologists have never thought to test the correlation between similar marking patterns and the social and academic characteristics of the group of examiners, so too, because they have not seen that the spontaneous docimology of teachers has its logic and its social functions, they can only fall back on puzzled indignation at the cool response their rational preaching gets from the teaching profession.

39. Sociodicy: justification of society; formed by analogy ·with theodicy (trans.).

40. D. A. Goslin, *The Search for Ability: Standardized Testing in Social Perspective*, New York, John Wiley & Sons, 1966, p. 191.

41. 'That an individual possesses the bachelor's degree may or may not prove that he knows, or once knew, something about Roman history and trigonometry. The important thing about his degree is that it helps him to secure a position which is socially or economically more desirable than some other position which can be obtained without the aid of this degree. Society has misgivings about the function of specific items in the educational process and has to make atonement by inventing such notions as the cultivation of the mind' (E. Sapir, 'Personality', in *Selected Writings of Edward Sapir in Language, Culture and Personality*, ed. D. G. Mandelbaum, Berkeley, University of California Press, 1968, p. 567).

42. This tendency, inherent in every school system, was grasped by Durkheim in the privileged case of the *ancien régime* college: 'To be sure, the *ancien régime* college produced no doctors, no priests, no statesmen, no judges, no lawyers, no professors; but, in order to become a professor, a lawyer, a judge, etc., it was considered essential to have been to college' (Durkheim, *L'évolution pédagogique*, II, p. 182).

43. This evolution, starting at the end of the last century with the setting up of the competitions for recruitment to Government departments which, in invoking the requirements of 'general culture', marked the decline of the specialist and technician trained 'on the job', in a sense culminates in the passing-out competition of the École Nationale d'Administration, which has peopled the Civil Service and ministerial cabinets with 'young gentlemen' combining the benefits of a bourgeois upbringing with those of the most general and most typically traditional academic training.

44. A good deal of research on mobility implicitly espouses this ideology and reduces the question of the reproduction of class relations to the question of the intergenerational mobility of individuals. Having done so, it is unable to understand everything that individual practices, particularly those contributing to or resulting from mobility, owe to the objective structure of class relations within which they take place. Thus, for example, the collective interest the dominant classes have in the preservation of the structure of class relations, hence in the evolution of the educational system towards ever closer subordination to the demands of the economy and economic calculation, an interest which entails, inter alia, sacrificing a proportion of the students from those classes, is now tending, because of their over-enrolment, to come into conflict with the individual interests of the members of those classes which incline them to expect the educational system to consecrate automatically the social pretensions of all members of the class.

4

DEPENDENCE THROUGH INDEPENDENCE

But first of all there came a hierophant who arranged them in order; then he took from the knees of Lachesis lots and patterns of life, and mounting upon a high pulpit, spoke as follows: 'Hear the words of Lachesis, the daughter of Necessity. Mortal souls, behold a new cycle of mortal life. Your genius will not choose you, but you will choose your genius; and let him who draws the first lot choose a life, which shall be his destiny (...) The chooser is answerable — God is justified.'

Plato,

The Republic

Whether one sets out to analyse the communication of the message, the organization of the exercise or the assessment and sanctioning of the effects of the communication and the exercise, i.e. pedagogic work as the prolonged action of inculcation through which the basic function of every educational system is accomplished, or whether one seeks to grasp the mechanisms by which the system overtly or tacitly selects the legitimate addressees of its message by imposing technical requirements which are always, to various degrees, social requirements, we have seen that it is impossible to understand the *dual objective truth* of a system defined by its capacity to employ the *internal logic* of its functioning in the service of its *external function* of social conservation, if one fails to relate all the past and present characteristics of its organization and public to the complete system of relations prevailing, in a determinate social formation, between the educational system and the structure of class relations. To grant the educational system the absolute independence which it claims or, on the contrary, to see in it only the reflection of a state of the economic system or the direct expression of the value system of 'society as a whole', is to refuse to see that its *relative autonomy* enables it to serve external demands under the guise of independence and neutrality, i.e. to conceal the social functions it performs and so to perform them more effectively.

The effort to catalogue the external functions of the educational system, that is, the objective relations between this system and the other sub-systems, for example the economic system or value system, remains fictitious whenever the relations thereby established are not brought into relationship with the structure of the relations prevailing at a given moment between the social classes. Thus we have had to bring university organization (e.g. the institutional conditions of pedagogic communication or the hierarchy of degrees and disciplines) into relationship with the social characteristics of its public, in order to avoid the empiricist dilemma which obliges common sense and a number of semi-scientific theories to alternate between condemnation of an educational system presumed to be the sole author of all the inequalities it produces, and denunciation of a social system bearing sole responsibility for the inequalities bequeathed to an intrinsically impeccable educational system. Similarly, it is necessary to determine the differential form which the relations between this or that sub-system take for each social class in a society characterized by a certain structure of class relations, in order to avoid the illusion, frequently found among economists, that the School, invested by 'Society' with a single, purely technical function, stands in a single, simple relation to the economy of that society; or the illusion favoured by culturalist anthropologists, that the School, invested by 'Society' with a single, purely cultural function of 'enculturation', does no more than express in its organization and functioning the hierarchy of values of the 'national culture' which it transmits from one generation to another.

Reducing the functions of the educational system to its technical function, that is, reducing the ensemble of relations between the educational system and the economic system to the 'output' of the School as measured against the needs of the labour market, prohibits rigorous use of the comparative method, condemning one instead to abstract comparison of statistical series divested of the significance which the facts measured derive from their position in a particular structure, serving a particular system of functions. The conditions for a fruitful application of the comparative method are only fulfilled when the variations in the hierarchical structure of the functions of the educational system (i.e. the variations in the functional weight of each function in the complete system of functions) are systematically brought into relation with the concomitant variations in the organization of the educational system. By making a critique of two approaches which concur in ignoring these requirements, one in the name of a sort of declaration of universal comparability, the other in the name of a belief in the irreducibility of 'national cultures', we can at least hope to state the conditions for the construction of a model which would enable each of the cases historically realized to be understood as a particular case of the transformations which the system of relations between the structure of functions and the structure of organization may undergo. The different types of structure of the educational system, i.e. the different historical specifications of the essential function of producing durable, transposable dispositions (habitus) incumbent on every educational system, do indeed only assume their full significance when brought into relation with the different types of structure of the system of functions, themselves inseparable from the different states of the balance of power between the groups or classes by whom and for whom these functions are realized.

THE PARTICULAR FUNCTIONS OF 'THE GENERAL INTEREST'

Never before has the question of the 'aims' of education been so completely identified with discussion of the contribution education makes to national growth. Even the preoccupations apparently most foreign to this logic, such as the ostentatious concern to 'democratize educational and cultural opportunity' increasingly draw on the language of economic rationality, taking the form, for example, of denunciation of the 'wastage' of talent. But are economic 'rationalization' and 'democratization' so automatically linked as well-intentioned technocrats like to think? The sociology and economics of education would not be so easily trapped in such a problematic if they did not dismiss the question that is objectively posed by all artificialist inquiries into the 'aims' of education, namely the theoretical question of the functions of the educational system that are *objectively possible* (i.e. not only logically but also socio-logically) and the correlated methodological question of the comparability of educational systems and their products.

The technocratic thinking which, reviving the philosophy of history of social evolutionism in its simplest form, claims to extract from reality itself a unilinear, one-dimensional model of the phases of historical change, obtains without much effort the yardstick of a universal comparison which enables it to hierarchize the different societies or educational systems univocally, according to their degree of development or 'rationality'. In reality, because the indicators of the 'rationality' of an educational system are less amenable to comparative interpretation the more completely they express the historical and social specificity of educational institutions and practices, this procedure destroys the very object of comparison by divesting the elements compared of all they owe to their membership in systems of relations. Consequently, whether one confines oneself to indicators as abstract as illiteracy rate, enrolment rate and teacher-pupil ratio, or takes into account more specific indicators of the efficiency of the educational system or of the degree to which it makes use of the intellectual resources potentially available, such as the role of technical education, the proportion of student intake successfully graduating, or the differential representation of the sexes or social classes in the different levels of education, it is necessary to reinstate these relations within the systems of relations on which they depend, in order to avoid comparing the incomparable or, more subtly, failing to compare the really comparable.

More profoundly, all these indicators rest on an implicit definition of the 'productivity' of the educational system which, in referring exclusively to its *formal, external* rationality, reduces the system of its functions to one of them, itself subjected to a reductive abstraction. Technocratic measurement of educational output assumes the impoverished model of a system which, knowing no other goals than those it derives from the economic system, responds optimally, in quantity and quality, and at minimum cost, to the technical demand for training, i.e. the needs of the labour market. For anyone who accepted such a definition of rationality, the (formally) most rational educational system would be one which, totally subordinating itself to the requirements of calculability and predictability, produced at the lowest cost specific skills directly adjusted to specialized tasks and guaranteed the types and levels of skill required for a given dateline by the economic system, using to this end personnel specially trained in handling the most adequate pedagogic techniques, setting aside class and sex divisions so as to draw as widely as possible (without stepping outside the limits of profitability) on the intellectual 'reserves' and banishing all vestiges of traditionalism so as to substitute for an education in culture, designed to form men of taste, an education capable of producing made-to-measure specialists according to schedule.[1]

The simplification to which such a definition subjects the system of functions is seen as soon as it is pointed out that the statistical relations most often invoked to demonstrate the existence of an overall correspondence between the degree of formal rationality of the educational system and the degree of development of the economic system take on their specific meaning only when reinserted into the system of relations between the educational system and the structure of class relations. An indicator as univocal in appearance as the number of certificate-holders at each level in each speciality cannot be interpreted within the formal logic of a system of juridical equivalences: the economic and social profitability of a given diploma is a function of its scarcity on the economic and symbolic markets, i.e. the value which the sanctions of the different markets confer on the different diplomas and different categories of diplomas. Thus, in a country with a high rate of illiteracy, the mere fact of literacy or, a fortiori, possession of an elementary diploma, is sufficient to ensure a decisive advantage in occupational competition.[2]

Similarly, because traditional societies generally exclude women from schooling, because the use of all intellectual capacities is demanded by the development of the economy, and because the entry of women into male occupations is one of the main social changes accompanying industrialization, one might be tempted to see the rate of feminization of secondary and higher education as an indicator of the degree of 'rationalization' and 'democratization' of the educational system. In reality, the Italian and French examples suggest that one must not be misled by a very high rate of feminization and that the educational careers girls are offered by the richest nations are often simply a more expensive and more luxurious variant of traditional upbringing or, to put it another way, a reinterpretation of the most modern studies for women in terms of the traditional model of the division of labour between the sexes, as is attested by female students' whole attitude towards their studies and, still more visibly, by the choice of discipline or the rate of vocational use of their diplomas, which are both a cause and an effect of their attitude. Conversely, even low rates of feminization may express a clear-cut break with the traditional definition of female upbringing in a Muslim country whose whole tradition tended to exclude women from higher education completely. More precisely, the overall rate of feminization has a different significance depending on the social recruitment of the female students and the distribution of the rates of feminization of the various faculties and disciplines. Thus, in France, the fact that the chances of university entrance are virtually the same for boys and girls does not imply the disappearance of the traditional model of the division of labour and the ideology of the distribution of 'gifts' between the sexes: girls are still consigned more often than boys to certain types of studies (Arts subjects in the main), the more so the lower their social origin. Even indicators as unequivocal at first sight as the proportion of women graduates making vocational use of their academic qualification are subject to the system effect: to measure adequately the social profitability of the diploma held by a woman, one must at least take into account the fact that the 'value' of an occupation (such as, in France, that of primary or secondary school teacher) steadily diminishes as it is feminized.

Another example: the apparently most unimpeachable indicator of an educational system's efficiency, the 'wastage' rate (defined by the number of students in a given intake who fail to complete the course successfully) remains meaningless until it is seen as the effect of a specific combination of the social selection and technical selection that an educational system always carries out inseparably. The 'waste product' is in this case as much a transformed product as is the finished product; consider the system of dispositions towards the educational institution, his occupation and his whole existence which characterizes the 'failure', as well as the technical and above all social profits accruing — unequally, depending on the society and the class — from the fact of having had some higher education, albeit intermittent or interrupted. What is the value of a comparison between the wastage rates of British (14 percent), American or French universities, if one fails to consider, in addition to the degree of selection before entry which distinguishes Britain from France or the US, the diversity of the procedures the different systems use to carry out selection and to cause its effects to be internalized, ranging from the categorical exclusion operated by French-style examination, especially the State competition, to the painless elimination ('cooling out') made possible in the US by the hierarchy of university establishments?[3] If it is true that an educational system always succeeds in obtaining from those it consecrates. and even those it excludes, a certain measure of adherence to the legitimacy of consecration or elimination and thereby of the social hierarchies, it can be seen that a low technical efficiency may be the price paid for the educational system's high efficiency in performing its function of legitimating the 'social order' — even when class-unconscious technocrats sometimes pat themselves on the back for condemning a wastage which they cannot assess without discounting the corresponding profits, by a sort of error in national accountancy.

In short, the technocratic notion of 'output' has the function of preventing analysis of the educational system's system of functions: if it were carried out, such an analysis would forbid recourse to the implicit or explicit postulate of the 'general interest', by showing that none of the functions of the educational system can be defined independently of a given state of the structure of class relations. If, for example, students from the different social classes are unequally inclined to recognize the verdicts of the School and, in particular, unequally disposed to accept without protest second-order courses and careers (i.e. the jobs in teaching or middle management for which they are destined by faculties or disciplines which offer for some a last refuge while others are relegated there by the mechanisms of streaming), this is because the relations between the school system and the economic system, i.e. the labour market, remain connected, even among apprentice intellectuals, to the situation and position of their social class of origin through the mediation of class ethos, the principle determining the level of occupational aspiration.

Failing to make this connection, one is led to reduce the whole system of relations governing the relationship of a category of individuals to their occupational future to a mechanical effect of the correspondence or non-correspondence between labour supply and demand. Schumpeter makes this sort of reduction when he claims to establish a clear and simple relation between over-production of graduates relative to jobs and the advent of the revolutionary attitude among intellectuals.[4] Similarly, undertaking to formulate a 'politics of education', M. Vermot-Gauchy starts by reducing this ambition to that of 'determining the nature and number of the career openings likely to become available to the rising generations and those now working';[5] to calculate these 'skill needs' it is apparently sufficient to proceed from the expected pattern of production to the foreseeable manpower needs of the various sectors, from prediction of the manpower use in a given sector to its 'skill needs', from these to the 'training needs' and finally from 'training needs' to the level and content of the qualifications educationally required in order to satisfy them.

Such a deduction, formally irreproachable (allowing for the approximations and the constancy hypotheses entailed by any 'projection'), rests on a definition of 'needs' which owes its credibility to nothing more than a superficial analogy: either one recognizes as 'needs' only those judged worthy of being satisfied by reference to a technocratic ideal of the economic worthiness of nations or one recognizes as 'needs' all the demands for education actually expressed.[6] There is nothing to prevent one opting for the first alternative and relating a determinate state of the School to a pure model of the educational system defined exclusively and univocally by its ability to satisfy the requirements of economic development. But, given that there is no society in which the educational system is reduced to the role of an industrial enterprise subject to exclusively economic goals, that production for the needs of the economy does not everywhere have the same weight in the system of functions and, more profoundly, that the specificity of an educational system and of its 'production' techniques is reproduced in the specificity of its products, it is only by sheer force of ideology that one can present the 'needs of the economy' or of Society as the rational, reasonable basis for a consensus on the hierarchy of the functions incumbent upon the educational system. In condemning as irrational the 'motivations' or 'vocations' which nowadays lead a proportion of students into 'unproductive' studies and careers, without seeing that these orientations are the product of the combined action of the School and class values, themselves objectively oriented by the action of the School, technocratic ideology betrays the fact that it knows no other 'rational' objectives than the goals objectively inscribed in a certain type of economy.[7] The technocrats are able to profess the sociologically impossible idea of an educational system reduced to its economic function alone, only because, having failed to relate the economic system (to which they subordinate the educational system) to a determinate structure of class relations, and taking for granted an economic demand conceived as independent of the power relations between the classes, they then, in all innocence under cover of its technical function, reintroduce the social function of the educational system and in particular its function of reproducing and legitimating the structure of class relations.

It is not surprising that this idealism of the 'general interest' fails to grasp the structural properties and operational characteristics that each educational system owes to the ensemble of its relations with the other sub-systems, i.e. to the system of functions which, in a determinate historical situation, derives its specific structure from the structure of class relations. It is still less surprising that this pan-econometric monism ignores the specific properties that the structure and functioning of the educational system owe to the function specifically incumbent upon it as the holder of the delegated power to inculcate a cultural arbitrary. Nor, finally, is it surprising that the ingenuous alliance between a utilitarian evolutionism and reformist voluntarism condemns its exponents to a negative sociology which, by the light of an exemplary rationality, can see only failures and shortcomings ('archaism', 'vestiges', 'backwardness', 'obstacles' or 'resistance') and can only characterize in terms of absence the pedagogic specificity and historical particularity of an educational system.

UNDIFFERENTIATED FUNCTIONS
AND INDIFFERENCE TO DIFFERENCES

Those who undertake to capture the originality of a culture in the signifying unity of its elements and who, like the configurationist school, show by the attention they give to the different forms of upbringing that they mean to avoid dissociating the analysis of a culture from the study of cultural transmission, might at first sight appear to escape the abstractions which arise from ignorance of the 'configurations'. But is it possible to take culture as a concrete totality, indivisibly responsible for its own causality and, on this basis, to relate the different aspects of a culture to a sort of generative formula, a 'spirit of the age' or 'national character', without running the risk of ignoring the specificity of the different sub-systems by treating each of them as if it did no more than manifest a single primordial dynamism, present everywhere and without mediation in each of its manifestations? When the requirement of totalization of particular relations is reduced to a philosophy of totality which sees the whole in every part, it leads one as infallibly as technocratic ideology to ignore, together with the specificity of the educational system, the *system effect* which gives its functional significance and weight to a function within the system of functions or to an element (organization, population, etc.) within the structure or the historical transformation of the structure. Whereas the technocrats reduce the relatively autonomous history of the educational system to the abstract schema of a unique, unilinear, universal evolution marked only by the stages of a morphological growth or the landmarks in a process of formal, external rationalization, the configurationists reduce the specificity which the system derives from its relative autonomy to the 'originality' of a 'national culture', with the result that they are equally well able to find a society's ultimate values reflected in its educational system or to point to an effect of education in the most characteristic and the most diverse features of its culture.

Thus, Jesse R. Pitts holds the 'group of school friends', described as a 'delinquent community', to be 'the prototype of the solidarity groups existing in France beyond the family nucleus and the extended family', seeing, for example, 'aggressivity towards parents and teachers' reappearing in 'the conspiracy of silence towards higher authorities'.[8] But this does not prevent him seeing in the pedagogic relation a pure reflection of 'cultural themes' of *la France éternelle:* 'in his relationship with the teacher, the child comes into contact with one of the most typical incarnations of French doctrinaire-hierarchical values'.[9] At school as in the family, in bureaucratic organizations as in the scientific community, there reappears, according to Pitts, as a 'constant characteristic of French society' or 'the French cultural system', a prevailing type of relationship to others and to the world, dogmatically characterized in a batch of abstract words, 'authoritarianism', 'dogmatism', 'abstraction', etc. Failing to analyse the specifically pedagogic mechanisms through which the School contributes towards reproducing the structure of relations between the classes by reproducing the unequal class distribution of cultural capital, the 'culturalist' sociologist is always liable to give way to his penchant for unexplained homologies, inexplicable correspondences and would-be self-explanatory parallelisms. The presumption that a leap of pure intuition can take one straight to the very principle of the cultural system is particularly ineffectual in the case of class societies, where it dispenses one from preliminary analysis of the different types or levels of practice and the different classes' differential relations to those practices.[10]

An educational system in fact owes its particular structure as much to the transhistorical demands which define its essential function of inculcating a cultural arbitrary as it does to the state of the system of functions which historically specifies the conditions in which this function is realized. Thus, to see a mere vestige of the 'aristocratic cult of prowess' in the charismatic ideology of 'giftedness' and virtuosity so widespread in France, among students and teachers alike, prevents one from· seeing that in its academic form this ideology (together with the practices it underpins or calls forth) constitutes one of the possible ways – doubtless the one best suited to a historical form of the demand for reproduction and legitimation of the class relations – of securing recognition of the legitimacy of pedagogic action, in and through pedagogic action itself. Moreover, in default of an analysis of the variations in this ideology according to the positions occupied by the different categories of agents in the structure of the school system (teachers or students, higher education or secondary education staff, Arts students or Science students, etc.) and according to the relationship these agents maintain with their position as a function of their class membership or social origin, one is condemned to explain a 'sociological' abstraction in terms of a 'historical' abstraction — to relate, for example, the professorial cult of verbal prowess to the national cult of artistic or war-like prowess, not without suggesting that ontogenesis can account for phylogenesis and biography for history:

> If we go back to the origins, a man achieved a feat of prowess when he performed an outstanding deed of valour, by a spontaneous, unforeseen decision while at the same time obeying clear, long-standing principles. At Roncevaux, Roland, borne up by his faith in the principles of chivalry, was able to seize the opportunity to transform adverse circumstances into a day of triumph for the spirit (. . .) So prowess can exist at all social levels. The creation of a piece of jewellery by a Parisian craftsman, the peasant's careful distilling of a liqueur, the civilian's stoicism in the face of Gestapo torture, Marcel Proust's affable courtesy in Madame de Guermantes's salon, are all examples of prowess in modern France.[11]

When one is trapped in the vicious circles of thematic analysis, tourist routes around 'common themes' which can only lead to 'commonplaces', the only way out, it seems, is to explain the implicit values of history manuals by a history worthy of a manual.

It might be thought that an analysis like Michel Crozier's, in which he endeavours to apply his theory of the 'bureaucratic phenomenon' to the French educational system, would escape the holistic syncretism of the culturalist anthropologists' bird's-eye view. But in fact, under the guise of correcting the abstraction inherent in generic description of bureaucracy by means of 'concrete' borrowings from culturalist descriptions of 'French culture', this analysis compounds the theoretical errors of culturalism with those of technocratic thinking. Ignoring the relative autonomy of the different sub-systems, Crozier inevitably finds in each of them, and particularly in the educational system, the projection of the most general characteristics of French bureaucracy, which are themselves obtained simply by combining the most general tendencies of modern societies with the most general tendencies of the 'national character'. To posit, at the outset, that 'the educational system of a given society reflects that society's social system' is summarily to reduce the academic institution to its generic function of 'social control', the common residue of all its specific functions, and to make it impossible . to perceive all that an educational system owes to its essential function, in particular its specific way of fulfilling its external functions in a given society at a given moment.[12]

Thus, for example, Crozier is only able to grasp characteristic features of the school institution, such as the ritualization of pedagogic action or the distance between master and pupil, insofar as he recognizes in them manifestations of the logic of bureaucracy, i.e. fails to recognize what is specifically scholastic about them, in that it expresses tendencies or requirements proper to all institutionalized educational systems, even when scarcely or not at all bureaucratized: the tendency towards 'routinization' of pedagogic work, which is expressed in, among other things, the production of intellectual and material instruments specifically devised by and for the School, manuals, corpuses, topics, etc., appears, alongside the first signs of institutionalization, in traditional schools like the rhetoric and philosophy schools of Antiquity or the Koran schools, which exhibit none of the features of bureaucratic organization.[13] And if one thinks of the *epideixis* of the Sophists, small-scale educational entrepreneurs still obliged to resort to prophetic techniques for capturing an audience in order to set up a pedagogic relationship, or the disconcertion techniques with which the Zen masters imposed their spiritual authority on an aristocratic clientele, it may be doubted whether teacherly 'prowess' and its distancing effect can be better understood in terms of 'the existence of a gap between the teacher and the pupil which reproduce the strata-separation of the bureaucratic system' than by reference to a functional requirement which is inherent in all pedagogic action insofar as this action presupposes and must produce recognition of the teacher's pedagogic authority, whether personal or delegated by the institution.

Similarly, when Crozier sees in the institutional guarantees of university 'independence' no more than a form of the guarantees statutorily written into the bureaucratic definition of official posts, he lumps together two facts as irreducible to one another as the systems of relations to which they belong, on the one hand the autonomy which teachers have claimed and obtained as civil servants subject to the common legislation of a Government department, and on the other hand, the pedagogic autonomy inherited from the medieval 'corporation'.[14] Only the characteristic tendency of every educational system, bureaucratized or not, to reinterpret and retranslate external demands in accordance with its essential function, and not some mechanical inertia or perverse persistence, can account for the resistance which a teaching corps tends to put up against any external definition of its tasks, in the name of an ethic of conviction which refuses to measure the consequences of practice by any criteria other than the corps's own values and in the name of an ideology of 'mastery' and its rights which draws strength from invoking the traditions of autonomy bequeathed by a relatively autonomous history. In short, if it is not acknowledged that a particular system of education is defined by a particular type and degree of autonomy, one tends to describe as simple specifications of generic processes, such as the tendency towards bureaucratization, characteristics of the functioning of the institution and of the agents' practice which stem from the power given to the School to fulfil its external functions in accordance with the principles defining its essential function of inculcation.

To express all the relations between the systems in terms of the metaphorical scheme of 'reflection' or, worse, of reflections reflecting each other, is to dissolve into undifferentiatedness the differential functions the different systems perform in their relations with the different social classes. Thus analyses of the bureaucracy and of its relations with the educational system which refer the practice and values of the administrative bodies of the State to the training given by the different grandes écoles ignore the fact that the ex-students of these schools bring into the State apparatus, which the system of grandes écoles enables them to monopolize, dispositions and values which they owe at least as much to their membership in certain fractions of the dominant classes (distance from role, flight into abstraction, etc.) as to their educational training. Similarly, one is bound to see no more than a product of bureaucratic organization in the most typical attitudes of the lower categories of administrative staff, whether it be the tendency to formalism, punctuality fetishism, or rigid adherence to the rules, so long as one fails to note that all these traits, which may also manifest themselves outside the bureaucratic situation, express, in the logic of that situation, the system of dispositions (ethos) — probity, meticulousness, propensity to moral indignation — which the members of the petty bourgeoisie owe to their class position and which would be sufficient to predispose them to espouse the values of public service and the 'virtues' demanded by the bureaucratic order even if administrative careers were not also their means par excellence of social advancement. By the same token, the disposition which middle-class students or middle-rank teachers, and a fortiori, students whose fathers are middle-rank teachers, manifest towards education — e.g. cultural willingness or esteem for hard work — cannot be understood unless the system of scholastic values is brought into relation with the middle-class ethos, the principle of the value the middle classes set on scholastic values. In short, only on condition that one mediates the structure of relations between the sub-systems through the structure of relations between the classes is it possible to grasp, beyond the too obvious similarities, the true homologies between the bureaucracy and the educational system, by bringing to light the homology of their relations with the social classes. Thus, by suggesting with the amorphous notion of 'social control' that the educational system performs an indivisible, undifferentiated function for 'society as a whole', all-purpose functionalism tends to conceal the fact that a system which helps to reproduce the structure of class relations indeed serves 'Society', in the sense of the social order', and through it the educational interests of the classes which benefit from that order.

But it is impossible to account fully for the success of all the holistic philosophies inspired by a common indifference to differences, without taking into account the specifically intellectual functions of their silences and reticences, denials and slips or, conversely, the displacements and transfers they make towards the themes of 'homogenization', 'massification' or 'globalization'. Thus obedience to the principles of the dominant ideology manages to impose itself on intellectuals in the form of obedience to the conventions and proprieties of the intellectual world. It is no accident that in present-day France reference to social classes tends to appear, depending on the group or the conjuncture, as an ideological slant which the distinguished guardians of polite-society objectivism adopt with an elegant pout; as the solecism of a provincial incapable of coming up to date, deplored by the licensed representatives of an imported sociology and left far behind by the shock-troops of every avant-garde, who ceaselessly scan the horizon of 'modernity' for fear of missing an ideological or theoretical revolution, ever ready to spot the newest-born of the 'new classes', 'new alienations' or 'new contradictions'; as a philistine sacrilege or Boeotian blunder deserving the commiseration of the proselytes of the new mysteries of art and culture; or as an indisputable platitude, unworthy of serious argument but liable to arouse the unpleasant dissensions so elegantly avoided by 'anthropological' talk of the profundities of the common treasury. If we did not know that the intellectual or even political significance of the ideology proper to a category of intellectuals can never be deduced directly from that category's position in the structure of class relations but always owes something to the position it occupies in the intellectual field, it would be impossible to understand how indifference to class differences, whose conservative function we have shown, can, without contradiction, pervade ideologies which make ostentatious sacrifice to ritual or incantatory invocation of the class struggle.

Some of the most radical 'critiques' of the educational system find in 'contestation' of the generic function of every educational system considered as an instrument of inculcation the means of masking the class functions which this function fulfils: in emphasizing the frustrations inherent in all socialization, not least, of course, sexual frustrations, much more than the specific form of the constraints or privations which, even the most generic ones, bear differentially on the different social classes, these ideologies lead to a concordial denunciation of pedagogic action conceived as an undifferentiated action of repression and so to an ecumenical revolt against the repressive action of 'society', reduced to an impressionistic superimposition of political, bureaucratic, university and family hierarchies. It is sufficient to see that these ideologies are all based on the search for and denunciation of *generic alienations,* spuriously specified by tragic reference to 'modernity', to perceive that in surrendering to a syncretic representation of the relations of domination which leads them to establish undifferentiated revolt against the mandarin-professor as the principle of a generalized subversion of hierarchies, they fail, like technocratic or culturalist thinking, to grasp the relative autonomy and dependence of the educational system with respect to the social classes.[15]

THE IDEOLOGICAL FUNCTION
OF THE EDUCATIONAL SYSTEM

Having discovered that it is possible to relate to the same principle all the inadequacies to be found in analyses of the educational system that are based on social philosophies as opposed, in appearance, as evolutionist economism and cultural relativism, one is obliged to seek the principle of a theoretical construction capable of rectifying and accounting for these inadequacies. But it is not sufficient to perceive the shortcomings common to both approaches in order to arrive at the objective truth of the relationship between the relative autonomy of the educational system and its dependence on the structure of class relations: how is one to take account of the relative autonomy the School owes to its essential function, without letting slip the class functions it necessarily fulfils in a society divided into classes? In neglecting to analyse the specific, systematic characteristics the educational system owes to its essential function of inculcation, is one not, paradoxically, prevented from posing the question of the external functions the educational system fulfils in fulfilling its essential function and, more subtly, the question of its ideological function of concealing the relationship between its essential function and the external functions of its essential function?

One of the reasons why it is not easy to observe simultaneously the educational system's relative autonomy and its dependence on class relations, is that a conceptual grasp of the class functions of the educational system has been associated, in the theoretical tradition, with an instrumentalist representation of the relations between the School and the dominant classes, while analysis of the structural and operating characteristics that the educational system owes to its essential function has almost always gone hand in hand with blindness to the relations between the School and the social classes, as if ascertaining the fact of autonomy presupposed the illusion of the educational system's neutrality. To believe that the meaning of any element in an educational system is exhausted merely by relating it directly to a reduced definition of the interests of the dominant classes, without inquiring into the contribution this system makes, qua system, towards reproducing the structure of class relations, is an easy way of obtaining, by a sort of pessimistic finalism, the facile answers of an explanation at once ad hoc and all purpose. Just as refusal to recognize the relative autonomy of the State apparatus leads one to ignore some of the best-hidden services this apparatus renders to the dominant classes in accrediting, thanks to its autonomy, the representation of the State as an umpire, so schematic denunciations of the 'class University' which posit, before any analysis, the identity 'in the last analysis' of school culture and the culture of the dominant classes, of cultural inculcation and ideological indoctrination, or pedagogic authority and political power, prohibit analysis of the mechanisms through which equivalences that structural lags, functional duplicities and ideological displacements make possible are indirectly and mediately brought about.

Durkheim, in conceiving the relative autonomy of the educational system as the power to reinterpret external demands and take advantage of historical opportunities so as to fulfil its internal logic, at least obtained the means of understanding the tendency to self-reproduction which characterizes academic institutions, and the historical recurrence of the practices linked to the demands inherent in the institution or of the tendencies inherent in a body of professional teachers.[16] In his preface to Durkheim's *L'évolution pédagogique en France*, Halbwachs saw the work's chief merit in the fact that Durkheim related the longevity of university traditions to the educational system's 'own life':

> The organs of education are, in every age, connected with the other institutions of the social body, with customs and beliefs, with the great currents of thought. But they also have a life of their own, an evolution which is relatively autonomous in the course of which they conserve many features of their former structure. Sometimes they defend themselves against the influences exerted on them from outside, leaning on their past for support. It is impossible to understand, for example, the division of the universities into faculties, the systems of examinations and degrees, boarding-school life, school discipline, without going back a long way into the past, to the period of the construction of the institution whose forms, once created, tend to persist through time, either by a sort of inertia or because they manage to adapt to new conditions. Considered from this standpoint, the pedagogical organization appears to us as more hostile to change, more conservative and traditional perhaps than the Church itself, because it has the function of transmitting to new generations a culture whose roots lie in a remote past.

Because pedagogic work (whether performed by the School, a Church or a Party) has the effect of producing individuals durably and systematically modified by a prolonged and systematic transformative action tending to endow them with the same durable, transposable training (habitus), i.e. with common schemes of thought, perception, appreciation and action; because the serial production of identically programmed individuals demands and historically gives rise to the production of programming agents themselves identically programmed and of standardized conserving and transmitting instruments; because the length of time necessary for the advent of a systematic transformation of the transformative action is at least equal to the time required for serial production of transformed reproducers, i.e. agents capable of exerting a transformative action reproductive of the training they themselves have received; because, above all, the educational institution is the only one in full possession, by virtue of its essential function, of the power to select and train, by an action exerted throughout the

period of apprenticeship, those to whom it entrusts the task of perpetuating it and is therefore in the best position, by definition, to
impose the norms of its self-perpetuation, if only by using its power to
reinterpret external demands; and finally because teachers constitute
the most finished products of the system of production which it is,
inter alia, their task to reproduce — it is understandable that, as
Durkheim noted, educational institutions have a relatively autonomous
history and that the tempo of the transformation of academic institutions and culture is particularly slow. The fact remains that if one fails
to relate the relative autonomy of the educational system and its
history to the social conditions of the performance of its essential
function, one is condemned, as Halbwach's text and Durkheim's very
undertaking show, to put forward a circular explanation of the relative
autonomy of the system in terms of the relative autonomy of its
history and vice versa.

The generic characteristics every educational system owes to its
essential function of inculcation and to its relative autonomy cannot be
fully explained without taking into account the objective conditions
which, at a given moment, enable an educational system to achieve a
determinate degree and particular type of autonomy. It is therefore
necessary to construct the system of relations between the educational
system and the other sub-systems, specifying those relations by reference to the structure of class relations, in order to perceive that the
relative autonomy of the educational system is always the counterpart
of a dependence hidden to a greater or lesser extent by the practices
and ideology authorized by that autonomy. To put it another way, to a
given degree and type of autonomy, i.e. to a determinate form of
correspondence between the essential function and the external functions, there always correspond a determinate type and degree of dependence on the other systems, i.e. in the last analysis, on the structure
of class relations.[17]

If the academic institution observed by Durkheim could appear to
him as even more conservative than the Church, this is because it was
enabled to push its transhistorical tendency to autonomization so far

only by the fact that pedagogic conservatism then fulfilled its function of social conservation with an efficacy that much greater because
it remained better concealed. Thus, failing to analyse the social conditions which made possible the perfect match, characteristic of traditional education, between the mode of inculcation and the content
inculcated, Durkheim was led to include in the essential function of
every educational system, defined as 'the conservation of a culture
inherited from the past', what is no more than a particular, although
historically very frequent, combination of the essential function and
the external functions.[18] When the culture that the School objectively
has the function of conserving, inculcating and consecrating tends to be
reduced to the relation to culture that is invested with a social function
of distinction by the mere fact that the conditions for acquiring it are
monopolized by the dominant classes, *pedagogic conservatism*, which in
its extreme form, gives the educational system no other goal than that
of conserving itself in self-identity, is the best ally of *social and political
conservatism*, since, under the guise of defending the interests of a
particular corps and autonomizing the aims of a particular institution, it
contributes by its direct and indirect effects to the maintenance of 'the
social order'. The educational system has never been able to present
more completely the illusion of absolute autonomy with respect to all
external demands, and in particular with respect to the interests of the
dominant classes, than when the consonance between its essential
function of inculcation, its function of conserving culture and its
function of conserving 'the social order' was so perfect that its dependence on the objective interests of the dominant classes could
remain unnoticed in the happy unconsciousness of elective affinities. So
long as nothing intervenes to disturb that harmony, the system can in a
sense escape history by enclosing itself in the production of its reproducers as in a cycle of eternal recurrence, since it is, paradoxically, by
ignoring all demands other than that of its own reproduction that it
most effectively contributes to the reproduction of the social order.[19]
Only the functional relationship between the pedagogic conservatism of
a system dominated by its obsession with its self-perpetuation and

social conservatism can explain the constant support which the con-servers of university order, for example the champions of Latin, the agrégation or the literary thesis, the traditional pillars of the literate relation to culture and of the pedagogy by default inherent in humanist teaching of the 'humanities', have always received and still receive in France from the most conservative fractions of the dominant classes.[20]

Given that the historical and social conditions defining the limits of the relative autonomy an educational system owes to its essential function define at the same time the external functions of its essential function, every educational system is characterized by a *functional duplicity* which is actualized in full in the case of traditional systems, where the tendency towards conservation of the system and of the culture it conserves, encounters an external demand for social conserva-tion. It is precisely its relative autonomy that enables the traditional educational system to make a specific contribution towards repro-ducing the structure of class relations, since it need only obey its own rules in order to obey, additionally, the external imperatives defining its function of legitimating the established order, that is, to fulfil simul-taneously its social function of reproducing the class relations, by ensuring the hereditary transmission of cultural capital, and its ideo-logical function of concealing that social function by accrediting the illusion of its absolute autonomy. Thus, the full definition of the relative autonomy of the educational system with respect to the in-terests of the dominant classes must always take into account the specific services this relative autonomy performs for the perpetuation of the class relations: it is precisely its peculiar ability to autonomize its functioning and secure recognition of its legitimacy by accrediting the representation of its neutrality that gives the educational system its peculiar ability to mask the contribution it makes towards reproducing the class distribution of cultural capital, the concealment of this service being not the least of the services its relative autonomy enables it to perform for the conservation of the established order.[21] The educa-tional system succeeds so perfectly in fulfilling its ideological function of legitimating the established order only because this masterpiece of social mechanics succeeds in hiding, as if by the interlocking of false-bottomed boxes, the relations which, in a class society, unite the function of inculcation, i.e. the work of intellectual and moral integration, with the function of conserving the structure of class relations characteristic of that society.[22]

So it is, for example, that, even more than the corps of State officials, the corps of teachers sets the moral authority of its pedagogic ministry — an authority all the greater for seeming to owe nothing to an academic institution which itself seems to owe nothing to the State or society — to work in the service of the ideology of academic freedom and scholastic equity. If teachers' pedagogic practices or professional ideologies are never directly or totally reducible or irreducible to those agents' class origin and class membership, the reason is that, as French educational history shows, they express in their polysemy and functional polyvalence the structural coincidence between the ethos the agents owe to their original and present social class and the conditions of actualization of that ethos which are objectively inscribed in the functioning of that institution and in the structure of its relations with the dominant classes.[23]

Thus, primary-school teachers have no difficulty in reformulating in the universalistic ideology of *l'Ecole libératrice* a Jacobin disposition towards an ethical demand for formal equality of opportunity which they derive from their class origin and class membership and which, in the social history of France, has become inseparable from its retranslation into the school ideology of social salvation through scholastic merit. Similarly, the representation of scholastic virtues and excellence which still guides pedagogic practices in French secondary education, even in the sciences, reproduces, not without bearing the mark of petty-bourgeois or academic reinterpretation, a social definition of intellectual and human excellence in which the generic inclination of the privileged classes towards the cult of manners is specified in accordance with the norms of an aristocratic tradition of fashionable elegance and literary good taste perpetuated by a system of education impregnated with Jesuit values. Like the scale of dominant values, the scholastic hierarchy of abilities is organized in accordance with the oppositions between the 'brilliant' and the 'serious', the 'elegant' and the 'laboured', the 'distinguished' and the 'vulgar', 'general culture' and 'pedantry', in short, between polytechnical ease and technical mastery[24] — dichotomies generated by a classificatory principle so powerful that, capable of specification for every field and moment, it can organize all the hierarchies and interlockings of hierarchies of the university world and consecrate social distinctions by constituting them as academic distinctions. The opposition between the student 'good at composition' and the student 'good at French' is just one actualization of the same principle of division which opposes the general specialists from the grandes écoles (ENS, Polytechnique, ENA) to the specialists produced by the second-rank schools, that is, the upper bourgeoisie to the petty bourgeoisie and the 'front door' to the 'back door'.[25]

As for higher education teachers, sons of petty bourgeois who owe their exceptional social advancement to their ability to turn a first-rate pupil's docile doggedness into academic ease by dint of doggedness and docility, or sons of middle or upper bourgeois who have had to exhibit at least the appearance of renouncing the temporal profits promised by their birth in order to impose the image of their university seriousness, their every practice reveals the tension between the aristocratic values imposed on the French educational system both by its own tradition and by its relations with the privileged classes, and the petty-bourgeois values that are encouraged, even in those teachers not drawing them directly from their social origin, by a system which, by virtue of its function and its position in relation to power, condemns its agents to occupy a subordinate rank in the hierarchy of the fractions of the dominant classes.[26] An institution which authorizes and encourages interchangeable transmitting agents to divert the authority of the institution so as to give the illusion of inimitable creation provides a particularly favourable terrain for the play of the compounded cross-censorships permitted by successive and sometimes simultaneous reference to the scholastic cult of brio and the academic cult of the golden mean. Higher education teachers thus find in the very ambiguities of an ideology in which are expressed both the social duality of recruitment to the teaching body and the ambivalence of the objective definition of the professional post, the instrument best adapted to repress, without self-contradiction, all deviations from two systems of norms which are contradictory in more than one respect. One sees how lordly contempt for the laboured virtues of the intellectual worker, the university retranslation of the aristocratism of talent — which itself retranslates the aristocratic ideology of birth in conformity with the requirements of bourgeois heredity — can be allied with moral reproval of success immediately perceived as worldly compromise, and with punctilious defence of status rights, even against the rights of competence — so many attitudes which express in a specifically university form the petty-bourgeois propensity to derive comfort from an apotropaic affirmation of universal mediocrity. Thus, all university norms, those which preside over the selection of students or the co-option of colleagues as well as those which govern the production of lectures, theses and even purportedly scientific works, always tend to favour the success, at least within the institution, of a modal type of man and work, defined by a double negation, i.e. brilliance without originality and heaviness without scientific weight, or, if you will, the pedantry of lightness and the coquetry of erudition.

Although it is almost always dominated by the bourgeois ideology of grace and giftedness, the petty-bourgeois ideology of laborious ascesis succeeds in profoundly marking scholastic practices and the judgements passed on them, because it encounters and reactivates a tendency towards ethical justification by merit which, even when relegated or repressed, is inherent in the dominant ideology. But the syncretism of university ethics remains inexplicable unless it is seen that the relationship of subordination and complementarity which is set up between petty-bourgeois and big-bourgeois ideology re-produces (in both senses), in the relatively autonomous logic of the academic institution, a relationship of antagonistic alliance, observed in other fields and particularly in politics, between the petty bourgeoisie and the dominant fractions of the bourgeoisie. Predisposed, by its two-fold opposition to the working classes and to the dominant classes, to serve the maintenance of the moral, cultural and political order, and through it those whom that order serves, the petty bourgeoisie is condemned by the division of labour to serve zealously in the subordinate and middle-rank posts of the bureaucracies responsible for maintaining order, whether by inculcating order or by calling to order those who have not internalized it.[27]

It is therefore necessary to bring the structural and operating properties an educational system owes to its essential function and to the external functions of its essential function into relation with the socially conditioned dispositions the agents (transmitters or receivers) owe to their class origin and class membership and to the position they occupy in the institution, in order to understand adequately the nature of the relationship between the educational system and the structure of class relations, and to bring to light — without falling into any metaphysics of the harmony of the spheres or providentialism of the best or the worst — correspondences, homologies or coincidences reducible in the last analysis to convergences of interest, ideological alliances and affinities between habitus.[28] Even if it is not feasible to construct the interminable discourse which would undertake in each case to run through the complete network of the relations which give each relation its complete meaning, it is sufficient to grasp, with respect to a particular relation, the system of circular relations which unite *structures* and *practices,* through the mediation of habitus, qua products of the structures, producers of practices and reproducers of the structures, in order to define the limits of validity (i.e. the validity within those limits) of an abstract expression such as 'the system of relations between the educational system and the structure of class relations'; by the same token one posits the principle of the empirical work which leads the way out of the fashionable, fictitious dilemma of mechanical pan-structuralism and affirmation of the inalienable rights of the creative subject or the historical agent.[29] Insofar as it defines the primordial conditions of production of the differences between habitus, the structure of class relations, regarded as a field of forces which expresses itself both in directly economic and political antagonisms and in a system of symbolic positions and oppositions, supplies the explanatory principle of the systematic characteristics which the practice of the agents of a determinate class takes on in the different areas of activity, even if that practice owes its specific form in each case to the laws proper to each of the sub-systems considered.[30] Thus, if it is not seen that the relationship between the various sub-systems is established only through the mediation of class membership, i.e. through the actions of agents disposed to actualize the same basic types of habitus in the most diverse practices (fertility, marriage, economic, political or educational conduct), one is in danger of reifying abstract structures by reducing the relationship between these sub-systems to the logical formula enabling any one of them to be derived from any other; or, worse, one is in danger of reconstituting the appearances of the real functioning of the 'social system', as Parsons does, only by giving the sub-systems the anthropomorphic shape of agents linked to one another by exchanges of services and so contributing to the smooth functioning of the system which is nothing other than the product of their abstract compounding.[31]

If, in the particular case of the relationship between the School and the social classes, the harmony appears to be perfect, this is because the objective structures produce class habitus and in particular the dispositions and predispositions which, in generating practices adapted to these structures, enable the structures to function and be perpetuated: for example, the disposition to make use of the School and the predispositions to succeed in it depend, as we have seen, on the objective chances of using it and succeeding in it that are attached to the different social classes, these dispositions and predispositions in turn constituting one of the most important factors in the perpetuation of the structure of educational chances as an objectively graspable manifestation of the relationship between the educational system and the structure of class relations. Even the negative dispositions and predispositions leading to self-elimination, such as, for example, self-depreciation, devalorization of the School and its sanctions or resigned expectation of failure or exclusion may be understood as unconscious anticipation of the sanctions the School objectively has in store for the dominated classes. More profoundly, only an adequate theory of the habitus, as the site of the internalization of externality and the externalization of internality, can fully bring to light the social conditions of performance of the function of legitimating the social order, doubtless the best concealed of all the functions of the School. Because the traditional system of education manages to present the illusion that its action of inculcation is entirely responsible for producing the cultivated habitus, or, by an apparent contradiction, that it owes its differential efficacy exclusively to the innate abilities of those who undergo it, and that it is therefore independent of class determinations — whereas it tends towards the limit of merely confirming and strengthening a class habitus which, constituted outside the School, is the basis of all scholastic acquirements — it contributes irreplaceably towards perpetuating the structure of class relations and, simultaneously, legitimating it, by concealing the fact that the scholastic hierarchies it produces reproduce social hierarchies.[32] To be persuaded that everything predisposes a traditional educational system to serve a function of social conservation, one only has to recall, among other things, the affinity between the culture it inculcates, its manner of inculcating it and the manner of possessing it which this mode of acquisition presupposes and produces, and between this set of features and the social characteristics of the public in whom it inculcates this culture, these characteristics themselves being interdependent with the pedagogic and cultural dispositions the inculcating agents derive from their social origin, training, position in the institution, and class membership. Given the complexity of the network of relations through which the function of legitimating the social order is accomplished, it would clearly be vain to claim to localize its performance in one mechanism or one sector of the educational system. However, in a class society in which the School shares the task of reproducing that product of history which constitutes at a given moment the legitimate model of the cultivated disposition with families unequally endowed with cultural capital and the disposi-

tion to make use of it, nothing better serves the pedagogic interests of
the dominant classes than the pedagogic 'laissez-faire' characteristic of
traditional teaching, since this action by default, immediately efficacious and, by definition, ungraspable, seems predestined to serve the
function of legitimating the social order.

It is clear how naive it would be to reduce all the functions of the
educational system to the function of political or religious indoctrination which can itself be carried on with varying degrees of latency,
depending on the mode of inculcation. This confusion, inherent in most
analyses of the political function of the School, is all the more perni-
cious in that the ostentatious refusal of the function of indoctrination
or, at least, of the most overt forms of political propaganda and 'civic
instruction' can in turn fulfil an ideological function in concealing the
function of legitimation of the social order when, as the French
tradition of the lay, liberal or libertarian University demonstrates particularly well, declared neutrality towards ethical and political creeds or
even flaunted hostility towards the State authorities enhances the
invisibility of the contribution the educational system is alone in a
position to render the established order.

Thus, to understand that the social effects of the common or learned
illusions which are sociologically implied in the system of relations
between the educational system and the structure of class relations are
not illusory, it is necessary to go back to the principle which governs
this system of relations. Legitimation of the established order by the
School presupposes social recognition of the legitimacy of the School, a
recognition resting in turn on misrecognition of the delegation of
authority which establishes that legitimacy or, more precisely, on
misrecognition of the social conditions of a harmony between structures and habitus sufficiently perfect to engender misrecognition of the
habitus as a product reproducing what produces it and correlative
recognition of the structure of the order thus reproduced. Thus, the
educational system objectively tends, by concealing the objective truth
of its functioning, to produce the ideological justification of the order
it reproduces by its functioning.

It is no accident that so many sociologists, victims of the ideological effect of the School, are inclined to isolate dispositions and predispositions towards education — 'hopes', 'aspirations', 'motivations', 'will-power' — from their social conditions of production: forgetting that objective conditions determine both aspirations and the degree to which they can be satisfied, they think themselves entitled to proclaim the best of all possible worlds when, after a longitudinal study of school careers, they find that, as if by a pre-established harmony, individuals hoped for nothing they have not obtained and obtained nothing they did not hope for. Reproving the academics who always feel 'a sense of guilt on reading the statistics of university students' social origins', M. Vermot-Gauchy retorts that 'it has not occurred to them that genuine democratization perhaps consists in favouring the development of those forms of education best suited to the characteristics and wishes of children from modest or uncultured backgrounds', and adds: 'It is of little consequence to them that by social tradition, aptitude acquired by virtue of belonging to a certain background, etc., the intellectually brilliant son of a labourer would rather aim for the old practical schools or old national vocational schools and (if he has sufficient ability) get a technician's or engineer's diploma from the *Arts et Métiers*, for example, while a doctor's son prefers a classical education with a view to entering the faculties.'[33] Blessed, then, are 'modest' folk who, when all is said and done, aspire in their modesty to nothing but what they have; and praise be to 'the social order' which refuses to hurt them by calling them to over-ambitious destinies, as little suited to their abilities as to their aspirations.

Is Dr Pangloss less terrifying as a planner than as a metaphysician? Convinced that calculation suffices to produce the best of all possible educational worlds in the best of all possible societies, the new optimistic philosophers of the social order return to the language of all sociodicies, which are designed to convince people that the established order is what it ought to be since the apparent victims of that order require no call to order (i.e. to what they ought to be) before they agree to be what they ought to be. Our optimists can only pass over in silence, because they tacitly assume it, the function of legitimating and conserving the established order which the School performs when it persuades the classes it excludes of the legitimacy of their exclusion, by preventing them from seeing and contesting the principles in whose name it excludes them. The verdicts of the academic tribunal are so decisive only because they impose simultaneously conviction and ignorance of the social grounds of conviction. For social destiny to be changed into free vocation or personal merit, as in the Platonic myth in which the souls which have chosen their 'lot' must drink the water of the river of oblivion before returning to earth to live out the destiny which has befallen them, it is necessary and sufficient that the School, 'the hierophant of Necessity', should succeed in convincing individuals that they have themselves chosen or won the destinies which social destiny has assigned to them in advance. Better than the political religions whose most constant function was, as Weber says, to provide the privileged classes with a theodicy of their privilege, better than the soteriologies of the hereafter which helped to perpetuate the social order by promising a posthumous subversion of that order, better than a doctrine like that of *karma*, which Weber saw as the masterpiece of the social theodicies, since it justified the social quality of each individual within the caste system by his degree of religious qualification in the transmigration cycle, the School today succeeds, with the ideology of natural 'gifts' and innate 'tastes', in legitimating the circular reproduction of social hierarchies and educational hierarchies.

Thus, the most hidden and most specific function of the educational system consists in hiding its objective function, that is, masking the objective truth of its relationship to the structure of class relations.[34] To be convinced that this is so, one only has to listen to a consistent planner, discussing the most reliable way of selecting in advance students likely to succeed academically and so of increasing the technical efficiency of the educational system:

Before looking at the constituent elements of selection policy, it is appropriate to consider which characteristics of a candidate for university admission may legitimately be taken into consideration in the selection process. (. . .) In a democracy, institutions supported out of public funds ought not directly and openly to select on the basis of some of them. Amongst the characteristics it would not normally be legitimate to pay attention to in the selection process are sex, sibling order, age above the minimum (or length of time spent at school), physical appearance, accent or intonation, socio-economic status of parent, and prestige of last school attended. Reasons for the inclusion of some of these characteristics in such a list are self-evident. Even if, for example, it could be shown that those with parents who were low in the social hierarchy tended to be 'bad risks' in terms of academic performance at universities, a direct and open bias of selection policy against such candidates would be unacceptable.[35]

In short, the time (hence money) wasted is also the price that has to be paid for the continued masking of the relationship between social origin and academic performance, since an attempt to do more cheaply and more rapidly what the system will do in any case, would bring to light and, by the same token, annul a function which can be carried on only if it remains hidden. It is always at the cost of expenditure or wasted time that the educational system legitimates the transmission of power from one generation to another by concealing the relationship between the social starting point and social point of arrival of the educational trajectory, thanks to what is, ultimately, merely a certification effect made possible by the ostentatious and sometimes hyperbolic length of apprenticeship. More generally, if the lost time is not to be written off as pure loss, this is because it is the site of a transformation of dispositions towards the system and its sanctions which is indispensable to the operation of the system and the performance of its functions. The difference between deferred self-elimination and immediate elimination on the basis of a forecast of the objective chances of elimination, is the time required for the excluded to persuade themselves of the legitimacy of their exclusion. If educational systems are nowadays increasingly resorting to the 'soft approach' to eliminate the classes most distant from school culture, despite its greater cost in time and material, the reason is that, as an institution of symbolic government condemned to disappoint in some the aspirations it encourages in all, the educational system must give itself the means of obtaining recognition of the legitimacy of its sanctions and their social effects, so that machinery and techniques for organized, explicit manipulation cannot fail to make their appearance when exclusion no longer suffices per se to impose internalization of the legitimacy of exclusion.[36]

Thus, the educational system, with the ideologies and effects which its relative autonomy engenders, is for bourgeois society in its present phase what other forms of legitimation of the social order and of hereditary transmission of privileges were for social formations differing both in the specific form of the relations and antagonisms between the classes and in the nature of the privilege transmitted: does it not contribute towards persuading each social subject to stay in the place which falls to him *by nature,* to know his place and hold to it, *ta heatou prattein,* as Plato put it? Unable to invoke the right of blood – which his class historically denied the aristocracy – nor the rights of Nature – a weapon once used against the distinctions of nobility but liable to backfire against bourgeois 'distinction' – nor the ascetic virtues which enabled the first-generation entrepreneurs to justify their success by their merit, the inheritor of bourgeois privileges must today appeal to the academic certification which attests at once his gifts and his merits. The unnatural idea of culture by birth presupposes and produces blindness to the functions of the educational institution which ensures the profitability of cultural capital and legitimates its transmission by dissimulating the fact that it performs this function. Thus, in a society in which the obtaining of social privileges depends more and more closely on possession of academic credentials, the School does not only have the function of ensuring discreet succession to a bourgeois estate which can no longer be transmitted directly and openly. This privileged instrument of the bourgeois sociodicy which confers on the privileged the supreme privilege of not seeing themselves as privileged manages the more easily to convince the disinherited that they owe their scholastic and social destiny to their lack of gifts or merits, because in matters of culture absolute dispossession excludes awareness of being dispossessed.

NOTES

1. This definition of formal educational rationality might be challenged on the grounds that the demands of the economic system are no longer formulated in terms of narrow specialization but that the emphasis is, on the contrary, on the aptitude for vocational re-adaptation. But this is in fact a new type of vocational speciality, required by a new state of the demand of the economic system. Despite this broadening of the definition, the capacity to produce occupationally usable skills remains the measure of the rationality of the educational system.

2. The formal equivalence between their university systems and diplomas makes comparison between France and Algeria particularly significant in this respect: 'In a society where 57% of the people have no certificate of general education and 98% no certificate of technical education, possession of a C.A.P. (trade proficiency certificate) or C.E.P. (primary school certificate) gives an immense advantage in economic competition; an infinitesimal difference of level, such as that between someone who can read and someone who can both read and write, produces a disproportionate difference in chances of social success' (P. Bourdieu, *Travail et travailleurs en Algérie*, Paris, Mouton, 1962, pp. 272-73). Similarly, for a girl, possession of a diploma has a very different value depending on the rate of schooling of the female population: for example, in Algeria in 1960, 70 percent of the girls with a CEP or a higher certificate were in non-manual jobs; the percentage of them not in employment was insignificant (ibid., p. 208).

3. What is true of statistical indicators is equally true of the seemingly most specific indices of the organization and operation of the school system: an analysis of the content of curricula and school manuals which ignored the real conditions of their implementation, or a study of State control of universities, university decentralization or the recruitment of administrators and teachers based solely on the juridical texts, would be as misleading as a study of religious behaviour which presumed to infer the believers' real practice from the canonical texts even when it is defined by formally identical texts.

'Academic freedom' is in reality a function of the relationships between the university system and political or religious power. In France, the appointment of a faculty lecturer is nominally a Ministry decision but, since it is a foregone conclusion that the candidate proposed by the Faculty Board will be appointed, recruitment is in fact based on co-option, with full-scale canvassing of colleagues. Conversely, in other countries, many academic elections are merely formal procedures ratifying choices already made. In Italy, recruitment officially takes place by competition, but this device barely conceals the play of cliques and influences inside and outside the university.

4. J. A. Schumpeter, *Capitalism, Socialism and Democracy*, London, Unwin, 4th edn, 1954, pp. 152-55.

5. M. Vermot-Gauchy, *L'éducation nationale dans la France de demain*, Futuribles, Monaco, Ed. du Rocher, 1965, p. 75.

6. The demand for education manifests itself in two phases, first at the point of entry to the school system as a demand for schooling, with the demands for the labour market, which sanctions superfluous graduates with unemployment or under-employment, manifesting themselves only at a later stage. The demand for schooling, which is reflected in a broadening of the social base of admissions and longer attendance, obeys regularities partially independent of the imperatives of number and skill which educational planning seeks to satisfy. It is this demand (closely tied to higher living standards and changing attitudes to education among the different social classes), which the Robbins Report, less confident than M. Vermot-Gauchy of the predictability of the technical demand of the labour market (dependent on the ups and downs of growth and on technological innovations unpredictable beyond the very short term), takes as a basis for forecasting student numbers (Great Britain Committee on Higher Education, op. cit., note 30, chapter 3).

7. Hence knowledge of the operation of the school system and of the different social classes' attitudes towards education provides the only basis for forecasting when one wants to know, not what the desirable distribution of the school population among the various types and levels of education might be, but what it is likely to be at a given date.

8. J. R. Pitts, 'Continuité et changement au sein de la France bourgeoise', *A la recherche de la France*, Paris, Ed. du Seuil, 1963.

9. Ibid., p. 288.

10. Thus the Japanese specialists who criticized Ruth Benedict's work, *The Chrysanthemum and the Sword*, mainly attacked the simplifications and approximations authorized by such use of the 'holistic' approach. Who, they ask, is the Japanese designated at some points as 'the proverbial man in the street' and elsewhere as 'everyone' or 'anybody'? Minima finds that 'most of her patterns apply to the military and the fascist cliques during the last war' and Watsuji considers that her patterns are not assignable to any concrete group in the national society' Most of the commentators are unsure how her cultural generalizations 'are related to the very evident heterogeneity of Japanese society' (J. W. Bennett and M. Nagai, 'The Japanese Critique of the Methodology of Benedict's *Chrysanthemum and the Sword*', *American Anthropologist*, 55, 1953, pp. 404-11, esp. 406-7).

11. Pitts, Continuité et changement', pp. 273 and 274.

12. M. Crozier, *The Bureaucratic Phenomenon*, London, Tavistock, 1964, p. 238. He continues: If our French model of organizational control is applicable,

we should find; in the French educational system, the main characteristic patterns of the bureaucratic system of organization which we have analyzed, since they all revolve around the problem of social control and could not remain in existence without being handed down and reinforced by education.'

13. The Sophists, the first professional teachers (Plato, *Protagoras*, 317 b: 'I acknowledge that I am a professional teacher – *sophistes* – an educator of men'), gave their pupils selected extracts from the great poets (*Protagoras*, 325 e) and started to distribute copies of their own writings as 'models' *(paradeigmata)* (see R. Pfeifer, *History of Classical Scholarship*, Oxford, Clarendon Press, 1968, p. 31).

14. 'French teachers received good tenure very early – they were probably the first in the world to do so. They have been able gradually to secure for themselves the most perfect independence, as long, of course, as they keep within the limits set by the rules' (Crozier, p. 240-41).

15. Sharing with their favourite enemy, technocracy, an indifference to differences, 'critical' ideologies differ from it only in the application they make of this disposition when, consigning sociology to the pursuit of generic alienations, they build up an ideological system in which the elements most frequently attested are a predilection for sociological categorizations capable of inducing the illusion of homogeneity ('readership', 'age group', 'youth', if not 'the users of hospitals, housing estates or public transport') or a fascinated interest in the homogenizing and alienating effects of television or the 'mass media', automation or technical objects and, more generally, 'technological civilization' or 'consumer society'.

16. For example, one finds some American sociologists reproaching their own academic institution with traditions or vices in its operation which many French authors, generally in the name of an idyllic vision of the American system, complain of in the French university, imputing what they regard as its unique features to the uniqueness of a national history. While they do not have to reckon with the vestiges of a medieval past or the survivals of State centralization, the American universities also succeed in expressing, perhaps less completely, some of the most characteristic tendencies of the university system, in features such as 'boning', the institutionalized obstacle-race to which the student's career is reduced; obsession with examinations, which steadily increases with the growing importance of their role in social success; furious competition for the titles and honours that will accompany an individual, especially if he becomes an academic, throughout his life; the 'intellectual servitude' to which instructors and assistants are subjected; the 'unbelievably picayunish' features of doctoral dissertations, which will gather dust on a library shelf; the unproductiveness of the professors who, once tenured, 'ease up' and ensconce themselves; the university ideology of contempt for management and teaching methods (see L. Wilson, *The Academic Man, A Study in the Sociology of a Profession*, New York, OUP, 1942).

17. Every school system, to varying degrees and in forms determined in each case by the structure of class relations, fulfils the totality of the functions corresponding to the totality of the possible relationships with the other systems, so that its structure and functioning are always organized in relation to a determinate structure of possible functions. Constructing the system of possible configurations of the system of functions would be a purely academic exercise if it did not enable each historical case to be treated as a particular case of the ideal totality of the possible combinations of functions, thereby bringing to light all the relations between the school system and the other sub-systems, not least, of course, the blank or negative relations which are by definition the best-hidden ones.

18. In including in the definition of the essential, hence transhistorical, function of the school system characteristics deriving from a historically determined state of the relations between the educational system and the class structure, Durkheim tends implicitly to present as a transhistorical law a relationship whose epistemological status is only ever that of 'accidental generalizations', historical regularities to which there has hitherto been no exception but whose opposite is sociologically possible. We are not endorsing the pedagogic Utopias based on the automatic compatibility of the essential function with any external function whatever, when we refuse to take products of history, however recurrent, for expressions of a historical nature ('no society is known in which . . .') or even a human nature ('men will always be men'). Knowing the tendency to justify the established order by reference to 'the nature of things' which characterizes conservative thought, one sees the use which pessimistic philosophies of history, always ready to transmute a historical regularity into a necessary and universal law, could make of the eternizing of the relation between schooling and conservatism.

19. Perhaps in no other system are pedagogic choices in syllabus, exercises and examinations so totally determined as in the French system by the requirements of the training of teachers who will correspond to the traditional norms. It is indeed the logic of a mode of teaching which tends to be organized exclusively with a view to preparing others to teach, that French teachers express when, in their pedagogic judgements and practices, they at least unconsciously measure all their students against the accomplished model of the student who is none other than the 'good pupil' they were and who 'promises' to become the teacher they are.

20. The relation of dependence through independence which links an educational system to the material and symbolic interests of the dominant classes or, more exactly, the dominant fractions of those classes, can be grasped in a survey in the form of the convergence or divergence of the opinions expressed on pedagogic problems by the different categories of teachers and the different classes or class fractions. For example, when one analyses the responses to a

questionnaire on, inter alia, the teaching of Latin, the agrégation, vocational training and the respective functions of school and family in children's upbringing, beyond the manifestations of the old alliance between the dominant fractions of the bourgeoisie and those teachers most attached (in both senses) to the traditional mode of recruitment and training, and by the same token, to the traditional conception of culture (the 'humanities'), one glimpses the first signs of a new alliance between those fractions of the dominant classes most directly tied to production and the management of the State apparatus and those categories of teachers capable of expressing their categorial interests of university conservation in the technocratic language of rationality and productivity (CSE nationwide survey through the press on the situation of the educational system).

21. If the relative autonomy of the school system can be treated as the necessary and specific condition for the performance of its class functions, this is because the successful inculcation of a legitimate culture and of its legitimacy presupposes recognition of the specifically pedagogic authority of the institution and its agents, i.e. misrecognition of the structure of social relations underpinning that authority. In other words, pedagogic legitimacy presupposes the delegation of an already existing legitimacy, but, in producing recognition of school authority i.e., misrecognition of the social authority underlying it, the institution produces legitimation of the perpetuation of class relations in a sort of circle of reciprocal priorities.

22. Thus, by a paradox which is the essence of its heuristic fertility but which most users of the notion of relative autonomy fail to grasp, it is necessary to draw out all the consequences of autonomy so as to lose none of the dependence which is realized through it.

23. For example, the proportion of teachers from the petty bourgeoisie declines steadily at higher levels of the hierarchy of the stages of education, i.e. as the contradiction inscribed in the professorial office is accentuated and as the primacy of the relation to culture characteristic of the privileged classes asserts itself more fully. Thirty-six percent of primary school teachers aged under 45 in 1964 were from the working classes, 42 percent from the petty bourgeoisie and 11 percent from the middle or upper bourgeoisie, whereas, among secondary and higher education teachers (taken together), 16 percent were from the working classes, 35 percent from the petty bourgeoisie and 34 percent from the middle and upper bourgeoisie. In the absence of statistics, one can get an idea of the social origin of higher education teachers by considering the social origin of the students of the École Normale Supérieure: 6 percent working class, 27 percent middle class, 67 percent upper class. While there is no doubt that the various categories of teachers owe a number of their characteristics to the position they occupy in the educational system, i.e. to the relations of competition or alliance, declared or tacit, which they maintain with the other categories, and to the

academic trajectory, with the corresponding type of training, which has brought them to that position, nonetheless these characteristics are closely linked to differences in social origin, so that categories of teachers who scarcely differ as regards their conditions of existence and professional situation may be separated, in their professional and extra-professional attitudes, by differences which are irreducible to oppositions between categorial interests and which relate back, beyond their present class, to their class of origin (see also 1971, 9; 1974, 3).

24. No doubt this system of specifically academic oppositions would not have the same degree of classificatory output and symbolic efficacy if it did not indirectly evoke the opposition between theory and practice in which the fundamental division between manual and non-manual labour finds expression (see 1977, 1). In systematically privileging one of the poles of a series of systematic oppositions (with the pre-eminence accorded to the theoretic disciplines, the literary cult of form and the taste for mathematical formalism or the absolute depreciation of technical education), the educational system privileges those on whom a family relatively freed from the pragmatism imposed by the urgencies of economic necessity has bestowed the privilege of the aptitude for symbolic, i.e. initially verbal, mastery of practical operations, and the detached, distant and 'disinterested' relation to the world and to others, hence to language and culture, which are demanded by the school, especially when it is a matter of acquiring dispositions as highly valued as the specifically aesthetic disposition or the scientific attitude (see 1971, 3).

25. In Flaubert's *Dictionary of Received Ideas* one reads: '*Composition*: At school, skill at composition shows application, whereas skill at translation shows intelligence. But out in the world, scoff at those who were good at composition'. It could easily be demonstrated that for the *grande bourgeoisie* of business and power, the *normalien*, who, in the teachers' ideology represents the ideal cultivated man, stands in much the same relation to the ENA graduate, the incarnation of an up-dated 'society' culture, as the 'student good at composition' *(le fort en thème)* does to the man cultivated according to the canons of the traditional School.

26. The structural discrepancy between an eminent position within the institution and the position outside the institution which results from the institution's inferior (or marginal) position within the power structure may well be one of the most potent principles explaining the practices and opinions of higher education teachers (similar in this respect, to high-ranking army officers).

27. The functions performed by the division of the work of domination between the petty and upper bourgeoisie, particularly the role of scapegoat and foil assumed by subaltern agents appointed to exert vicarious physical or symbolic coercion, may be indicated by enumerating some of the most significant realizations of this functional opposition: the colonel, 'father of his regiment', and the sergeant-major, 'scourge of the barrack-room'; the judge and the 'cop'; the 'boss'

and the foreman; the senior official and the clerk facing the public; the doctor and the nurse, or the psychiatrist and the warder; and, within the French school system, the *proviseur* (headmaster) and the *surveillant general* (in charge of discipline) or the teacher and the *'pion'* (cf. in England the role of the prefect and the proctor – trans.). One sees the double game authorized in the school system by the duality of functions and staffs; open or tacit disparagement of the bureaucracy of educational administrators and disciplinary officials constitutes one of the surest and most economical springs of institutional charisma.

28. To appreciate the distance separating the analysis of concrete mediations from the theoretical formulation which at best summarizes it and, at worst, dispenses with it, the reader only has to look back at some of the analyses in this book, which, reduced to an abstract shorthand, would present themselves as, for example, 'the system of communicative relations between transmission levels and reception levels systematically defined by the relations between the educational system as a communication system and the structure of class relations' (Chapters 1 and 2); or as 'the system of relations between the system of school values defined in its relationship to the values of the dominant classes and the value system deriving from the original and present class membership of the corps of agents' (Chapter 4).

29. On the role of the concept of the habitus in breaking out of this prescientific dilemma which, even in its avant-garde forms, recalls in more respects than one the old debate on social determinisms and human freedom, see *Outline of a Theory of Practice* (1977, 1).

30. There is, for example, every reason to think that the same ascetic ethos of social upgrading underlies the conduct of a part of the middle classes as regards both fertility and attitudes towards education. Whereas in the most fertile social categories, such as farm workers, farmers and manual workers, the chances of entering sixième decrease steadily with each additional child, in the least fertile categories – craftsmen, traders, clerical workers and middle management – they fall dramatically in families with four or more children, i.e. those which are distinguished from the group as a whole by their high fertility. Instead of seeing in the number of children the causal explanation for the fall in rate of enrolment, it has to be supposed that the will to limit the number of births and the will to give the children a secondary education express one and the same ascetic disposition in those categories which combine them. For an analysis of the relationship between class ethos and fertility, see P. Bourdieu and A. Darbel, 'La fin d'un malthusianisme', in Darras, *Le partage des bénéfices*, Paris, Minuit, 1966, pp. 134-54.

31. Although they assert the immanence of the structure of class relations at all levels of social practice, the structuralist readers of Marx, carried away by their objectivist reaction against all idealist forms of the philosophy of action, will acknowledge agents only as 'supports' of the structure and are obliged to ignore

the question of the mediations between the structure and practice, because they fail to confer on structures any other content than the power — a very mysterious one in the last analysis — of determining or over-determining other structures.

32. To give a concrete sense of the concordance of the effects of school action and selection with the effects of the pre-school or para-school education that is given anonymously by the conditions of existence, even if it is specified and invested with its specifically pedagogic meaning by the pedagogic authority of a family group, it is sufficient to point out that, from sixième to Polytechnique, the hierarchy of schools in terms of the academic prestige and social profitability of the qualifications they lead to, corresponds strictly with the social composition of their intake.

33. M. Vermot-Gauchy, *L'éducation nationale*, pp. 62-63.

34. Few institutions are so well protected as the educational system against sociological inquiry. If it is true that the School has the function of hiding the external functions of its essential function and that to perform this ideological function it has to hide the fact that it performs it, then scientific sociology must, in this case, in order to find its object, take as its object that which stands in the way of the construction of the object. To refuse such a project is to consign oneself to blind or complicitous adherence to the given as it gives itself, whether this theoretical surrender be masked under the flaunted rigour of empirical procedures or legitimated by invocation of the ideal of "ethical neutrality", a mere non-aggression pact with the established order. If there is no science but of the hidden, then the science of society is, per se, critical, without the scientist who chooses science ever having to choose to make a critique: the hidden is, in this case, a secret, and a well-kept one, even when no one is commissioned to keep it, because it contributes to the reproduction of a 'social order' based on concealment of the most efficacious mechanisms of its reproduction and thereby serves the interests of those who have a vested interest in the conservation of that order.

35. R. K. Kelsall, 'University Student Selection in Relation to Subsequent Academic Performance — A Critical Appraisal of the British Evidence', in *Sociological Studies in British University Education*, The Sociological Review: Monograph No. 7, ed. P. Hamos, Keele, Oct. 1963, p. 102.

36. The French educational system which in its traditional form demanded and obtained recognition of unchallengeable verdicts expressing an always univocal hierarchy (even when concealed under a set of interlocking hierarchies) contrasts in this respect with systems like the American university, which provides for the institutional resolution of the tensions resulting from the disparity between the aspirations it helps to instil and the social means of realizing them. If one considers the limiting case, one imagines universities which, accepting quasi-explicitly their role as institutions of symbolic government, would equip them-

selves with all the institutionalized instruments (tests, plus a system of branch lines and sidings making up a university subtly hierarchized under the guise of diversity) and specialized personnel (psychologists, psychiatrists, guidance councellors, psychoanalysts) required for the discreet, friendly manipulation of those whom the institution condemns, excludes or relegates. This Utopia enables it to be seen that 'rationalization' of the technical and institutional tools for exclusion, channelling, and inculcation of acquiescence in channelling and exclusion, would enable the school system to fulfil more efficiently, because more irreproachably, the functions it performs today when it selects and, by concealing the principles of its selection, wins acquiescence in that selection and in the principles underlying it.

APPENDIX

The Changing Structure of
Higher Education Opportunities:
Redistribution or Translation?

The 'democratization' of university admissions is one of those questions so closely integrated into an ideological problematic predetermining, if not the possible answers, at least the possible readings of those answers, that we hesitate to give so much as the appearance of intervening, even with scientific reasons, in a debate where scientific reason has so little place. It is amusing to note, for example, that those who were the first to proclaim the advent of 'democratization' without a scrap of statistical evidence or on the basis of hasty, tendentious comparison of simple percentages of the representatives of each social category in the student body,[1] are today eager to denounce as the effect of an ideological obsession any attempt to measure scientifically the changing structure of the chances of access to the various levels and types of education relative to social origin. For a full appreciation of this paradox, one needs to know that measurement of the evolution of educational opportunity over a sufficiently long period has only been possible since the Bureau Universitaire de Statistique began publishing statistical series broken down into relatively pertinent categories.[2] As opposed to simple manipulation of the levels of representation of the various categories of students within the whole student body (implicitly treated as an empire within an empire), construction of the objective probabilities of enrolment attached to the different social categories requires us to relate the proportion of selection-survivors in each category to their category of origin as a whole. It therefore provides one of the most effective ways of empirically grasping the system of relations, at a given moment in time, between the education system and the structure of the social classes, and of measuring its transformation over a period of time.[3]

This construction is, at all events, the only means of avoiding the errors which result from autonomizing a population of survivors who owe their essential characteristics much less to the *social composition* of the group they constitute than to their objective relations with the category of which they are the scholastic representatives, relations which are expressed, for example, in the differential selection rates according to social class and sex.[4] More generally, it is only by systematically applying the *relational mode of thought* that one can avoid the error of seeing substantial attributes in the properties attached to a category, having failed to observe that the adequate significance of each of the terms of a relation (e.g. that between political positions and field of study) can only be fully established within the system of the relations which they cover and conceal. Consider, for example, the 'sociologists'' literature on the role of sociologists in May 1968, or the naiveties that are inspired by the relatively high proportion of working-class students in Science Faculties, when this fact is not seen in relation to the privileged classes' quasi-monopoly on the major scientific grandes écoles, i.e. when the problem of social recruitment is not posed at the level of the whole system of science courses.

Vigilance against the temptation of treating the elements independently of the relations which constitute them into a system is particularly necessary when comparing different periods. Thus, to grasp the social significance of the different social categories' share in the different faculties or disciplines, one has to take into account the *position* this or that faculty or discipline occupies at a given time within the system of faculties or disciplines. Otherwise one succumbs to the illusions of monographic history which, implicitly arguing from the identity of the names to the substantial unity through time of the corresponding institutions or features, is bound to compare the incomparable and to fail to compare elements which, though incomparable when apprehended in and for themselves, constitute the true terms of comparison because they occupy homologous positions in two successive states of the system of educational institutions.[5]

For the benefit of those who conclude from the growth in the total number of students in higher education that there has been a 'democratization' of faculty intake, it must be pointed out that this morphological phenomenon may correspond to a perpetuation of the status quo or even, in certain cases, to a decline in the representation of the disadvantaged classes[6] as well as to a broadening of the social base of admission. An increase in the rate of schooling of a particular age group can in fact take place to the almost exclusive advantage of the social categories who were already the most schooled, or, at least, in proportion to the previous distribution of inequalities in schooling. More generally, expanded enrolment is the resultant of factors of several different orders: while, in France, the increased number of students reflects (at least since 1964) both the greater strength of the cohorts (following the post-1946 rise in birth rates) and the rise in the enrolment rate of the 18-plus age group, the distribution of this overall rate among the enrolment rates of the different socio-occupational categories is likely to have changed much less than the constant rise in the overall rate of higher education enrolment would lead one to suppose.

More precisely, in order to get a numerical approximation to the structure of the socially conditioned chances of university entrance, and especially in order to analyse the evolution of this structure over time, it is desirable to interrelate the whole membership of a socially defined category of students with the whole membership of the cohort of young people of the same age endowed with the same social characteristics. An increase in the proportion of students from a particular social category may reflect not the increased likelihood of adolescents from that category entering higher education, but a simple change in the numerical weight of that category in the active population. This is why calculation of the probability of higher education entry according to socio-occupational category of origin, sex, or any other criterion provides the most accurate formulation of the order of magnitude of the inequality of socially conditioned educational opportunities and their range.

The table of the likelihood of access to higher education (table 10) revealed, in 1961-62, considerable disparities between the different social categories. Thus, a farm worker's son had a 1.2 percent chance of entering higher education, and the son of an industrialist a better than even chance. This measure of the range of inequalities shows that at that time the educational system tended purely and simply to eliminate working-class youngsters from access to university education.

Between 1962 and 1966, the chances of access to higher education rose for all social categories. But if 'democratization' is taken to mean what it always implicitly suggests, namely the process of equalization of educational opportunities for children from the different social categories (perfect equality of opportunity presupposing that all subcategories should have a rate of opportunity equal to the overall rate of enrolment for that age group), then the empirically ascertained increase in the chances of all categories does not in itself constitute a sign of 'democratization'.

Furthermore, in order to be sociologically rigorous, analysis of the evolution of the structure of chances presupposes that one should also take into account the social significance of the evolution of that structure as a whole. Restricting ourselves to the extreme cases, we observe that the chances of access to higher education for workers' sons more than doubled over this period, whereas the chances of senior executives' sons were multiplied by only 1.6; but it is obvious that the doubling of a very low rate of probability does not have the same significance or the same social effects as the doubling of a rate thirty times greater. For an accurate assessment of the social consequences of these numerical changes which, as the graph shows, amount to an *upward translation*[7] of the structure of the educational chances of the different social classes (see figure 2, p. 92), one would strictly speaking have to be able to establish the *thresholds* which, in the different

TABLE 10

Trend of Educational Opportunities According to Social Origin and Sex Between 1961-62 and 1965-66

Father's socio-occupational group	Year	Objective chances (probability of access)		Conditional probability Science		Arts		Law		Medicine		Pharmacy	
		1961-62	1965-66	1961-62	1965-66	1961-62	1965-66	1961-62	1965-66	1961-62	1965-66	1961-62	1965-66
Farm workers													
M		1.2	3.0	44.0	53.3	36.9	26.4	15.5	16.3	3.6	3.3	0	0.5
F		1.0	2.3	26.6	33.7	65.6	55.4	7.8	8.6	0	3.3	0	1.2
Combined		1.1	2.7	34.7	45.0	50.0	38.0	12.5	12.0	2.8	3.3	0	0.8
Farmers													
M		3.8	8.5	44.6	45.0	27.2	24.4	18.8	20.3	7.4	7.9	2.0	2.2
F		3.0	6.7	27.5	31.8	51.8	48.5	12.9	10.9	2.9	3.9	4.9	4.6
Combined		3.4	8.0	37.0	39.2	38.1	35.0	16.2	16.1	5.6	6.2	3.1	3.3
Manual workers													
M		1.5	3.9	52.5	50.0	27.5	24.8	14.4	17.8	5.0	6.6	0.6	0.6
F		1.2	2.9	29.3	31.0	56.0	54.4	10.4	10.2	2.6	2.7	1.7	1.4
Combined		1.3	3.4	42.8	41.7	39.9	37.0	12.3	14.6	3.6	4.9	1.4	0.9
Office workers													
M		10.0	17.9	46.0	37.7	17.6	21.6	24.6	26.7	10.1	11.8	1.6	1.7
F		7.8	14.3	30.4	22.3	44.0	53.4	16.0	14.3	6.1	5.7	3.5	4.0
Combined		9.0	16.2	39.4	31.1	28.6	35.5	21.1	21.5	8.6	9.2	2.3	2.7
Employers in industry and commerce													
M		14.6	25.0	40.3	37.2	24.9	17.1	20.5	26.6	11.0	15.4	3.3	3.3
F		13.3	21.2	21.8	22.4	55.7	47.4	11.7	15.7	4.8	7.6	6.0	6.7
Combined		13.9	23.2	31.8	30.5	39.1	30.6	16.4	21.6	8.1	12.0	4.6	4.8
of which Industrialists													
M		52.8	74.0	28.5	34.3	25.2	11.6	22.0	32.3	20.0	17.8	3.9	4.0
F		56.9	68.6	13.2	18.4	57.8	42.5	11.2	19.8	10.8	9.8	6.8	9.2
Combined		54.4	71.5	21.1	26.6	41.1	26.0	17.0	26.5	15.5	14.0	5.3	6.4
Middle management													
M		24.7	38.2	38.3	41.2	30.2	21.0	21.0	23.2	8.5	12.6	2.0	1.6
F		25.4	31.4	22.2	25.5	61.9	52.6	9.1	11.3	3.4	6.4	3.4	3.9
Combined		24.9	35.4	30.5	34.0	45.6	37.2	15.2	18.0	6.0	9.8	2.7	2.7
Professions and senior executives													
M		38.7	61.0	40.0	35.7	19.3	13.7	21.8	26.8	14.7	20.1	4.2	3.5
F		36.9	51.2	25.7	22.8	48.6	43.5	11.6	15.0	6.5	11.1	7.6	7.4
Combined		38.0	58.7	33.3	30.0	33.2	27.0	16.9	21.5	10.8	16.2	5.8	5.2

regions of the scale of probabilities, are likely to produce significant changes in the agents' systems of aspirations. We know that to different objective probabilities correspond different sets of attitudes towards school and school-assisted social mobility. Even when they are not the object of conscious estimation, educational chances, which may be presented to intuitive perception in the group belonged to (neighbourhood or peer group), e.g. in the concrete shape of the number of known individuals who are still at school or already working at a given age, help to fix the social image of university education which is in a sense objectively inscribed in a determinate type of social condition. Depending on whether access to higher education is collectively felt, even in a diffuse way, as an impossible, possible, probable, normal or banal future, everything in the conduct of the families and the children (particularly their conduct and performance at school) will vary, because behaviour tends to be governed by what it is 'reasonable' to expect. Because quantitatively different levels of the rates of collective opportunity express themselves in *qualitatively* different experiences, a social category's collective chances constitute, through the process of internalization of the category's objective destiny, one of the mechanisms through which that objective destiny is realized.

Thus, rising from 52.8 to 74 percent, the likelihood of university entry for the sons of industrialists was multiplied by only 1.4; but the rate thereby attained (74 percent) places them at a point on the scale of probability to which there can only correspond an experience of the quasi-certainty of higher education, with the new advantages and new contradictions associated with that experience. It has to be borne in mind that a large number of industrialists' sons are enrolled in the classes préparatoires and the grandes écoles (hence are not counted in the figures used to calculate the rate); and allowance also has to be made for the fee-paying schools not included in these statistics but mainly frequented by members of this category. Thus it can be assumed that virtually all the sons of industrialists capable of attending courses are in fact in education well beyond the age of eighteen, and that the first signs of a class *over-enrolment* are beginning to appear.

In short, through the general increase in rates of probability of access to university, the evolution of the structure of educational opportunities between 1962 and 1966 consecrated the cultural privileges of the upper classes. Indeed, for three categories (sons and daughters of industrialists, sons of senior executives), the chances of access were equal to or greater than 60 percent, not counting the students in the grandes écoles. For a senior executive's son in 1961-62, continued education after the baccalauréat was a probable future; in 1965-66 it was a typical future. By contrast, the increase in the probabilities of access for working-class children has not been sufficient to lift them decisively out of the region of objective chances where the experience of resignation is shaped, or, exceptionally, the experience of the 'wonderboy', miraculously saved by the School. The fact that a manual worker's son has a 3.9 percent chance of going to university, instead of 1.5 percent, is not sufficient to modify the image of higher education as an unlikely, if not 'unreasonable' future, and one that is, so to speak, unlooked for. As for the middle classes, it is probable that certain fractions (especially primary-school teachers and junior Civil Servants) have reached a threshold where higher education tends to appear as a normal possibility and where the image of education ending with the baccalauréat is tending to fade.

In other words, the conception of education so long accepted by the upper classes, in which the baccalauréat is simply a ticket to higher education (stated negatively in the formula, 'the *bac* means nothing') is tending to spread to the level of the middle classes: the image which formerly induced many to withdraw from education after the baccalauréat, especially the sons of middle-rank managerial staff and above all the sons of clerical workers, who confined their ambitions to overcoming the barrier that had held back their fathers' careers ('you can't do anything without the *bac*'), is tending to give way to the opposite image ('the *bac* gets you nowhere nowadays'), a conception founded, moreover, on real and realistic experience, given that the baccalauréat which has become the sine qua non for access to many jobs which the previous generation was able to reach 'by the back door', i.e. very often after primary education, is no longer sufficient to ensure automatic accession to higher executive positions. One sees in this case how what is, to a large extent, merely a translation of aspirations can be experienced by the individuals concerned as a radical change or, as those observers who refuse to mince their words would say, a 'mutation'.

But inequality in the chances of university entrance still only very partially expresses the socially conditioned educational inequalities. The table of conditional probabilities shows that male and female students of different origin are far from evenly distributed among the various disciplines. If social origin or sex acted as a differential sieve only for higher education, and if, on entering university, unequally selected contingents had equal chances of entering the different courses — in short, if the distribution of students among the various faculties depended only on individual 'vocations' and 'tastes' (considered as natural propensities unaffected by social determinisms) — then for a hundred students of a given origin, we should expect to find a distribution of conditional probabilities which, in each social category, purely and simply reflected the different disciplines' share of the total number of students, i.e. Arts 31.5, Science 32.4, Law 16.5, Medicine 15.6 and Pharmacy 4 percent in 1961-62 and, in the same order, 34.4, 31.4, 19.9, 10.7 and 3.5 percent in 1965-66. Compared with the random distribution which would result from the 'free play of natural faculties', the actual distribution exhibits a systematic distortion due, by and large, to the fact that students of less well-to-do origin gravitate towards the Arts and Science Faculties and students from the wealthier classes towards the Faculties of Law and Medicine. Indeed, this *social specialization* of the faculties tended to become more pronounced between 1961-62 and 1965-66.

In 1961-62, working-class students mainly went in for Arts or Science whereas a higher proportion of upper-class students took up Law or Medicine: 84.7 percent of the children of farm labourers, 75.1 percent of the children of farmers, and 82.7 percent of the children of manual workers were enrolled in Arts or Science; this was the case for only 66.5 percent of the children of senior executives, and 62.2 percent of the children of industrialists (who were strongly represented in the scientific grandes écoles). In short, the lower a student's social origin, the more his access to higher education had to be paid for by a *restriction on choice,* even to the extent of the more or less compulsory *relegation* of the least favoured categories into Arts or Science. The evolution of conditional probability rates between 1962 and 1966 shows that the distribution remained virtually unchanged, with the different social categories ranged in the same hierarchy with respect to the 'choice' of Arts or Science subjects. The higher proportion of law students in the overall number is reflected for all socio-occupational categories in a decline in the conditional likelihood of studying Arts or Science subjects but this decline is particularly marked in the case of the higher categories. Whereas in 1966 the farm workers' children had an 83 percent chance of enrolling in Arts or Science, the farmers' children 74.2 percent (0.9 percent less than in 1962) and the manual workers' children 79.3 percent (3.4 percent less), the children of senior executives now had only a 57 percent chance (9.5 percent less) and the industrialists' children 52.6 percent (9.6 percent less); thus the gap between the workers' children and the senior executives' children widened during this period from 15 to 22 percent.

If we look more closely at the figures for male students we find a decline in the likelihood of entering the Arts Faculty for all categories (except the sons of clerical workers) but the decline is much greater in the upper classes than in the working and middle classes. The rate of probability for workers' sons fell from 27.5 to 24.8 percent but for senior executives' sons from 19.7 to 13.7 percent and for industrialist's sons from 25.2 to 11.6 percent.

We know that access to secondary education was extended to new fractions of the working classes only at the cost of relegation into establishments or sections (e.g. the 'modern' stream) objectively situated at the bottom of the academic hierarchy, a relegation which channels them almost inevitably into the Science Faculties, as opposed not only to the other faculties but also to the scientific grandes écoles.[8]

And so it is not surprising that one finds an increased conditional probability for working-class students of enrolling in science, whereas upper-class students more frequently take up Law or Medicine. Thus the probability of Arts enrolment for farmworkers' sons decreased by 10.5 percent over this period, while the probability of their enrolling in Science rose by 9.3 percent. For senior executives' sons, on the other hand, the probability of Arts enrolment fell at the same time as the probability of Science enrolment (by 5.6 and 4.3 percent, respectively), while the probability of their doing Law or Medicine rose by 5 and 5.4 percent.

In general, for students from the working and middle classes (farm labourers, farmers, manual workers, clerical staff and middle management) the conditional probability of studying Law remained much the same; the highest increase was only 2.8 percent, for the middle-management category. But the chances increased considerably for the children of senior executives (4.6 percent), and especially for the children of industrialists. The same is true of Medicine: the chances of entry remained static or increased very slightly for working-class students but rose by 5.6 percent for upper-class students.

It may be concluded that the slight improvement in working-class children's chances of entering university has in a sense been offset by a strengthening of the mechanism tending to relegate the survivors into certain faculties (and this in spite of the reforms intended to 'rationalize' the organization of studies in the Faculties of Law and Medicine, which were put into effect during the period of this survey).

The principle of statistics interpretation that is implied and required in calculating the conditional probabilities relative to the different faculties only has to be applied to other internal differentiations of the educational system (e.g. those separating the disciplines within the same faculty [see figure 3, p. 96, and table 9, p. 98], and especially those opposing the grandes écoles, themselves rigorously hierarchized, to the system of faculties), in order to give one the means of grasping in the statistics measuring the evolution of the structure of the chances of access to a given level and type of education, what is perhaps the fundamental law of the transformation of the relations between the educational system and the structure of the social classes. An approach which takes as its unit the individual student, ignoring the position that the establishment or course receiving him occupies in the overt or hidden hierarchy of the academic institution, misses the doubling-up of privilege stemming from the fact that the categories with the best chances of entering a given level of education are also the categories with the best chances of entering the establishments, sections or subjects conferring the best chances of subsequent success, both academic and social. Furthermore, such an approach cannot show that the translation of the structure of the probabilities of access to an educational system capable of exploiting pre-existing differentiations or creating new ones is necessarily accompanied by a continuous redefinition of the criteria of the academic and social rarity of academic credentials.[9] This systematic bias leads one to underestimate the educational system's capacity to neutralize the effects of a translation of the structure of opportunity, by means of a ramifying differentiation which conceals its own hierarchical structure, in other words, its capacity to set up in place of the black-and-white oppositions between admission and exclusion which characterized an earlier state of the system, the artfully contrived and shrewdly dissimulated gradations which run from full recognition of academic citizenship to the different shades of relegation.[10]

NOTES

1. These percentages are generally taken directly, without any thought for method, from statistics established in terms of categories disparate in time or space and referring to ill-defined or changing sub-sets of the student population. Thus, in an extreme case, one finds an article which settles the question of the democratization of education (reduced, by a play on words, to the question of

the social composition of the student body) on the basis of statistics which, for the sake of establishing chronological series, have to combine junior, middle and senior executives in a category termed 'civilian and military functionaries'; this breakdown is all the more casual in that it purports to back up an 'analysis' seeking to show the transition from a 'bourgeois intake' to an 'average intake'.

2. In 1963 we had to be content with calculating, for a single year the likelihood of entry to higher education and the conditional likelihood of entry to the different faculties in relation to social origin and sex (a calculation never previously made in this form). This was because until 1958 the statistics for the student body, by socio-occupational category of origin, by sex and by faculty, which were available for previous periods grouped together in the same category all civilian and military functionaries, regardless of rank. See P. Bourdieu and J.-C. Passeron, 1964, 1, pp. 15 ff. (table of probabilities) and pp. 139 ff. (note on the method used to construct the table).

3. Thus, as soon as the trend of the proportion of middle-class students in the student body is compared with the trend of the relative proportion of the middle classes in the French working population, it is immediately clear how much fiction there is in analyses which tend to interpret the slightly increasing weight of this category of students (identified by the father's occupation *at the time of university enrolment*) as an indication of the increased share of these classes in the benefits of higher education. Between 1962 and 1968 it was, in fact, precisely the most numerous and most representative categories of the middle classes which expanded most in the working population, i.e. + 34.2 percent for middle management as a whole (+ 67 percent for teachers and literary and scientific occupations) and + 26.4 percent for clerical staff, as against, for example, + 4 percent for employers in industry and commerce (− 1.9 percent for industrialists proper). *Economie et statistique,* no. 2, June 1969, p. 43.

4. For other examples, see above, Chapter 3, pp. 159-61.

5. Thus, for example, because the system of grandes écoles cannot be conceived outside the relations which link it to the other institutions of higher education, and because any particular school cannot be conceived outside its relations with the other schools, i.e. in abstraction from the position if occupies at a given moment in time within the system of the grandes écoles, a social history of the Ecole Polytechnique or the Ecole Normale Supérieure (more precisely, a history of the social backgrounds, the careers, or even the political and religious attitudes of their students) which ignored the position of each within the grandes écoles system, and therefore, everything stemming from their *positional value* in the structure of relations between the grandes écoles system and the power system, if only by virtue of the establishment of the Ecole Nationale d'Admin-istration, would be quite as fallacious as a history of Saint-Cyr [the military college] which remained at the level of idiography and failed to notice that other

schools (e.g. the Agronomy Schools) are tending to take the place of Saint-Cyr in the system of functions fulfilled by the system of grandes écoles.

6. This hypothesis is not ruled out – at least for a particular type of education – even in an expanding school system and in a situation of economic growth. An indication of such a tendency is perhaps to be seen in the trend of Medical Faculty admissions.

7. 'Translation' – in the mathematical sense: a change of place without change of shape (trans.).

8. See M. de Saint Martin, 1968, 2.

9. The statistics on income relative to age on terminating education show that the economic profitability of an extra year's study rises sharply after the age-bracket approximately coinciding with the average age of entry to higher education, i.e. at an educational level from which the working classes are more or less totally eliminated. There is every reason to think that this threshold must have steadily risen as access to a given level of education lost its scarcity value because of the transposition of the structure of chances.

10. In this context, to leave out the grandes écoles – whose intake has tended to rise socially since the beginning of this century, the proportion of upper class students at the ENS increasing, for example, from 49 percent between 1904 and 1910 (or 1924-30) to 65.9 percent in 1966 on the Arts side, and from 36 percent between 1904 and 1910, to 49.6 percent between 1924 and 1930 and 67.6 percent in 1966 on the Science side – is to make a mistake out of all proportion to the numerical weight of their clientele, since these institutions, carrying the highest positional value in the educational system and even in the system of its relations with the power apparatus, are the virtual monopoly of the privileged classes.

GLOSSARY OF INSTITUTIONS
AND TITLES

Other terms are defined ad hoc in the text or notes. In general, the following list offers 'juridical' definitions; the sociological realities of prestige and opportunity cannot be summarized here.

agrégation	a *concours* (q.v.) in each subject, for a small number of teaching posts in secondary education as *agrégé de l'Université* (in fact a sine qua non for a post in higher education).
Arts et métiers	a further education college training technicians *(Conservatoire National des Arts et Métiers)*.
baccalauréat ('bac')	the national school examination taken at about 18; there are several types corresponding to different curricula; most – but not all – give access to the *facultés*.
CAPES	*Certificat d'Aptitude au Professorat de l'Enseignement Secondaire*: giving access to a post in secondary education as *professeur certifié*, a category of lower status than the *agrégés*; awarded by *concours* (q.v.).
cacique'	*(normalien* jargon) the candidate who comes top in a major *concours* (also: *'major'*).
CEG	*Collège d'Enseignement Général*: a secondary school giving a short 'modern' course.
CES	*Collège d'Enseignement Secondaire*: a secondary school giving the various types of secondary schooling under one roof.
CET	*Collège d'Enseignement Technique*: a secondary technical school giving a vocational course after age 14.
classes préparatoires	classes in the most important *lycées*, preparing candidates for the *concours* of the *grandes écoles* (q.v.).
concours	an annual, national, competitive examination, e.g. for the *agrégation* or the *CAPES*. Each of the major *grandes écoles* has its own recruitment *concours*.

235

Concours Général	a national competition for secondary school pupils (for a prize).
doctorat d'état	the highest university degree; see *thèse d'état*.
ENA	the *Ecole Nationale d'Administration*: a *grande école* training future high-ranking Civil Servants.
ENS	the *Ecole Normale Supérieure* (rue d'Ulm): the *grande école* leading the academic hierarchy of the *grandes ecoles;* its two sections, *lettres* (Arts) and *sciences,* each recruit by *concours* (see *classes préparatoires*), about 50 students a year, most of whom will become secondary or higher education teachers or research scientists.
grandes écoles	opposed to the *facultés* in the bi-partite university system, the *grandes écoles* differ considerably amongst themselves (e.g. in age at entry) but are generally characterized by selectivity, superior facilities and guaranteed professional outlets. They include ENS Ulm (q.v.) and several other ENS, *Polytechnique* (q.v.), *HEC* (q.v.) 'Sciences Po' (the Political Science Institute), the *Ecole Centrale* and the *E.N.S. des Mines.* As well as these *'super-grandes'* the term is also applied to a large number of less prestigious engineering schools.
HEC	the *Ecole des Hautes Etudes Commerciales*, a *grande école* whose graduates take up senior managerial posts in industry and commerce.
licence	approximately the 'bachelor's' degree.
lycée	the traditional type of State secondary school (cf. *CEG*, etc.); there are now also *lycées techniques* and *lycées modernes.*
maitrise	the 'master's' degree.
'major'	see *'cacique'.*
normalien	a student of the ENS.
Polytechnique	the *Ecole Polytechnique*, a *grande école* whose students *(polytechniciens)* are trained for State administrative posts; they tend to move sooner or later into the private sector.
thèse d'état	long thesis required for the *doctorat d'état* (q.v.).
section	in secondary education, denotes one of the types of curriculum ('classical', 'modern', 'general', 'practical' – also subdivided) leading to the *baccalauréat* (q.v.) or a certificate of vocational training, etc.
sixième	the first year of secondary schooling, the subsequent years (counted downwards) leading to *première, terminale,* and the *classes préparatoires* (q.v.).

BIBLIOGRAPHY

A selective list of works on the sociology of education and culture by members of the Centre for European Sociology.

ABBREVIATIONS

Actes	Actes de la recherche en sciences sociales
AES	Archives européennes de sociologie
CSE	Centre de sociologie européenne
ISSJ	International Social Science Journal
RFS	Revue française de sociologie
SSI	Social Science Information
TM	Les temps modernes

1964

Book

1 P. Bourdieu and J.-C. Passeron, *Les héritiers, les étudiants et la culture*, Paris, Minuit, 1964.

1965

Books

1 P. Bourdieu, L. Boltanski, R. Castel and J.-C. Chamboredon, *Un art moyen, essai sur les usages sociaux de la photographie*, Paris, Minuit, 1965; new enlarged edn, 1970.
2 P. Bourdieu, J.-C. Passeron and M. de Saint Martin, *Rapport pédagogique et communication*, Paris – The Hague, Mouton, 1965 (Cahiers du CSE, 2).

1966

Book

1 P. Bourdieu and A. Darbel, with D. Schnapper, *L'amour de l'art. Les musées d'art européens et leur public*, Paris, Minuit, 1966; new enlarged edn, 1969.

Articles

2 P. Bourdieu, 'L'école conservatrice, les inégalités devant l'école et devant la culture', *RFS*, 7, 1966, pp. 325-47; trans. 'The School as a Conservative Force', in *Contemporary Research in Sociology of Education* ed. J. Eggleston, London, Methuen, 1974, pp. 32-46.

3 P. Bourdieu, 'Champ intellectuel et projet créateur', *TM*, 246, nov. 1966, pp. 865-906; trans. 'Intellectual Field and Creative Project', in *SSI*, 8 (2), April 1969, pp. 89-119; also in *Knowledge and Control* ed. M. F. D. Young, London, Collier-Macmillan, 1971, pp. 161-88.

1967

Book

1 P. Bourdieu, translation of and afterword to E. Panofsky, *Architecture gothique et pensée scolastique*, Paris, Minuit, 1967; new enlarged edn, 1970.

Article

2 P. Bourdieu, 'Systems of Education and Systems of Thought', *ISSJ*, 19 (3), 1967 pp. 338-58; repr. in *Knowledge and Control*, ed. Young, pp. 189-207.

1968

Articles

1 P. Bourdieu, 'Outline of a Theory of Art Perception', *ISSJ*, 20 (4), pp. 589-612.

2 M. de Saint Martin, 'Les facteurs de l'élimination et de la sélection différentielles dans les études de sciences', *RFS*, 9, numéro spécial, 1968, pp. 167-84.

1969

Mimeographed

1 P. Bourdieu with Y. Delsaut and M. de Saint Martin, *Les fonctions du système d'enseignement: classes préparatoires et facultés*, Paris, CSE, 1969.

1970

Articles

1 P. Bourdieu and M. de Saint Martin, 'L'excellence scolaire et les valeurs du système d'enseignement français', *Annales*, 25 (1), janv.-fév. 1970, pp. 147-75; trans. 'Scholastic Excellence and the Values of the Educational

System', in *Contemporary Research,* ed. Eggleston, pp. 338-71.

2   Y. Delsaut, 'Les opinions politiques dans le système des attitudes: les étudiants en lettres et la politique', *RFS,* 11 (1), janv.-mars 1970, pp. 45-64.

1971

Books

1   C. Grignon, *L'ordre des choses. Les fonctions sociales de l'enseignement technique,* Paris, Minuit, 1971.

2   M. de Saint Martin, *Les fonctions sociales de l'enseignement scientifique,* Paris – The Hague, Mouton, 1971 (Cahiers du CSE, 8).

Articles

3   P. Bourdieu, 'Disposition esthétique et compétence artistique', *TM,* 295, 1971, pp. 1345-78.

4   P. Bourdieu, 'Champ du pouvoir, champ intellectuel et habitus de classe', *Scolies,* 1, 1971, pp. 7-26.

5   P. Bourdieu, 'Genèse et structure du champ religeux', *RFS,* 12 (3), 1971.

6   P. Bourdieu, 'Une interprétation de la sociologie religieuse de Max Weber', *AES,* 12 (1), 1971, pp. 3-21.

7   P. Bourdieu, 'Reproduction culturelle et reproduction sociale', *SSI,* 10 (2), 1971, pp. 45-79; trans. 'Cultural Reproduction and Social Reproduction' in *Knowledge, Education and Social Change,* ed. R. Brown, London, Tavistock, 1973, pp. 71-112.

8   P. Bourdieu, 'The Thinkable and the Unthinkable', *Times Literary Supplement,* 15 Oct. 1971, pp. 1255-56.

9   P. Bourdieu, L. Boltanski and P. Maldidier, 'La défense du corps', *SSI,* 10 (4), 1971.

1972

Book

1   P. Bourdieu, *Esquisse d'une théorie de la pratique, précédé de trois études d'ethnologie kabyle,* Geneva, Droz, 1972; trans, with additions 1977, 1.

Articles

2   P. Bourdieu, 'Les stratégies matrimoniales dans le système des stratégies de reproduction', *Annales,* 4-5, juill.-oct. 1972, pp. 1105-27; trans. 'Marriage Strategies as Strategies of Social Reproduction', in *Family and Society: Selections from the Annales,* ed. R. Forster and P. Ranum, Baltimore, Johns Hopkins U.P., 1976, pp. 117-44.

3 V. Karady, 'Normaliens et autres enseignants à la Belle Epoque. Note sur l'origine sociale et la réussite dans une profession intellectuelle', *RFS*, 13 (1), janv.-mars 1972, pp. 35-58.
4 J. Testanière, 'Crise scolaire et révolte lycéenne', *RFS*, 13 (1), janv.-mars 1972, pp. 3-34.

1973
Articles

1 L. Boltanski, 'L'espace positionnel. Multiplicité des positions institutionelles et habitus de classe', *RFS*, 14 (1), 1973, pp. 3-26.
2 P. Bourdieu, 'Le marché des biens symboliques', *L'Année sociologique*, 22, 1973, pp. 49-126.
3 P. Bourdieu, 'Les doxosophes', *Minuit*, 1, 1973, pp. 26-45.
4 P. Bourdieu, L. Boltanski and M. de Saint Martin, 'Les stratégies de reconversion', *SSI*, 12 (5), 1973, pp. 61-113.
5 V. Karady, 'L'expansion universitaire et l'évolution des inégalités devant la carrière d'enseignant au début de la IIIe République', *RFS*, 14 (4), oct.-déc. 1973, pp. 443-70.

1974
Articles

1 P. Bourdieu, 'Avenir de classe et causalité du probable', *RFS*, 15 (1), janv.-mars 1974, pp. 3-42.
2 P. Bourdieu, 'Les fractions de la classe dominante et les modes d'appropriation des oeuvres d'art', *SSI*, 13 (3), 1974, pp. 7-32.
3 J.-M. Chapoulie, 'Le corps professoral dans la structure de classe', *RFS*, 15 (2), avril-juin 1974, pp. 155-200.
4 C. Suaud, 'Contribution à une sociologie de la vocation: destin religieux et projet scolaire', *RFS*, 15 (1), pp. 75-115.

1975
Articles

1 L. Boltanski, 'La constitution du champ de la bande dessinée', *Actes*, 1, janv. 1975, pp. 37-59.
2 L. Boltanski, 'Pouvoir et impuissance: projet intellectuel et sexualité dans le *Journal* d'Amiel', *Actes*, 5-6 nov. 1975, pp. 80-108.
3 P. Bourdieu, 'L'invention de la vie d'artiste', *Actes*, 2, mars 1975, pp. 67-94.
4 P. Bourdieu, 'L'ontologie politique de Martin Heidegger', *Actes*, 5-6, nov. 1975, pp. 109-56.

5   P. Bourdieu, 'Le langage autorisé. Note sur les conditions sociales de l'efficacité du discours rituel', *Actes*, 5-6, nov. 1975, pp. 183-90.
6   P. Bourdieu and L. Boltanski, 'Le titre et le poste. Rapports entre le système de production et le système de reproduction', *Actes*, 2, mars 1975, pp. 95-107, trans.: 'Formal Qualifications and Occupational Hierarchies: The Relationship Between the Production System and the Reproduction System', in *Reorganizing Education: Management and Participation for Change* ed. E. King, London, SAGE, 1977.
7   P. Bourdieu with L. Boltanski, 'Le fétichisme de la langue', *Actes*, 4, juillet 1975, pp. 2-32.
8   P. Bourdieu with Y. Delsaut, 'Le couturier et sa griffe: Contribution à une théorie de la magie', *Actes*, 1, janv. 1975, pp. 7-36.
9   P. Bourdieu and M. de Saint Martin, 'Les catégories de l'entendement professoral', *Actes*, 3, mai 1975, pp. 68-93.
10 J.-C. Chamboredon and J. Prévot, 'Changes in the Social Definition of Early Childhood and the New Forms of Symbolic Violence', *Theory and Society*, 2 (3), 1975, pp. 331-50.
11 C. Grignon, 'L'enseignement agricole et la domination symbolique de la paysannerie', *Actes*, 1, janv. 1975, pp. 75-97.
12 F. Muel, 'L'école obligatoire et l'invention de l'enfance anormale', *Actes*, 1, janv. 1975, pp. 60-74.

1976

Articles

1   P. Bourdieu, 'Le champ scientifique', *Actes* (2e année), 2-3, juin 1976, pp. 88-104; trans. 'The Specificity of the Scientific Field and the Social Conditions of the Progress of Reason', *SSI*, 14 (6), 1975, pp. 19-47.
2   P. Bourdieu and L. Boltanski, 'La production de l'idéologie dominante', *Actes* (2e année), 2-3, juin 1976, pp. 4-73.
3   P. Bourdieu with M. de Saint Martin, 'Anatomie du goût', *Actes* (2e année), 5, oct. 1976.
4   C. Grignon, 'L'art et le métier, école parallèle et petite bourgeoisie', *Actes* (2e année), 4, août 1976, pp. 21-46.

1977

Book

1   P. Bourdieu, *Outline of a Theory of Practice*, Cambridge, CUP (trans. of 1972, 1 with additional chapters).

INDEX

Abegglen, J. C., 168.
abilities, *see* competence; natural, *see* natural.
academicism, anti-academic, 39, 128; *see also* literary, mandarin, manner.
access, probabilities of, *see* probabilities.
action, *see* pedagogic action.
advertizing, 20, 25.
age group, 94, 104, 215, 223.
agrégation, agrégés, 150-1, 162, 168, 171, 172, 235; defence of, 144, 199; *Société des,* 150.
affinity: elective, 78, 198; structural, *see* structural.
'alienation', 23-4; generic, 194.
amateurism, 128; *see also* literary.
apprentice intellectuals, *see* intellectuals.
apprenticeship, *see* learning.
arbitrariness, x-xiii, 5-11; of content imposed, 8; and gratuitousness, 8; of imposition, 6; link between two, 9-10, 15-16; and sociological necessity, 8.
arbitrary, cultural: distance between, 16, 25-6, 30-1; dominant, 9, 10-11; dominated 23-4, 42; system of, 23.
aristocracy, 9, 115, 129-30, 149, 201-2, 210; *see also* feudalism.
'aspirations', 102, 134, 207, 226, 228.
asylum, 18, 37, 44.
attitudes, *see* disposition.
auctor 25, 63; and *lector,* 58, 59.

authority, x; argument of, 67; pedagogic 3, 11-31, 36-7, 108-10, 111, 124-5, 147, 190, 195, (and personal) 20-1, 62-3, 65, 190; school, 3, 63-6, 108, 110, 124-5, 200.
autonomization: methodological, 88, 101, 105-6, 159, 222; tendency to, 60, 149, 151; *see also* inertia.
autonomy, 111, 172, 197; absolute, illusion of school system's, 66, 177-8, 198, 199; limitation of, 26-7, 199; relative (of school system), 11-12, 60, 100, 126, 132, 145, 152, 165, 178, 189, 191, 194-9, (of State), 195, 200; social conditions of, 149-50, 197-9.

baccalauréat, 88, 144, 146, 149, 154, 170, 227, 235.
Balazs, E., 139.
Bally, C., 117.
Bardy, G., 64.
Benedict, R., 212.
Bennett, J. W., 212.
Benveniste, E., 107.
Bernstein, B., xvi, 133.
bilingualism, and biculturalism, 12.
biography, 37, 89, 160-1; *see also* trajectory.
biology, and pedagogy, 7, 10, 32; *see also* reproduction..
Blanchard, R., 172.
Bloomfield, L., 136.
Bouglé, C., 103, 175.
bourgeoisie, 14, 139, 161, 169, 202, 210; big, 139, 147, 201-4; petty, 134, 139, 145, 149, 192, 200-4, 215.
brilliance, 111, 118, 121, 131, 143, 161, 170-1, 201-2; *see also* man-

THE EDUCATIONAL CAREER
AND ITS SYSTEM OF DETERMINATIONS*

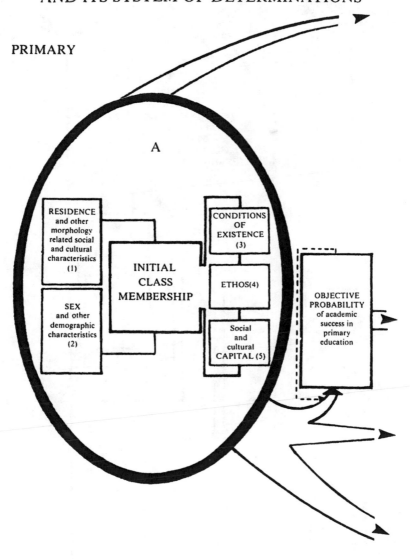

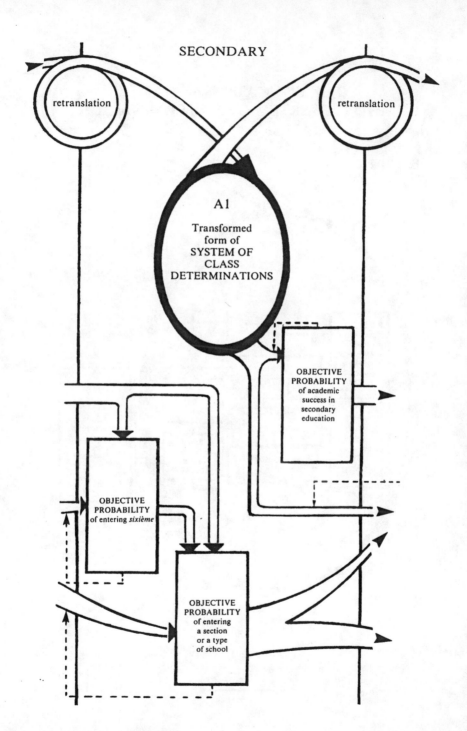

SECONDARY

retranslation

retranslation

A1

Transformed
form of
SYSTEM OF
CLASS
DETERMINATIONS

OBJECTIVE
PROBABILITY
of academic
success in
secondary
education

OBJECTIVE
PROBABILITY
of entering *sixième*

OBJECTIVE
PROBABILITY
of entering
a section
or a type
of school

7974

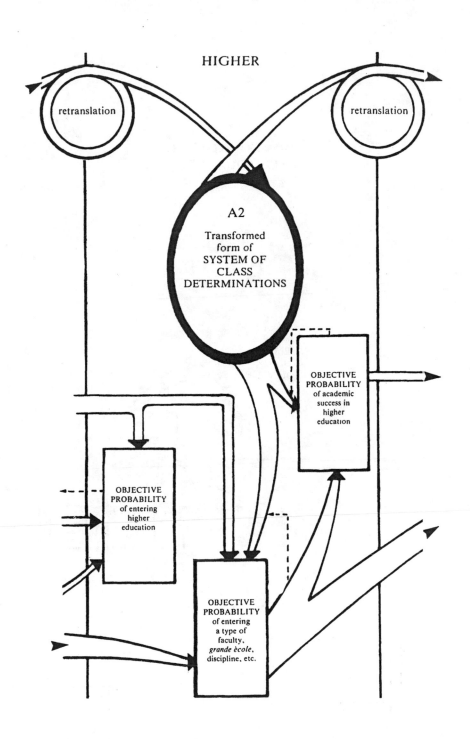

VOCATIONAL USE OF
ACADEMIC QUALIFICATION

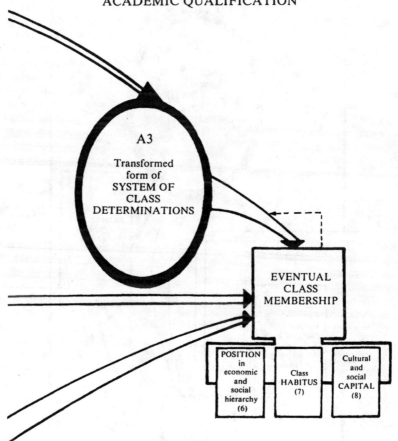

*This diagram is intended to suggest the logic by which the system of determinations attached to class membership (circle A) acts throughout an educational career, restructuring itself as a function of the varying weight of any given factor (e.g. cultural capital or income) within the structure of factors at the different stages of the passage through education, broadly distinguished here as primary, secondary (A1), higher (A2) and post-graduation (A3). It must be borne in mind that, within this system of factors constantly restructured by its own action, the relative weight of the determinations due to initial class membership steadily declines to the advantage of the academic determinations which retranslate them. The lines indicate correlations between variables and the arrows indicate genetic processes. The dotted arrows are used to suggest the determinations which operate through the internalization of objective probabilities in the form of subjective expectations. In other words, the diagram seeks to represent some of the mechanisms through which the structure of class relations tends to reproduce itself by reproducing those habitus which reproduce it.

(1) Distance from centre(s) of cultural values (concentration(s) of intelligentsia) and from educational and cultural facilities; structure of academic and cultural opportunities of groups belonged to (neighbourhood, peer group). (2) Other demographic characteristics (sibling order, family size, etc.) specified by class membership (differential selection) and social definition. (3) Security of employment; income and income prospects; environment and working conditions; leisure, etc. (4) Dispositions towards school and culture (i.e. vis-à-vis learning, authority, school values, etc.); subjective expectations (of access to school, of success, of advancement by means of school); relation to language and culture (manners). (5) linguistic capital; previous knowledge; capital of social connections and prestige (testimonials); information on educational system, etc. (6) Average income; average income at beginning and end of career; speed of promotion; position in economic and social structures, particularly in the various fields of legitimacy and in power structure. (7) Relation to class origin and education, depending on academic record and eventual class membership. (8) Diploma; old boy network.

LaVergne, TN USA
03 April 2010
178052LV00001B/36/A